LOCKHEED
P-38 LIGHTNING

Other titles in the Crowood Aviation Series

CROWOOD

AVIATION SERIES

LOCKHEED
P-38 LIGHTNING

JERRY SCUTTS

The Crowood Press

First published in 2006 by
The Crowood Press Ltd
Ramsbury, Marlborough
Wiltshire SN8 2HR

www.crowood.com

British Library Cataloguing-in-Publication Data
A catalogue record for this book is available from
the British Library.

ISBN 1 86126 770 3
EAN 978 1 86126 770 2

Typefaces used: Goudy (*text*),
Cheltenham (*headings*).

Typeset and designed by
D & N Publishing
Lambourn Woodlands, Hungerford, Berkshire.

Printed and bound in Great Britain by CPI Bath.

Acknowledgements

In putting together this record of the P-38 I would like to thank the following individuals to and organizations:

Aeroplane Monthly; Ian Carter; Richard Franks; Phil Jarrett; Lockheed Aircraft Corporation; Alain Pelletier; Imperial War Museum Photographic Library; Richard L. Ward; the United States Air Force and website data posted by the Smithsonian Institution via John Anthony and Terence Geary.

Contents

Introduction

When the prototype Lockheed XP-38 was shown to the US press and public for the first time, in 1938, there was universal praise for its incredibly sleek lines. The US Army Air Corps had never seen anything like it; certainly no single-seat fighter was ever that big. And when its performance was announced, the praise for Lockheed approached adulation. To a great extent this faith in the company's product never waned, which in some ways clouded judgement. Under the impetus of war and rapid technical advances the fact that the long-range P-38 could actually be outpaced by a single-engine fighter took some time to grasp. The Lightning could certainly escort American bombers to Berlin – it was the first American fighter to do so – but the tragic fact was that it could not always get back. This was not a flaw that could be attributed to Burbank's brilliant engineers, but a problem that was beyond anyone's control; one that could literally be blamed on the weather. But ask any pilot posted to the South Pacific and faced with flying for several hours over water, impenetrable jungle and murderous enemy troops what he preferred, and the answer would come down firmly on the side of Lockheed's twin-boom killer.

From almost any angle the Lightning looked the part; a deadly, menacing and purposeful warplane with a distinctive and unique layout. Small wonder then, that on D-Day, in June 1944, the Supreme Commander wanted P-38s to be first over the Normandy invasion beaches, on the grounds that nobody, not even the greenest naval gunner, could fail to recognize them.

This narrative retells the P-38 story with the intention of bringing the reader a few facts and figures, and photographs, that have not been fully explored elsewhere. Certainly the P-38 can stand further exposure, so deeply was it ingrained in the combat philosophy of the wartime US Army Air Forces.

JERRY SCUTTS
London, 2005

OPPOSITE PAGE:
A magnificent study of 44-25415, one of the 2,520 P-38L-5s, the last and best model of the Lightning. The aluminium skin had at least seven different tonal values, ex-factory. Lockheed

THIS PAGE:
Lockhead designed a fighter and also turned it into the top US reconnaissance aircraft of the war. Leading here is an F-5B-1 with a P-38J-5 behind. Lockheed

CHAPTER ONE

Burbank's Beauty

The twin-engine fighter enjoyed an important but somewhat chequered career as a combat aircraft in the inventory of the fighting powers during the Second World War. Starting, operationally at least, with the Messerschmitt Bf 110 *Zerstorer*, the 'heavy fighter' was mythologized by Luftwaffe Commander-in-Chief Hermann Goring as being so capable that it would sweep all before it as an essential element of *Blitzkreig*. When Germany attacked Poland in 1939 Hitler's propaganda machine had successfully legitimized this class of aircraft, but as it transpired this was somewhat premature. However, designers around the world were hardly surprised at the Bf 110's testimonial, as they had been advocating the worth of such aircraft for some time.

One reason why a twin-engine layout was popular was because many aero engines of the pre-war period, irrespective of their country of origin, were hard-put to produce more than 1,000hp (746kW). The potential to obtain more power certainly existed, and test engines had been developed and run in several countries, but mass

production of advanced powerplants lay some time in the future. Therefore the use of two relatively low-powered engines not only doubled the available horsepower, but enabled such a design to cope with the corresponding increase in weight of a larger airframe. Also, there was the undeniable crew safety factor inherent in twin engines.

The *Zerstorer*'s operational debut proved to be rather less spectacular than Goring had boasted. Few Bf 110 sorties were actually flown over Poland, and those that were hardly met any challenge in aerial combat. Moreover, Poland's fighter force was not equipped with the kind of firepower that the opposing fighters of other nations would soon bring to bear on the *Zerstorer* crews.

A twin-engine fighter embodies the classic compromise of airframe weight being hopefully cancelled out by engines powerful enough to maintain a contemporary (circa 1938–39) top speed goal of around 300–350mph (480–560km/h) and a manoeuvrability on a par with that of single-engine fighters. Only in a few cases

was this ideal ever achieved, most twin-engine fighters being forced to concede a superior agility to smaller fry.

Few twins could hope to turn as tightly as a single-seater, bringing the distinct drawback that the larger aircraft, needing a wider turning circle, could be 'cut off' in a pursuit curve. This danger could be cancelled out if the twin's speed could be maintained long enough to pull away during the turn, or to outstrip an adversary in a high-speed dive. These and other factors represented a substantial engineering challenge for designers. The Lockheed Aircraft Company, in tendering for a United States Army Air Corps (USAAC) requirement of 1937, decided that a twin-engine layout would provide adequate power for the 300mph (480km/h)-plus interceptor fighter required by the Air Corps.

Even before the Second World War began, few service chiefs had clear ideas as to how fighters would be deployed. The important defence/offence role of the short-range single-seaters developed fairly rapidly, but twins were in many ways 'orphans

In an age of transition the XP-38 had a huge impact on the US aviation scene, making even the radical Bell Airacuda look pedestrian. The port Allison lacks a manifold fairing. Lockheed

of the storm'. The concept of fighters escorting single, poorly-armed photographic-reconnaissance (PR) machines had been explored over the trenches during the First World War, but very little had been done to determine the practicality of deploying substantial numbers of fighters to protect even larger formations of bombers. The fighter 'circuses' so favoured by the Germans in that conflict advanced aerial combat, and much of the tactical doctrine of the second global conflict remained rooted in that of the last year or so of the 'war to end wars'.

Numerous expedient tactical formations, such as the 'finger four', the Lufbery circle and the Immelmann turn had emerged during the earlier conflict, and the trick was to adapt these to a generation of far heavier and faster fighters. The doldrums of the 1920s and 1930s and underfunding for the military brought relatively few changes. Fighter speeds advanced, but the biplane continued to be the yardstick and, as bomber performance also improved, the belief that 'the bomber will always get through' left the fighter without a definite role outside short-range target defence and the interception of hostile aircraft.

Not until Britain's perceived need for nightfighters materialized in the Bristol Beaufighter did that country really have a clear picture of a primary operational requirement for a fast, well-armed twin large enough to accommodate a crew of two. Several other aircraft emerged that provided ample space for a second or third crew member, including the Bf 110, but Lockheed was almost alone in providing its P-38 with but a single seat.

None of a number of French and Italian twin-engine designs featured single-pilot operation, showing that the American approach stayed the course when few others did so. Germany toyed with the Focke-Wulf Fw 187, but only in its early form did this experimental type have a single seat.

In Britain, the nearest equivalent to the P-38 was the sleek Westland Whirlwind, a promising fighter design that proved the lethality of grouping a battery of heavy guns in the nose, ahead of the pilot. The Whirlwind first flew in October 1938, and its concentrated firepower enabled it to strafe with greater accuracy than would have been possible if allowance had to be made for the wider spread of wing-mounted guns. The Whirlwind's operational career pointed the way for this class of aircraft. It proved to be a useful fighter-bomber, and in this instance it took something of a

lead. Let down by unreliable engines and subsequently allowed to fall by the wayside, the Whirlwind never had its potential fully exploited.

A first-line fighter with twin booms like the Lightning was never seriously considered in Britain for the RAF, although some manufacturers, notably Miles Aircraft, had explored the configuration. Numerous European designers, including Anthony Fokker, had proposed a twin-boom layout as practical, insofar as it freed a short central fuselage nacelle or 'pod' for the pilot, who would be right behind a battery of guns and therefore able to aim the weapons with great accuracy. A central pod would also provide adequate space for ammunition stowage and, in some instances, the nosewheel of a tricycle undercarriage. A further advantageous factor in twin-boom designs was ease of ammunition replenishment and gun access. A nosewheel configuration was the 'wave of the future', and Fokker went one stage further. The Dutch company's D.XXIII was the first fighter to mate a cockpit pod to both tractor and pusher engines. Unfortunately it existed only as a prototype in 1939, and there was insufficient time to exploit its potential before war came.

Fokker had previously developed the one operational European fighter that was

of similar configuration to the P-38, namely the G.I of 1937. Although twin-fuselage designs had also been popular during the First World War, the configuration had generally fallen from favour. The appearance of the prototype G.I at the 1936 Salon Internationale de l'Aéronautique in Paris was noteworthy, and its radical appearance, with its attendant advantages, generated great interest.

But the radial-engined G-1 with its tail-wheel undercarriage looked pedestrian compared with the graceful XP-38, which was an inspired exercise in aesthetics and streamlining. Here was a completely new fighter with an unconventional rather than revolutionary twin-boom layout using a tricycle undercarriage. Nonetheless, however good the Lockheed fighter looked, and however great its promise, there still remained the question of finding an effective combat role for it.

As the P-38 and the Whirlwind had no second seat, the most useful role for a twin-engine type, that of nightfighter, was not seriously considered for either, at least at conception.

This did not prevent some Lightnings being used in the nocturnal role in the Pacific as a stop-gap measure, but the radar-equipped night interceptor was generally believed to be too demanding for one man

Epitomizing grace and streamlining, the YP-38s were real crowd-pullers when they were rolled out of the old brewery building Lockheed had acquired to gain space at Burbank. IWM

to handle effectively, at least in the early years of the war. The British in particular never really explored the single-pilot, multi-duty philosophy, despite an experimental installation of a Mk IV airborne interception (AI) set in a Hawker Typhoon and, reportedly, in a handful of Hurricanes in 1941.

Although the Americans later proved that such an arrangement was perfectly feasible (and practical in operation) in the Grumman F6F Hellcat and Vought F4U Corsair, the pilot's workload on a relatively short-range patrol was marginally less in these aircraft than it would have been when flying a twin. In the latter case the pilot had to monitor the performance of both engines, navigate, observe the sky around him at all times, maintain contact with a ground controller and watch a tiny radar screen that was prone to static and other 'clutter'. And he could never afford his let his attention become too fixed on the scope.

Playing it safe when adapting the Lightning into a nightfighter as the P-38M, Lockheed engineers eventually opted to introduce a second seat for a radar operator. Without radical redesign, room was found for the operator in the barely adequate space behind the pilot where radio equipment was installed in the standard single-seat P-38.

Earlier model P-38s had pointed the way to the M version. Units in the field had found that a second occupant could squeeze into the space behind the pilot's seat, normally taken up by the radio. With the set removed and a rudimentary seat installed, the so-called 'piggy-back' Lightning proved a useful liaison aircraft and served as a pattern for the nightfighter.

With the Lightning, Lockheed created the world's only single-seat, multi-engine fighter to go into mass production and stay the course throughout the crucible of combat. That alone endowed the P-38 with almost mythical qualities and made it something very special.

Into the Unknown

In common with numerous other aircraft manufacturers the world over, Lockheed had never built a fighter (and had built very few military aircraft at all from the ground up) before it responded to a circular proposal for an experimental pursuit intended for 'the tactical mission of interception and attack of hostile aircraft at high altitude'. This was Air Corps Specification X-608, issued in February 1937. Among the fairly broad requirements was a minimum true air speed of 360mph (580km/h) at altitude, and a time to climb to 20,000ft (6,000m) of under 6min. Armament was to be twice as heavy as that of existing fighters, a 25mm shell-firing cannon being mentioned, and the winning design would be fitted with the most powerful engines available, enabling the aircraft to fly at full throttle for over an hour.

Despite the enormous challenge of meeting the specification without the existence of an engine capable of the 1,600hp (1,200kW) required for such an aircraft, Lockheed decided to bid. The company's association with what became the Lightning began at that point, with several rival concerns also bidding for an X-608 contract. In the standard procedure of the time, a design competition would decide which submission had the most merit under a points system. In reality there was little direct competition for Lockheed. Bell submitted its single-engine XP-39 proposal, and Vultee offered its XP-1015 (Experimental Interceptor Pursuit), a twin-engine design that apparently progressed no further than the 'paper' stage. Boeing, Curtiss and Douglas were invited to take part in the X-608 competition, but

Consolidated declined. Little is known of the rival proposals; none progressed as far as the prototype stage.

Lockheed had established its reputation with medium-capacity airliners, the most famous of which was probably the Lockheed 14. With war clouds looming in Europe, the company's management realized the desirability of bidding for lucrative military contracts, particularly from European nations. Foreign cash would help fund the production facilities necessary to build aircraft in unprecedented quantities, and Lockheed moved quickly to adapt the Model 14 into a patrol bomber for the RAF. The resulting Hudson was the first of many thousands of US aircraft to cross the Atlantic for war service with Britain and the Allied nations. Projecting the militarized airliner further, Lockheed developed the larger PV-1 Ventura and, ultimately, the drastically redesigned PV-2 Harpoon.

While the Model 14 derivatives were not new designs, but were based on tried and tested layouts perfected by Lockheed engineers, they were all multi-seat aircraft. A single-seat fighter was radically different, and in bidding to build such an aircraft the company took a gamble that it could find a suitable engine and fulfil production contracts, should they materialize. The only possible powerplant around

This view emphasizes the size of the YP-38. Among the guests are USAAC chief 'Hap' Arnold (in white hat), Lockheed company President Robert Gross and National Defense Commission director William Knudsen. The aircraft has small propeller blade cuffs and the twin 'machine-guns' are empty blast tubes. IWM

which to design a fighter had been built by the Allison Division of General Motors. This was the V-1710-C8, which had not even been run at 1,000hp (746kW) by February 1937.

Compared with Bell's design submission, the XP-39, which was itself quite radical, Lockheed's Model 22 not only showed similar innovation but was some three times larger. This appeared not to matter overmuch, as the competition was very much an open book. At that time the USAAC's Wright Field Pursuit Projects Office was headed by Lt Benjamin S. Kelsey. He had to resort to some sleight of hand insofar as the conservative Air Corps was concerned. What the Air Corps needed was a fighter, but Kelsey reckoned that calling it an interceptor would open up the competition to encompass some new, exciting possibilities.

At Lockheed, Clarence 'Kelly' Johnson's team under Hall L. Hibbard perfected the P-38 layout at Burbank after considering several designs, some of which were quite complex. Johnson and Hibbard considered themselves co-inventors of the Model 22, and filed patents to that effect after the XP-38 had flown. Army chiefs wanted Lockeed's fighter built in quantity; as many as the factories could produce as fast as possible, and no wonder. Lockheed had turned the relatively slow 'heavy fighter' concept on its head and produced a fast and manoeuvrable aircraft with the safety factor of two engines, which had always been a strong testimonial in such designs. The P-38 began to take on an aura as the very embodiment of a fighter of the future.

Contract Issued

Kelsey's ruse paid off handsomely. The Army liked what it saw, and Lockheed was rewarded with War Department Contract AC9974, company identification Model 22, military designation XP-38.

By the late 1930s fighter speeds were steadily rising, enough to challenge the theory that the bomber, owing to its size, speed and armament, was all but invulnerable to interception and destruction. That mythical invulnerablity, which was never really tested outside war games and exercises, was gradually being eroded as each new interceptor prototype took to the air. By 1940 Bell, Curtiss, Republic and North American had all but cornered the American market in single-engine types, other

A YP-38 on test, probably being flown by Lockheed pilot Milo Burcham, who put in many hours at the controls of pre-production and operational Lightnings. IWM

manufacturers submitting both conventional and some very radical designs with very little contractural success.

Despite these 'also-rans' falling by the wayside, keen competition and publicity not only kept the industry in the forefront of aviation development, but resulted in the USA setting the standards that the rest of the world would eventually follow.

Advanced Features

In the days when variable-pitch propellers, enclosed cockpits and self-sealing fuel tanks were all still relatively new, US companies gradually moved into the lead with a general acceptance of tricycle undercarriages for certain categories of aircraft, particularly bombers. In fighters, Bell had taken a national lead by incorporating a nosewheel in its P-39 Airacobra, and Lockheed adopted a similar layout for its new twin-engine fighter.

The Model 22 went through several quite advanced design studies. Aviation was on the threshold of a new era, and many innovations were thought to be practical for future combat aircraft for the armed forces. Windtunnel testing of models and examination of mock-ups often proved that, while major departures from the 'tried and tested' formulae such as buried engines, propellers driven via extension shafts and flying-wing and canard layouts would and did work, ease of mass production and field

maintenance might have been very problematical. But with the 1940s fast approaching, the most pressing obstacle to lengthy development became time itself.

In realistic tests many proposed fighter designs failed to meet their promised performance because they relied on engines that were not fully developed. Often physically larger than their predecessors, such power units offered a potentially significant increase in top speed; if and when the engines were proven and built. Shortly before the war European interceptor fighters were operating at maximum speeds of 300–400mph (480–640km/h) in level flight, and while there was an understandable desire on the part of US manufacturers to better that speed range by 20 per cent or more, achieving it proved far more difficult than many aeronautical engineers imagined.

Therefore, in selecting its new combat aircraft, the USAAC tended to opt for designs that were conventional and easy to manufacture. Single-seaters still generally had their engine in front of the pilot, armament was housed in the mainplanes, and there was a single fuselage and a recognizable tail-surface grouping with twin or single fins. The use of two wing-mounted engines allowed centreline guns in the nose of the fuselage, which thus had room for a one-, two- or three-man crew. Doubling the power of available engines of around 950hp (710kW) hardly offered any surfeit of performance, as the inevitable weight penalty of a larger airframe and associated military equipment had to be absorbed.

Although official conservatism in procurement was often criticized it proved sound enough, and for another half-decade after 1940 most of the world's air arms relied on aircraft powered by reciprocating engines in conventional airframes fitted with 'straight' rather than swept wings. All of that was understood at Burbank, but, if he could, Kelly Johnson wanted to explore other possibilities.

Much brainstorming led to the final configuration of the Model 22, which was chosen from six layouts put forward by Johnson. These encompassed a conventional single-fin aircraft with elongated engine nacelles and the pilot positioned right forward in a bomber-type nosecone; a similar layout, but with extremely slim engine nacelles that were not carried aft of the wing; a twin-boom, twin pusher with two endplate vertical fins; twin booms with the pilot's cockpit in the port-side boom, the other being 'clean'; and twin booms with a central nacelle incorporating tractor and pusher engines. The sixth exercise was unmistakably the P-38 configuration, and was the one chosen by the USAAC. The layout favoured by Johnson was not the least complex of his six ideas, but was quite distinctive and unlike any previous fighter design accepted for production.

Lockheed Progress

For the Model 22 Lockheed managed to counter the omnipresent weight spiral by having a single cockpit in a short fuselage pod containing the cockpit and the fixed weapons. Long twin 'fuselage' booms spread the weight and carried the tail surfaces.

The Model 22 was an inspired design, practical in operation and meeting the desire of engineers and airframe designers who wanted the company stamp on something just radical enough to stand out from the crowd. Lockheed achieved that in considerable measure.

The design team opted to use two supercharged, 12-cylinder Allison V-1710 liquid-cooled in-line engines for the new fighter. This choice was also something of a gamble, for it had still not achieved a sustained 1,000hp output by 1938, though a higher output was promised.

Boosting Power

The Model 22's twin booms were streamlined but made deep enough to provide space for a separate turbosupercharger (as against the integral, mechanical type) and intercooler aft of each engine, as well as cooling intakes and the necessary internal ducting to feed air to the turbine. The main supercharger housings, with their characteristic turbine-wheel cores, were installed on top of the booms at approximately the mid-point of each wing.

The US industry considered superchargers to be essential for sustained high-altitude flight, and Kelly Johnson later commented on this philosophy insofar as it affected the P-38. He stated that by the time the engineers had strung together long turbosupercharger ducting, added radiators and the undercarriage bay, the design had stretched so much that a twin-boom layout was almost the only logical way to go.

To minimize the effects of engine torque, which could induce a dangerous swing to right or left on take-off in other twin-engine aircraft, Lockheed chose to fit the P-38 with propellers that counter-rotated outwards. This effectively dampened any tendency for the aircraft to wander off-line during take-off before sufficient speed had built up for the flying controls to take effect.

On 23 June 1937 the USAAC issued Contract 9974, authorizing Lockheed to build one XP-38 prototype. This was some five months ahead of the Bell XP-39 Airacobra. Construction of the Lockheed aircraft began in July 1938, and it was completed that December. It was allocated the military serial number 37-457.

Structure

What emerged from the old brewery building purchased by Lockheed as part of an expansion plan at Burbank was an aircraft with an all-metal structure and a single-main-spar wing with a double-'I'-section beam box at the centre section and a single 'I' beam member in the outer panels. The wing spanned 52ft (15.85m) and had an area of 327.5sq ft (30.4sq m). The entire airframe was covered in a smooth, flush-riveted light-alloy stressed skin. The wings, which were built in three main sections, had sharply tapered leading and trailing edges and incorporated Lockheed-Fowler-type split trailing-edge flaps in four sections, between the ailerons and booms and inboard of the nacelles. The wingtips were

Swinging the compass of a P-322-B at Burbank. Seen to advantage are the intake fairings below the engine nacelles, which were different from those of the YP-38s. P. Jarrett

detachable. Each fuselage boom was a 37ft 10in (11.53m) long all-metal structure with stressed-skin covering and incorporating the fins, the rudders and the fabric covered elevator. A sheet-metal covering was soon adopted for the control surfaces, though the elevator and rudder trim tabs were made of metal from the start.

Cooling

Lockheed made every effort to keep the XP-38's airframe surface ultra-smooth and as uncluttered as possible by drag-inducing air intakes. The supercharged Allisons required no conventional ejector exhausts, only small bullet-shaped intakes on each side of the cowlings being necessary. A further intake rammed air into the carburettors on top of each boom, and to prevent the engine oil from overheating the XP-38 had retractable cooling scoops below each engine nacelle. Small radiator air scoops were fitted into the sides of the tail booms, there being a separate, retractable port for the exhausts on the top of each boom. When all the air scoops were 'closed' the airframe was indeed remarkably smooth, but, as subsequent events showed, Lockheed had perhaps been too conservative in this respect.

Each unit of the tricycle undercarriage retracted rearwards into its respective bay in the central nacelle and each fuselage boom, the main legs being of the single oleo-pneumatic, shock-absorbing type. The nosewheel was self-centreing, and there were brakes on the main wheels. The Curtiss metal three-bladed propellers were of the constant-speed, fully-feathering type, with opposite rotation to counter torque. Lockheed figures put the empty weight of the XP-38 at 11,507lb (5,220kg), and maximum loaded weight at 15,416lb (6,993kg).

The Model 22 prototype differed in several respects to subsequent examples, particularly in the cockpit area. The first canopy included a frameless, rounded windscreen attached to a humped centre section. In production P-38s a flat bulletproof windscreen with additional bracing was fitted, and a wind-down window section was provided on each side of the pilot's seat to aid entry to the cockpit. Each side window had distinctive cross-bracing.

Inside, the cockpit was dominated by a large half-wheel device that the pilot used to control the aircraft. This somewhat

cumbersome design, which reflected the 'muscle power' required to haul the P-38 around the sky, was later replaced.

Entry to the aircraft entailed the pilot clambering up via a pull-down fuselage 'stirrup' and dropping sideways and down into the seat over the rolled-down side window. Some attempts to enter the cockpit by this 'direct' route ended in an embarrassing tumble back on to the tarmac, especially if the would-be pilot was encumbered with a parachute. Pilots soon learned to throw their 'chute up on to the wing root first, but the Lightning remained a difficult aircraft to get into. Soon after production began, a retractable three-step

ladder was provided in the rear of the central nacelle. The pilot could thus gain access by stepping across the trailing-edge wing root. However, it was still, as one pilot put it: 'One hell of a way to get into an airplane'.

Climbing into the machine was one thing, but the problem that preoccupied a great many would-be pilots was how to get out of it in a hurry. The top section of the canopy hinged open sideways in early aircraft, but even with the later rear-hinged roof section the Lightning was not the easiest aircraft to exit in an emergency. The recommended procedure was to roll the aircraft on to its back to enable the pilot to drop out of the top of the canopy, but under

certain flight conditions that would have proved difficult, if not impossible. Pilots were also well aware that baling out of an aircraft of the P-38's configuration carried the inherent risk of striking the tailplane.

Extremely snug cowlings enclosed each 960hp (716kW) Allison V-1710 engine (a 1710-11 and a 1710-15 were initially fitted). The external lines tended to belie the hidden power of each V12; in fact, the highly polished XP-38 resembled a racing aircraft rather than a warplane. The USAAC national insignia was applied, including the underwing wording 'U.S. Army', and the then-current red-and-white stripes adorned the rudders.

One of the first batch of 'castrated' Lightnings after completion. British serials were generally retained as call signs for the P-322s used as trainers in the USA. P. Jarrett

At the roll-out ceremony the 'hand-built' XP-38 looked extremely sleek, dramatically futuristic and huge for a fighter, dwarfing every other 'pursuit' type then in inventory. Its dimensions were closer to those of a contemporary twin-engine attack bomber, as it was only about 13ft (4m) less than a Hudson in span, and some 6ft (1.8m) shorter.

Having announced its new baby to the world, Lockheed disassembled 37-457 and loaded it on to three trucks. Shrouded by canvas covers, the aircraft was driven to March Field, where it arrived in the early hours of New Year's Day, 1939. By 9 January it was reassembled and ready for its first flight, and Ben Kelsey prepared for an historic take-off.

The differences between the P-322-B and production P-38s can be fully appreciated in this view of AE979. The main changes were in the engine cowlings and exhausts, the P-322s lacking superchargers. Lockheed

Maiden Flight

Weather and brake problems delayed the first flight of the XP-38 until 27 January. Kelsey actually lost braking power on one test and ran the aircraft into a ditch, but thereafter all went smoothly. Kelsey taxied out and took off for the maiden flight. Almost immediately he sensed trouble. Both sets of flaps began to vibrate during the climb-out; all but one of four aluminium support rods had failed. This allowed the flaps to extend out to their stops and flail up and down, trying to tear themselves loose in the slipstream. Kelsey considered abandoning the aircraft, but immediately reconsidered. After all, this was the

project on which he had worked ceaselessly for some thirty months. Also, the XP-38 was brim-full of fuel, worrying for the pilot if any fire developed, but lethal to anyone on the ground if the pilotless aircraft could not be directed away from any residential area into which it might crash. Kelsey brought the XP-38 sufficiently under control to slow it right down for a landing. Worried that the brakes might fail, he adopted a steep, 18-degree angle of attack and eased the aircraft in with the control wheel pulled right back. As it touched, the XP banged its fin bumpers in a shower of sparks, but held its ground run in a straight line. Once the aircraft had stopped, Kelsey climbed down and inspected the damage,

which was easily repairable. He had not retracted the undercarriage during the 34min flight, and none of the planned objectives had been realized.

On 5 February Kelsey took the XP-38 up for a second time. A hand pump for the brakes had been installed, plus new Rusco brake linings. The flight lasted 36min and was far more positive than the first, although the increased brake pressure could still not completely cope with the thrust of the Allisons. Flight three also revealed some longitudinal instability. Kelly Johnson attributed this to insufficient area of the tailplane, which hardly extended outboard of the vertical surfaces. This was soon rectified, and all subsequent aircraft had 7sq ft (0.65sq m) greater area in the form of stub tailplanes outboard of each fin.

Despite the teething troubles Kelsey was clearly delighted with the XP-38 and later said in a letter to Wright Field, which had requested performance figures: 'It goes like hell and flies swell'. It was just what everyone at Lockheed believed.

Having taken the aircraft up several more times, Kelsey gradually overcame the bugs that arise with nearly all prototypes. Early flights were conducted with a very clean airframe virtually devoid of paint, but about this time black anti-glare panels were painted on the nose and the inside face of each nacelle directly in the pilot's line of sight.

After 5hr flying at March Field the XP-38 was ready for a move to Ohio for its USAAC tests. Kelsey took off at 06.12hr on 11 February and headed east. He landed to refuel at Amarillo in Texas, which took 23min. It was 03.07hr Eastern Standard Time before Kelsey touched down at Wright Field, having flown at an average true air speed of 360mph (579km/h).

The possibility of flying on to Mitchel Field, New York, had previously been put forward, and in discussion with Gen Henry

H. 'Hap' Arnold this was decided upon. The Air Corps chief thought that a complete transcontinental dash by the XP-38 would make some great headlines and show the world that the US aviation industry had successfully weathered years of isolationist neglect. Millionaire Howard Hughes had set the previous record in January 1937 with a coast-to-coast' time of 7hr 28min. Arnold felt there was no better way than beating Hughes's record to demonstrate that the USA could design and build world-class fighters and, more importantly, to convince Congress to increase funding for the USAAC. There was reportedly some reluctance by Lockheed to let a valuable prototype loose on what amounted to a publicity stunt, but 'Hap' was the boss. As for the stir it would undoubtedly create, looks alone would have sold the XP-38 to the most die-hard critic of pursuit aviation.

Prestige Flight

Ben Kelsey took off from Wright Field and set course for New York. He made his landing approach 11hr 2min after leaving Burbank. Unfortunately the final phase of the

flight did not go according to plan. As he waited in the landing pattern the XP-38's engines had to be throttled back. Cleared to land, Kelsey shoved the throttles forward, but there was no response from the Allisons. Try as he might, he could not gain enough power or speed to clear trees in his path. He touched the trees at around 100mph (160km/h) and the aircraft dropped on to its belly, wheels up, sliding along on golf-course turf rather than the runway that was a mere 2,000ft (610m) away. Kelsey had to sit and wait until the prototype Lightning lost momentum and finally ground to a halt. The aircraft was wrecked in the forced landing, though Kelsey was able to climb out unhurt.

The loss of a valuable prototype greatly annoyed the Lockheed engineers, who had been apprehensive about the record flight from the outset, and they could hardly keep the event out of the press although they tried to steer reporters away. At the crash scene the news hounds were implored not to publicize the demise of the XP-38, but to no avail. The accident made headline news.

Despite this setback, Kelsey's flying time was impressive. It was poorly timed officially, but worked out at 6hr 58min with two en-route stops. Hughes had flown non-stop in a specially prepared 'flying fuel tank' so the XP-38 had performed admirably. The above figures were Kelsey's own; the USAAC set the flying time at 7hr 2min, but even so the record had been beaten by the prototype of what was to be a standard Service aeroplane. The investigation into Kelsey's crash determined that the engine failure had resulted from idling back on the throttles and consequent carburettor icing.

It seemed, however, that Lockheed would now face an enormous setback, but the crash indirectly brought the company some unexpected compensation. In April 1939 an Army order was placed for thirteen YP-38 evaluation aircraft (39-689 to 39-701) and one structural test airframe, valued at $2,180,725. It was believed that, had the prototype not been destroyed in such a spectacular fashion, the initial order would have been delayed until a full flight evaluation had been completed. So the fact that, for a time, Lockheed had no aircraft to show for its efforts, was not the disaster it may at first have seemed. One drawback was that, although Burbank later tooled-up to complete P-38 contracts as fast as possible, the YPs had to be practically hand-assembled.

Specification – XP-38 (Lockheed Model 22)	
Powerplant:	One Allison V-1710-11 (port) and one V-1710-15 (starboard) providing 1,150hp (860kW) each for take-off and 1,000hp (746kW) at 20,000ft (6,000m).
Weights:	Empty 11,507lb (5,220kg); gross 13,500lb (6,120kg); maximum 15,416lb (6,993kg).
Dimensions:	Span 52ft 0in (15.85m); length 37ft 10in (11.53m); height 9ft 6in (2.90m); wing area 327.5sq ft (30.4sq m).
Performance:	Maximum speed 413mph (655km/h) at 20,000ft (6,000m); cruising speed 350mph (563km/h) at 16,000ft (4,880m); time to 20,000ft (6,000m) 6.5min; service ceiling 38,000ft (11,580m).
Armament:	None.

Parked on the Boscombe Down grass, P-322-B (AF106) awaits either another test flight or ferrying to an Eighth Air Force depot. The ultimate fates of the three RAF test Lightnings are unknown. Author

Tooling for mass production as such did not exist. And although the YPs undoubtedly benefited from the data Lockheed had accumulated from the XP-38 test flights, this was incomplete and there were several unanswered questions.

Even though the Army order was encouraging, the crash of the prototype meant a concurrent loss of development time with actual hardware. Burbank was inevitably short of full data on the performance of the new fighter, and this, according to some reports, put the whole project back by some eighteen months to two years. To add to the company's problems, the YP-38 proved demanding to manufacture, and the first example of the pre-production batch did not fly until Marshall Headle took it up on 17 September 1940. It was to be June 1941 before the thirteenth aircraft was delivered to the Army. By September 1939 the Army had increased its order by sixty-six aircraft, covering the P-38, XP-38A and P-38D.

However, building the YP-38s gave Lockheed valuable experience; several improvements were made, despite the aircraft looking externally similar to the prototype. These changes included adding mass balances above and below the elevator to counter the effects of flutter. Some tail buffeting had occurred during test flights, and although the balances provided some reassurance they apparently did not cure the problem completely. Kelsey always maintained that they were superfluous, anyway. The tail buffeting was later eradicated by fitting larger wing-root fillets. (It was argued by Kelsey and others, however, that tail buffeting was never really a problem with the P-38.)

The P-38 order book increased again in August 1940, the Army requiring 410 P-38E and -F fighters and F-4, F-4A, F-5 and F-5A PR derivatives. That created a rather interesting situation at Burbank, Lockheed

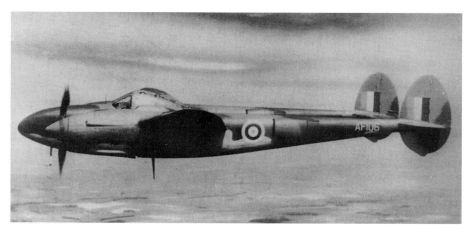

The dark brown, dark green and sky RAF scheme of the early P-322s conformed well to directives regarding camouflage patterns. APN

having a total of 686 fighters to build and deliver when work on the pre-production aircraft had barely started.

Testing Hazards

Test flying has always carried hazards for pilots, and the development of the P-38 was no exception. On 4 November 1941 Ralph Vinden was killed in a crash following high-speed-dive tests in a YP-38. Compressibility or 'shock stall' was the suspected cause of the aircraft shedding its tail, though few people understood why the accident had happened, or what could be done to prevent a recurrence.

Modern (1940s) military aircraft such as the P-38 were entering a hitherto unexplored regime of high-speed flight. These machines could easily exceed 550mph (885km/h) in a dive and encounter air pressures that normal aircraft control surfaces could barely overcome. Designers were at the beginning of a learning curve, and only experience would provide some

understanding and, perhaps, a solution. Windtunnel tests could reveal only so much, and were no real substitute for actual flying time.

The plain fact was that the P-38 and its reciprocating-engined contemporaries were the last of their kind. They had to have a brake put on their potentially lethal dive performance before they were battered to destruction and their pilots killed by forces that were barely understood. It would take an entirely new form of propulsion to thrust them safely through these invisible 'barriers' in the atmosphere.

Later it was realized that only turbojets had the punch to take such aircraft through the compressibility and 'sound' barriers. While designs that could do so existed even as the early P-38s were being tested, Lockheed and other manufacturers had to supply conventional piston-engined aeroplanes for a war that demanded ever-greater performance, preferably without killing Service pilots en masse. Kelly Johnson and his counterparts faced an almost impossible compromise at the most significant technical crossroads in aviation history.

Lockheed only partly overcame the compressibility problem with a gradual understanding of the forces at work on a fast-diving aircraft and the introduction of temporary remedies that protected it under extreme conditions. The quickest way was to impose severe performance restrictions on the aircraft, particularly with regard to high-speed dives at steep angles. It was not the ideal way to introduce a warplane into the demanding combat arena of the Second World War, but how easy is it to overcome the unknown?

Specification – YP-38 (Lockheed Model 122)	
Powerplant:	One Allison V-1710-27 (port) and one V-1710-29 (starboard) providing 1,150hp (860kW) each for take-off.
Weights:	Empty 11,171lb (5,067kg); gross 13,500lb (6,120kg); maximum 14,348lb (6,508kg).
Dimensions:	Span 52ft 0in (15.85m); length 37ft 10in (11.53m); height 9ft 10in (3.00m); wing area 327.5sq ft (30.4sq m).
Performance:	Maximum speed 405mph (652km/h) at 20,000ft (6,000m); cruising speed 350mph (563km/h); time to climb to 20,000ft (6,000m) 6min; service ceiling 38,000ft (11,580m); range (normal) 650 miles (1,050km); range (maximum) 1,050 miles (1,850km).
Armament:	One 37mm cannon, two 0.50in machine-guns, two 0.30in machine-guns.

Compressibility

When the Army Air Forces demanded ever-higher performance from a new breed of aircraft in the early 1940s, aviation engineers were cast on to the horns of a dilemma. The better they did their jobs, the more trouble they got into, for every extra mile of speed and every thousand feet of altitude revealed new frontiers of unknown and unconquered elements of the universe. They ran into laws of physics that no aircraft had then touched, as no pre-war type was able to fly high enough or fast enough to encounter them.

A prime example was compressibility, the strange behaviour of air when it is moving at somewhere near the speed of sound. This does not mean that the aircraft itself must be going at 700mph (1,125km/h), for compressibility can occur at much lower speeds. When the air forced upwards by a wing meets the air forced aside by the fuselage, these two converging air masses are compressed as though they were passing through a nozzle. The only way that the air can get around this 400mph (640km/h) bottleneck is by accelerating to 700mph (1,125km/h), thus creating compressibility at the fillet which joins the wing to the fuselage.

At that point the engineer was in trouble, as Lockheed found with the P-38, because he had first to diagnose the problem, which no one had encountered before, and then fix it. He encounters new laws of aerodynamics. One of them is that air, at slow speeds, acts like water, which is non-compressible, but at ultra-high speeds it behaves like air. There is a region between these two extremes in which the air burbles from one behaviour to another or is utterly 'lawless', and this is the compressibility range. While it is burbling past the wing/fuselage fillet the force it exerts on the fillet may change from pressure to suction, and back to pressure again, hundreds of times per second. Unless the fillet is sturdily built it will tear away in that 700mph reversible gale. Build it sufficiently heavy to remove all doubt and the aircraft will not fly fast enough to encounter the phenomenon, or win the war, but if the fillet problem is solved the aircraft may gain enough extra speed to run into compressibility somewhere else.

SOURCE: Frank J. Taylor and Lawton Wright, *Democracy's Air Arsenal*, 1947.

During their Service test period the YP-38s received fin numbers in the style seen here on the first aircraft so identified. P. Jarrett

Guns

The YP-38 airframe was lightened compared with that of the XP-38 by 1,500lb (680kg) as per the USAAC requirement, and mated to more powerful Allison 1710-27 and -29 engines of 1,150hp (860kW) each. Alterations were made to the cowlings, and on the underside the characteristic 'step' where the two kidney-shaped air intakes were located was retained on all subsequent models up to the P-38H. The YPs also had their handed propellers rotating outwards instead of inwards, as in the XP-38. Although not all of the YPs were fitted with guns, they were the first to have the nose section cut to take the barrels of two 0.50in and two 0.30in machine-guns and a single Oldsmobile 37mm cannon. Developed by Madsen of Denmark, the cannon was licence-built by the US company more usually associated with automobile manufacture.

The ammunition quota for the YP-38's machine-guns and cannon was a variable 200, 500 and 15 rounds respectively, stored in 'vertical' magazines accessed by two hinged doors that fully exposed the feed mechanism and working parts of the weapons.

The 37mm gun did not last long as a primary P-38 weapon, mainly because the calibre of ammunition was to a non-US standard size. Widely believed by United States Army Air Corps (USAAC) planners to be useful for a number of aircraft installations, the big cannon had also been earmarked for the Bell P-39 Airacobra and experimental versions of the Douglas XA-26 Invader. In the event it proved more practical to substitute a lighter and smaller 20mm weapon in the YP-38. The 37mm cannon was relegated to 'experimental' status and was only fitted (and actually used in combat) in one front-line US aircraft, the Bell P-39 Airacobra.

Assembly-line construction took various forms depending on the manufacturer, the size of aircraft and available space in the plant. In the case of P-38 fighters (referred to as 'armament ships' in technical manuals, to distinguish them from PR conversions) Lockheed eventually opted to build them in seven major subassemblies:

wing, tailplane, fuselage and centre-section, forward booms and aft booms, undercarriage and powerplant. Alternative nose sections, primarily those intended for the reconnaissance role, became an eighth factory sub-section.

At the start of P-38 assembly the Burbank plant employed a conventional rolling line with each near-complete aircraft being moved out of the covered area on its wheels. A three-track line was introduced as the production tempo increased and more people were hired to work shifts, enabling P-38s to be built round the clock. Lockheed was fortunate in that the Californian climate allowed much of the final fitting-out to take place in the open air without fear of corrosion through excessive rainfall, for example. During production of the P-38F a conveyor system was installed at Burbank whereby a 'crawler' cradle carried each suspended Lightning along to permit easy access to the aircraft's underside. This proved to be a convenient way of completing the final fitting-out of each aircraft.

Foreign Orders

As was common before the war, foreign governments, most notably those of France and Britain, went shopping abroad for aircraft. With its own aviation industry undergoing an upheaval in a semi-nationalized state, France appeared to be in a dangerous position should Hitler's Germany declare war before current production orders at home had been fulfilled. Modern war materiel was badly needed to increase the strength of the French armed forces, and numerous aircraft types were ordered from American companies, among them the P-38, which had been of interest to the *Comité du Matériel* and the *État Major* since the spring of 1938. French purchasing of US aircraft had begun earlier, on 26 January that year, with 115 Martin Maryland medium bombers. By the end of the year the order book had swelled to over 2,000 aircraft.

The French missions unwittingly annoyed the Americans, who faced a dilemma. On the one hand they were very pleased to except foreign funding to boost their industry, but on the other they wanted to ensure that the USAAC had 'first refusal' on new projects such as the XP-38. The country was also neutral, and until France was actually at war the ban on foreign sales was publicly adhered to. There were ways to circumvent the ban, provided the French went through the proper channels and kept President Roosevelt fully informed. The president, although mindful of the threat of war in Europe, continued to face a powerful isolationist lobby, and the tricky situation was not helped by the fatal crash of the Douglas DB-7 prototype on 23 January 1939. It was revealed that one of the victims was a French observer who had been on board without anyone's knowledge of the fact. Then, on 1 July, the French aviation journal *L'Air* published a silhouette and full details of the XP-38, which Lockheed and the USAAC felt was premature, at the very least. 'Hap' Arnold remained of the opinion that new aircraft should not be sold overseas until his own force had been re-equipped, and that would take time. No amount of French money could speed up the process of aircraft manufacture, and there was limited capacity to build the hundreds of fighters and bombers on order in the timescale required by France.

However, the French government saw the P-38 as something of a cornerstone of a future *Armée de l'Air* inventory. It was envisaged as an eventual replacement for three types, the Breguet 700, Potez 671 and Sud-Est S.E.100 twin-engine fighters, all of which were then under development. These types were designed to meet the C.2 (two-seat fighter) and CN.2 (two-seat nightfighter) government requirements and none had yet flown.

The *Armée de l'Air* further anticipated operations by P-38s taking place at low to medium levels, one reason why the French did not specify the fitting of the General Electric turbosuperchargers that were a significant feature of the design. There

might ostensibly have been the option of the engines having integral (mechanical) superchargers, as in British practice, though Allison did not produce any such engine during the war. The French version, which had a faired air-intake cover fitted in place of the turbine wheels, was given the suffix 'F' for 'France' and further identified by Lockheed as the Model 322-61-03. The powerplant chosen for the French export version comprised two Allison V-1710-C 15s, rated at 1,090hp (810kW) at 14,000ft (4,250m) and driving unhanded propellers. This combination was 'guaranteed' by Lockheed to provide a top speed of 400mph (645 km/h) at 16,900ft (5,150m). The aircraft were to be fitted with French radio, armament, instrumentation and engine throttle operation, which functioned in the opposite manner to American practice.

War had broken out in Europe in September 1939, but there was a lull in the fighting after Poland capitulated and there appeared to be a breathing space for the combatant powers in Western Europe to take delivery of US equipment.

Busy April

When the French Commission visited Lockheed in April 1940 it was able to see YP-38 production at first hand. Had a complete example been available the ban on foreign pilots flying new and 'secret' US aircraft may not have prevented a French test pilot from flying the YP-38, but members of the Commission were apparently able to gather enough data to confirm that the P-38 could serve their country well. In any event, the Frenchmen clearly liked what they saw and heard. It was unfortunate that none of the visitors, or their American hosts, had any clear idea of the time available for the completion and delivery of aircraft to Europe. All that was certain was that Hitler would make a move and probably strike in the West against France. Had Lockheed been aware of what was to happen the very next month, it would almost certainly not have had any French visitors that April.

Had there been no French order, foreign interest in the P-38 would not necessarily have evaporated. During that same April the British Purchasing Commission (BPC) signed a joint agreement with the French to purchase a combined total of 667 P-38s. The examples intended for Britain were ordered under the designation Model 322-

B (for 'Britain'), alias Model 322-61-04 or simply 322-61 in Lockheed records. The shorter and more convenient designation P-322 was subsequently used.

Time Runs Out

Before Germany attacked France and the Low Countries on 10 May 1940, American factories attempted to meet a backlog of European orders, but the 'Phoney War' was about to end. France was still awaiting many US aircraft when the German onslaught began, and the nation quickly proved unable to counter the enemy's *Blitzkreig* tactics. From America the *Armée de l'Air* had received the Curtiss Hawk 75, Martin 167 Maryland and Douglas DB7 light bomber in time to see combat in 1940, but these, plus some excellent indigenous warplanes, proved inadequate to the task.

A scant nine months since the war's beginning had proved far too short a time for US industry to gear up for mass production on the scale required. Lockheed's promising new fighter became an incidental casualty of the Battle of France, as no Model 322-Fs had been built, let alone shipped, before France was obliged to agree an armistice with Germany on 22 June 1940. Lockheed and other companies had gained from foreign orders, as these early cash sales funded the beginnings of the 'arsenal of democracy' that became so vital to Allied victory.

British Interest

The armistice left the Model 322-F without a replacement customer, but French enthusiasm for the aircraft had led the BPC to arrange for flight tests (the details of these do not appear to have survived) and for reports on the YP-38 to be made available. With the war on the Continent going alarmingly against the Allies, Britain further agreed, on 5 June 1940, to purchase all 667 export models ordered jointly with the French. This eleventh-hour transfer of all French and Anglo-French orders to Britain was completed by payment of a symbolic $1.

As Lockheed 322-61s, these 'castrated Lightnings', as they were disparagingly known at Burbank, were unsupercharged and had both propellers rotating in the same (right-hand) direction. The latter feature came about because Britain and France had desired gearing commonality with the Allison engine fitted into the

Curtiss H.81A Tomahawk, which both countries had ordered, but Lockheed thought this a poor arrangement. One can appreciate the scepticism. The company had designed a potentially good high-altitude fighter that was gradually being compromised for a completely different role. Nevertheless, the early 'export' examples intended for Britain became known by the designation Lightning Mk I, and were completed at Burbank as specified.

Although estimates had suggested that the Model 322-61 would have performed well enough without superchargers below 20,000ft (6,000m), as subsequently proved to be the case, actual tests apparently refuted the fact. Poor higher-altitude performance figures were not lost on Britain's representatives, who noted that the Model 322-61 was said to be particularly disappointing when fitted with the specified Allison C15 engine.

Had the perceived technical difficulties been overcome, the RAF would almost certainly have at least attempted to fit the Lightning into its order of battle, although it is difficult to envisage quite how, given the situation Britain faced in 1940. While awaiting the turn of events and the building of a Fighter Command ground-attack force in late 1940–41, there might well have been room for a second fast, well-armed twin-engine fighter as a companion to the Westland Whirlwind, but it was not to be the Lockheed Lightning. Had the RAF taken delivery, the first 143 Model 322 Lightning Mk Is would have been followed by 524 Lightning Mk IIs, fitted with superchargers and counter-rotating propellers.

Although the lack of turbocharging has been cited as one of the reasons for non-acceptance of the P-38 by Britain, they were not specified by France. A story also went round at the time that the Americans were reluctant to share their turbocharger technology with a foreign power, or could not produce enough of them to fit foreign aircraft, but this has no basis in fact either. More realistic was the possibility that General Electric would have been hard-put to supply enough turbochargers to equip all the Lightning Mk Is and American P-38s.

Too Hot?

British test pilots had apparently commented somewhat negatively on American flight-test reports (presumably for both the XP-38 and YP-38) and decided that the P-38 exhibited unacceptable 'high-altitude/high-speed characteristics', which seems a contradiction in terms for an interceptor fighter. Had their comments referred to high-altitude flying without the benefit of superchargers, it might have been understandable, although other drawbacks cannot be ruled out. The Lightning was potentially very fast for its day, to the point where some doubts were raised as to whether the pilot could control it under all flight conditions. This also strikes a somewhat discordant note, as the aircraft was 'red-lined' at a modest 300mph (480km/h). The reported comment may have reflected Lockheed's apprehension over the effects of compressibility, which, as was later confirmed, could prevent a propeller-driven fighter from safely exceeding 500mph (800km/h) in a dive without airframe modification or some form of aerodynamic braking.

Doubts were also voiced as to how a tricycle-undercarriage aircraft would take to operating from the traditional British grass runways, but this may have been a thinly-veiled excuse to mask the conclusion that nobody in the BPC really seemed to like the Lockheed Lightning.

Added to this general reluctance were some contractural difficulties with Lockheed, which led to Britain finally cancelling the entire Model 322 order. Here one can sympathize with the customer's reluctance, as before the passing of the Lend-Lease Bill of 1941 Britain would have had to pay millions of pounds in hard currency for a substantial number of French-derived P-38s it had not actually ordered, and in a configuration it did not really want.

The USAAC emerged the clear winner from the European P-38 episode. It gained plenty of new fighters that became useful low-altitude trainers, aircraft that would have been time-consuming and costly to adapt to US front-line standards. In addition, the P-38 acquired its enduring name. It was originally to be called the Atlanta, but Lockheed opted for the British-favoured Lightning, a more appropriate choice.

Three to Britain

When Lockheed had completed the first few Model 322-Bs, British test pilots had a chance to examine the aircraft. The date of this encounter has gone unrecorded, but it appears that the company initiated production of the foreign-order aircraft at much the same time as the YP-38s were being built for the USAAC, one reason why American fighter squadrons did not receive more than a few dozen examples before the end of 1941.

The Model 322-B's tricycle undercarriage and cockpit design were praised by British pilots, particularly the engine controls, which were colour-coded in green and red for easy readability. This may have been a precaution stemming from some perceived confusion with French control layout and operation.

The balance of the initial batch of 143 Lightning Mk Is intended for Britain (22 aircraft serialled AE978–AE999, and 121 identified as AF100–AF220) were completed at Burbank with the originally French-specified Allison V-1710- C15 engines.

When the British order was cancelled, these aircraft were absorbed by the USAAC/USAAF under the designation Lockheed RP-322 (R for Restricted). The 524 Lightning Mk IIs (AF221–AF744) followed suit and were brought up more or less to P-38F standard and powered by turbocharged Allison V-1710-F5Ls and -F5Rs.

In the meantime, three of the original production Lightning Mk Is, AF105, AF106 and AF108, were shipped to England by sea, arriving in March 1942. It appears that the Royal Aircraft Establishment (RAE) at Farnborough was the earliest recipient, carrying out unspecified trials with AF108. This aircraft was passed to the USAAF in Britain on 2 December 1942. Cunliffe-Owen took delivery of AF105 and similarly passed it to the USAAF on 1 July 1943.

On 30 April 1942 AF106 arrived at the Aeroplane and Armament Experimental Establishment (A&AEE) at Boscombe Down, Wiltshire, for brief handling trials. The aircraft was unarmed and carried a speed restriction of 300mph (480km/h). Flight trials were brief, as the RAF had little further interest in the type, but pilot reports were generally positive, stating that handling was pleasant, though elevator movement was described as heavy. The aircraft stalled at 78mph (125km/h) with flaps and undercarriage down, the approach to the stall being described as straightforward. Single-engine flight down to a speed of 115mph (185km/h) was also recorded as comfortable. With the trials completed, AF106 was also transferred to the USAAF, on 10 July 1943. Further use (if any) of this trio of hybrid Lightnings in the UK appears to have gone unrecorded.

Most, if not all, of the P-322s had been given green/brown/sky camouflage at the factory and had RAF roundels and serial numbers applied, the latter marking being retained for some time, even after the US national insignia was substituted. These aircraft were almost unique in the US inventory in having no USAAF serial number identification, although other types, such as Airacobras and P-40s, carried this indicator of their 'foreign order' origins. British serials were retained on the P-322s and used as radio call signs. This further stamped them as being a bit different, and when they were later repainted during their service as trainers the serials continued to be used, though there is some evidence that a numerical system was later introduced, in line with standard USAAF practice.

Out to grass in 1945–46, an appropriately numbered early P-38 awaits its inevitable fate at the hands of the scrap dealers. On the right is P-38F (no suffix) 41-7524. WTL via R.L. Ward

Worthy Trainer

By all accounts the castrated Lightning, far from being a widely-reported dud, was a 'hot ship' that proved very valuable in the low-level-training role, a role that USAAF fighters increasingly adopted as the nature of the tactical war changed in the various overseas theatres. Joining some of the many units attached to the USA-based 1st, 2nd, 3rd and 4th Air Forces the RP-322s ended up in locations as wide apart as San Bernardino, California, Syracuse, New York, and Williams Field in Arizona (see Appendix 4). The early 'RAF' Lightnings served mainly with advanced flying training squadrons, an assignment that some individuals, particularly instructors, would have viewed as tougher than combat on occasion.

Pilots found the RP-322 significantly lighter compared with other P-38s and considerably easier to handle. It was an unusual situation, wherein cadet Service pilots were given the chance to fly a fighter unhampered by weighty GFE (Government Furnished Equipment) that was the norm when they reached a combat unit. The RP-322s displayed the fine handling characteristics usually experienced and enjoyed only by test pilots. Their lighter weight was partly due to the reduced armament of two 0.30in and two 0.50in machine-guns, no cannon being fitted, reportedly.

At Williams Field student pilots generally flew the North American AT-6 and twin-engine Curtiss AT-9 Jeep before transitioning to the RP-322 to complete the course as fighter or PR pilots. The training curriculum changed in line with the requirements of front-line units, and by late 1943/early 1944 the Arizona base was the USA's only remaining P-38 flight school.

When their part in the supply of combat pilots had been completed, some of the Stateside training units closed down in 1944, and most of the Lockheed twins were stricken from USAAF charge ('surveyed' in American nomenclature). In most instances this meant a short delay in a journey to the smelters, and although numerous 'Limey Lightnings' did survive to the end of hostilities in 1945, they too were unceremoniously scrapped.

Significant Dates, Early P-38s	
AC Type Specification X-608 issued	19 Feb 1937
First flight (XP-38)	27 Jan 1939
Coast-to-coast dash (XP-38)	11 Feb 1939*
First USAAC YP-38 order (13 a/c)	27 April 1939
Model 22 details published in France	1 July 1939
First USAAC order (66 a/c)	20 Sept 1939
French order for Model 322-F	April 1940
German invasion of France	10 May 1940
British 'to purchase' Model 322-B	5 June 1940
France signs armistice	22 June 1940
Follow-on USAAC order (410 a/c)	30 August 1940
First flight of YP-38	17 Sept 1940
First YP-38 delivered to USAAF	March 1941
Total P-38s in US service (4)	31 March 1941
BPC views P-38E at Wright Field	8 April 1941
Last YP-38 delivery	June 1941
YP-38 lost in dive test	4 Nov 1941**
RAE tests (of AF107)	Dec 1941 – March 1942
A&AEE tests of AF106 (from)	30 April 1942

* Prototype destroyed
** Test pilot Ralph Vinden killed

CHAPTER TWO

Angels in Overalls

The heading for this chapter was a slogan used during the Second World War to emphasize the P-38's 'maid-of-all-work' ability to undertake various roles painted in the drab USAAF camouflage universally adopted for combat aircraft in 1940. These roles increased when Lightning production got into its stride after a slow start, boosted by the first overseas order. At a time when military aviation was making rapid advances in both passive and offensive capability, all US companies put in a lot of work to stay competitive. Lockheed attempted to broaden the base of the Lightning by exploring various alternatives to the

basic fighter/fighter-bomber role, but most of these would be overtaken by events. The aircraft was to see service only as a land-based fighter and the USAAF's principal PR aircraft for the duration of the war.

Test-Pilot Team

Lockheed needed a small army of production test pilots to fly every P-38 that came off the line before delivery to the customer. Among the intrepid souls who undertook this work were Avery Black, Charlie Brennen, Tom Kennedy, Jimmy Mattern,

Herman R. 'Fish' Salmon and Nick Nicholson, Lockheed production test pilot. Milo Burcham remained chief production test pilot for Lockheed throughout the P-38 programme, and Ben Kelsey stayed at Burbank until he entered the Service and went to England. Also hired on a temporary secondment were USAAC pilots, most of whom were drawn from the initial Service unit, the 1st Pursuit Group. Major Signa Gilkey of the USAAF also undertook numerous early test flights.

Further from home for much of the war were the company's field representatives, who advised on any technical changes

The business end of a P-38 in England, showing to advantage the grouping of the gun barrels. The central white spot in the panel below the nose cap was the gun-camera port on early aircraft. *Aeroplane*

Sergeant H. L. Southwood feeds ammunition into the magazine of a P-38F-1 at the Goxhill press day on 29 July 1942, while Cpl Warren C. Grider shoulders the belt. IWM

that combat units might have wanted to make to the P-38. The Lockheed 'tech reps' worked, often with their counterparts from engine manufacturer Allison, to ensure that any revisions to configuration were within design limitations and would not endanger pilots or aircraft.

Lockheed's tech rep in England was Tony LeVier, who was a great asset to the company as both an engineer and pilot. LeVier joined Lockheed as a test pilot in 1942, making his first flight in a P-38 on 1 July that year. By combining technical knowledge and flying skill LeVier made an ideal company representative, though this dual ability created a small problem for him. As tech reps were not usually pilots, LeVier occupied a unique position, one he complicated further by gaining first-hand knowledge of Lightning operations. Spending a period with the 55th Fighter Group (FG) in England, he flew on at least ten combat missions. While he was overseas LeVier also developed the habit of saluting everyone of rank to avoid awkward questions about exactly who he was and what he did, as an individual wearing USAAC uniform devoid of any insignia inevitably caused a few raised eyebrows!

Model Numbers

Lockheed allocated six separate model numbers to the P-38 programme, plus one covering the XP-38A. In general, model numbers were changed only when the extent of modification of the basic design was significant enough to warrant it. Thus several similar variants were covered by one model number. The breakdown was: Model 22 (XP-38); Model 122 (YP-38); Model 222 (P-38D to P-38H); Model 422 (P-38J and P-38L). Model 322 covered the French/British contract aircraft, and the 'one-off' XP-38A was the Model 622. A type-by-type breakdown of P-38 variants follows.

XP-38

Startlingly futuristic by 1939 standards, the XP-38 was powered by Allison V-1710-11/-15s enclosed by extremely close, tapering cowlings that terminated in pointed spinners. Below each nacelle was a retractable oil-cooler intake, and the small straight-edged boom intakes for the superchargers were less than half the size of the bulbous units fitted to subsequent models. A separate pipe for the turbo exhaust was situated on the top of each boom, to the rear of the turbine wheels.

YP-38

Compared with the prototype, the thirteen pre-production YPs differed in several respects, though the changes were subtle and virtually indistinguishable. The V-1710-27/-29 engines had B-2 superchargers and spur reduction gear instead of the former epicyclic type, which required the engine thrust line to be raised. Twin elliptical cooling intakes replaced the lip intakes of the XP-38's much slimmer cowlings, the aircraft consequently taking on the familiar shape of most of the early Lightning models. The radiator intakes on each side of the tail booms were also widened and greatly enlarged to incorporate the turbo exhausts. The originally specified armament installation of a quartet of Colt Browning 0.50in machine-guns was changed to two 0.30in (with 500 rounds per gun (rpg)) and two 0.50in machine-guns (210rpg) plus a 37mm cannon with fifteen rounds. The YPs were fitted with armament during a lengthy programme of Service test flying, most of this being undertaken by the Army. The second YP-38, 39-690, went to the National Advisory Committee for Aeronautics (NACA) test site at Langley, Virginia, on 27 November 1941, and remained there until 4 February 1942.

P-322

Wider-spaced teardrop or 'pen-knib' intakes with distinctive fairings were a feature of the foreign-contract P-322s, which were otherwise externally similar to the YPs but were powered by the Allison 'C' series engine. The new cowlings introduced a third re-contouring of the Model 22 in this area. Several internal changes including the French-derived instrumentation and the specified 'reverse' action of some of the

In flight, the YP-38 looked every inch the war winner the Lightning would eventually be, but it took time to get it into service in the required numbers. *Aeroplane*

controls, but very few aircraft would have incorporated these after the need for them expired.

P-38

As was not uncommon with initial production runs of US aircraft, Lockheed built the first batch of P-38s without any suffix apart from the company designator. Thus the next twenty-nine aircraft built (40-744–40-761 and 40-763–40-773) after the YPs were known simply as P-38-LOs. No change in powerplant was made, the Allison V-1710-27/29 installation of the YP-38 being retained.

The one-piece 'clear' windscreen of the YPs gave way to a framed section which curved round at the sides, forward of the roll-down side windows. As part of the additional 'combat equipment' a separate bullet-proof windscreen was added subsequently, this being set inside the screen directly in front of the pilot. The very pointed spinners of the YP-38s were slightly rounded off to make them easier to manufacture.

The armament fitted to the P-38 comprised a 37mm cannon and four 0.50in machine-guns. Armour plate, bullet-proof glass and fluorescent instrument lighting for night flying were also added. Not intended for combat, the P-38s were given an RP (Restricted Pursuit) prefix in 1942.

One interesting experiment with the first P-38, 40-744, concerned an asymmetric cockpit location. With the turbocharger removed there was just enough room to install a cockpit in the port boom. In this unique aircraft the second seat was usually occupied by a flight surgeon, who was able to monitor the occupant of the standard cockpit in the central nacelle. Only one conversion was carried out.

XP-38A

There was no P-38A model as such. However, the nineteenth P-38, 40-762, became the XP-38A, with which Lockheed sought to increase the high-altitude capability of the Lightning by adding a pressure cabin. Powered by Allison V-1710-27 and -29 engines, the aircraft was modified to offset the weight of the pressurization equipment by increasing the length of the tail booms. It was planned to replace the 37mm cannon with a lighter 20mm weapon in this variant, but in the event no armament was fitted. Under the direction of project engineer M. Carl Haddon the project proved

Specification – P-38D (Lockheed Model 222)	
Powerplant:	One Allison V-1710-27 (port) and one V-1710-29 (starboard) providing 1,150hp (860kW) each for take-off.
Weights:	Empty 11,780lb (5,343kg); gross 14,456lb (6,557kg).
Dimensions:	As previous models.
Performance:	Maximum speed 390mph (628km/h); time to climb to 20,000ft (6,000m) 8min; range (normal) 400 miles (640km).
Armament:	One 37mm cannon, two 0.50in machine-guns, two 0.30in machine-guns.

to be a useful exercise, yielding valuable data for the XP-39. Joe Towle undertook manufacturer's trials between May and December 1942, after which the XP-38A was passed to the USAAF. No appreciable advantage was envisaged in fitting a pressure cabin to standard P-38s, however.

P-38B and P-38C

These designations were reserved for two versions proposed by Lockheed in November and October 1939 respectively, but neither was proceeded with. It appears that both variants would have failed to conform to US War Department criteria as combat aircraft, and Lockheed passed on to the D model, which was a step towards that goal.

The introduction of the 'D' designator is understood to have been an attempt by the USAAC to identify several early models of US warplanes such as the P-38D, Consolidated B-24D and Republic P-47D as suitable for combat operations. This would help explain the 'missing' P-38B and -C designations.

P-38D-LO

Striving to offer the P-38 as a true combat-worthy fighter, Lockheed initiated production of the P-38D in August 1941. This variant, differing from previous models only in internal equipment, derived further benefit from combat reports from the war in Europe. A 20mm AN-M1 cannon (Hispano-Suiza pattern, licence built by Bendix) was installed in place of the heavier 37mm gun in the P-38-LO. This change enabled the modest fifteen-round ammunition load of the larger cannon to be increased to a much more practical 150 rounds.

The guns were sighted via a Lynn Instrument Company Model L-3 optical reflector gunsight, and a Type AN-N-6 gunsight-aiming point camera was mounted in the bomb shackle pylon on the port

side. Distinguished by a 'step' in the leading edge to enable access to the film magazine, this modified pylon was later fitted to all subsequent P-38 models. Earlier aircraft had the gun camera mounted in the extreme nose, but the film suffered from vibration when the guns were fired, hence the change in location.

Self-sealing fuel tanks were installed, and a low-pressure oxygen system was fitted, as was a circular landing light that retracted into the underside of the port wing.

The P-38D's engines were Allison V-1710-27/29s with the carburettor air scoops still covered by fairings forward of the turbo wheel on top of each boom. Normal fuel capacity remained at 210US gal (795ltr). Maximum internal fuel capacity was reduced from 410 to 300US gal (1,552 to 1,136ltr). Most of the thirty-six P-38Ds (40-774–40-809) were deployed as combat trainers in the USA under the designation RP-38D.

Lightning production remained frustratingly slow. By 15 August 1941 only thirty-nine aircraft had been delivered to the USAAF despite a gradually expanding workforce at Burbank. In September the Lightning was nevertheless available to participate in the important manoeuvres held by the Army in Louisiana to test current USAAF tactics and equipment.

By the time of Pearl Harbor the USAAF inventory of front-line combat aircraft included sixty-nine P-38Ds, some of which were issued to the 1st and 14th FGs as an expedient measure.

P-38E

With the USA at war, Lockheed further improved production rate to produce the P-38E. In November 1941, shortly before the 'Day of Infamy', the company was able, undoubtedly with some relief, to announce that an E model had become the one-hundredth Lightning off the production line.

It was an important milestone in the development of a fighter that, with subsequent 'war emergency' changes, had inevitably grown in complexity compared with the prototype and the YP-38s. An assembly line usually more associated in the USA with vehicle manufacture had been introduced to build the P-38E, Burbank laying down three moving lines in the factory.

As is usually the case with a mass-produced aircraft, the P-38 airframe was broken down into sub-sections to ease manufacture and assembly. On the factory line the aircraft was built in eight major engineering sections; the wing, tailplane, fuselage and centre section, the two forward booms, the aft booms, the undercarriage

incidence to improve handling qualities. Detail changes included improved instrumentation, revised hydraulic and electrical systems and winterization equipment.

The large upper airscoops atop each boom were eliminated and replaced by two 'bullet'-fairing intakes for supercharger cooling and a third small central intake that took in air for cabin heating. Concurrent with this modification was the fitting of an inboard strake adjacent to each turbine wheel to deflect some of the flying metal away from the cockpit in the event of the turbo disintegrating.

The three-blade Hamilton Standard hollow steel propellers were replaced by Curtiss Electric dural 'solid' types on late

4, 6 and 2in (25, 101, 152 and 50mm). This allowed a more direct feed for the belted ammunition and alleviated the jamming sometimes experienced on earlier models.

Several E models were among the first Lightnings to be made capable of carrying external fuel tanks on Interstate D-820 bomb shackles attached to the main spar, the necessary pylons being fitted under the inboard wing panels and stressed to take overload tanks of up to 300US gal (1,136ltr), which were often fin-stabilized. Normal external tank capacity was 155/165US gal (586/625ltr) Wing pylons were among the most important modifications introduced for the P-38, and the extra fuel brought total fuel tankage up to 410US gal (1,552ltr).

Individual P-38Es were used for a variety of manufacturer's tests, including the 'beard' radiator configuration adopted for the P-38J. The P-38E used for the radiator tests was 41-1983, which also flew with other items of equipment later incorporated into the P-38J and the sole P-38K prototype. One P-38E, 41-1986, was adapted with a raised tailplane in connection with the Sea Lightning floatplane proposal described later.

Another P-38E, 41-2048, was radically modified to gather data on laminar-flow wing sections. The central nacelle was stretched to accommodate a second seat, resulting in the only Lightning to have full dual controls. The wing and fuselage modifications brought about the name 'Swordfish', as also described later.

Although Britain had cancelled its 'main order' for P-38s, its association with the aircraft did not end completely. An example of the then-current production P-38E was made available to the BPC at Wright Field on 8 April 1941. While the results were by then of little more than academic interest, the British view of the P-38 appears to have become more positive. In part, the resulting test report stated that the aircraft exhibited pleasant-enough handling characteristics, and although the elevator appeared heavy, the stall at 78mph (125km/h) with flaps and undercarriage extended was straightforward. Single-engine flying with the installed Allison V-1710-C15s was also stated to be 'comfortable'. Even if the British tests had been even more positive, it is doubtful whether the RAF would ever have flown the P-38 in action, principally because of the difficulties Lockheed would have faced in supplying it in sufficient numbers.

Lockheed P-38F-1 41-7586 was part of a batch built early in 1942 and probably retained for training in the USA, like most of the early Lightnings. MAP

and powerplant. The fuselage section included all the armament, communications equipment, instruments and systems, so that a complete unit could be mated with the rest of the airframe as it was completed. This system also enabled various parts to be subcontracted outside Lockheed, specialist firms supplying components to the main contractor.

The P-38E was the first major production model to reflect the process of 'war emergency' refinement, and 210 were completed. Bendix/Hispano M-1 cannon armament was standardized, and the ammunition for the four 0.50in guns was increased from 200rpg to 500rpg. Cannon ammunition remained as before, at 150 rounds. A major but invisible revision to the P-38E was a change to the tailplane

production P-38Es. Radio communication was by an SCR-274N set.

All models up to and including the P-38E had a right-hand, sideways-opening top canopy section, but this was hinged at the rear on all subsequent models. The pitot head was still mounted under the fuselage nose in the E model, before being moved out below the port wing on the P-38F. The P-38E was also the last model to have the original long nosewheel door that extended forward of the oleo leg in the down position. This door was shortened from the P-38F onwards, to align with the oleo when viewed from the side.

Whereas the machine-gun arrangement had been symmetrical on earlier versions, it was staggered on the P-38E, the muzzles protruding from the nose approximately 1,

The cockpit of the early P-38s changed little, with the half-wheel control dominating. A cannon button is on the right arm, above the dive-limitation warning chart.
Aeroplane

P-38F

Having revised the P-38 as a result of comprehensive tests of early models, Lockheed turned its attention to what was to be the first of the breed to see widespread combat, the P-38F. As the P-38F-LO, the first aircraft, 41-2293, made its maiden flight in March 1942, and deliveries started immediately. Orders totalling 527 aircraft comprised 377 ordered by the USAAF and 150 of the ex-French/British order aircraft brought up to this standard.

All of the P-38Fs were powered by 1,325hp (988kW) Allison V-1710-49/53s and had standard armament, though further detail changes necessitated five different production blocks. There were 128 P-38F-LOs, followed by 149 P-38F-1-LOs, the latter being modified after completion

to carry two 155/165US gal (586/625ltr) drop tanks or two 1,000lb bombs on the wing-centre-section hardpoints. The F-1 was fitted with an N-3 gunsight and, as it became standard practice to update radios, the P-38F-1 was fitted with SCR-535 and SCR-522 sets incorporating identification friend or foe (IFF).

Seeking an answer to the compressibility problem that, at very least, was damaging the reputation of the P-38, NACA's Ames Aeronautical Laboratory at Moffett Field, California, took delivery of P-38F-1 41-7632 on 30 December 1942. Subjecting the aircraft to a thorough series of tests in the laboratory's 16ft (4.9m) windtunnel did not yield a sure remedy, but the figures gained added weight to the practicality of installing dive flaps in later-model Lightnings. Ames' engineers, who had no magic

cure for aeronautical mysteries, confirmed that 'tuck-under' (a strong tendency for a dive to steepen, especially at high Mach numbers, that was a manifestation of compressibility) occurred only when the P-38 was dived at Mach numbers above 0.6. The windtunnel test results further showed that the problem was due to the build-up of shock waves on the wings and fuselage, and Lockheed introduced redesigned wing fillets as a remedy.

The 100 P-38F-5s completed all had provision to carry drop tanks or bombs fitted as standard. The racks could also carry a 'smoke curtain' installation usually consisting of a teardrop-shaped M-10 smoke (or cylindrical M-33 chemical) canister on each wing rack, the nozzles of which were able to lay a dense screen when dispensed from low altitude. Despite this capability, the actual use of smoke tanks was limited.

P-38F-5s also had revised landing lights, desert (tropical) equipment and other changes, including the N-3B gunsight, which was to remain the standard sighting instrument up to the P-38J-5. From this model onwards three identification lights coloured amber, green and red, reading from front to back, were set in a removable inspection panel in the fuselage underside. White navigation lights were set into the outer face of each fin surface and were retained on all models. The twenty-nine P-38F-13s and 121 P-38F-15s were the remaining ex-British-order Lightning Mk IIs (Model 322-60-19s) brought up to 'F standard in terms of equipment, with superchargers and handed propellers.

The P-38F-15 also introduced an 8-degree flap position. This so-called 'manoeuvre setting' for the Lockheed-Fowler flaps was an actuator modification that enabled the flaps to be deployed at indicated air speeds of up to 250mph (400km/h) thereby inducing a significant increase in the machine's ability to turn without stalling. The P-38 was renowned for its gentle turn characteristics, and could be wracked round impressively tightly to maintain the turn at 1,000ft (300m) altitude with as little as 100mph (160km/h) 'on the clock'. The aircraft gave plenty of warning when on the edge of a stall, and rarely, if ever, snapped into a spin.

The opening top section of the cockpit canopy was provided with a rear hinge during the latter end of P-38F production, the wind-down side windows remaining the same as before.

Specification – P-38F (Lockheed Model 222)	
Powerplant:	One Allison V-1710-49 (port) and one V-1710-53 (starboard), providing 1,150hp (860kW) each at 25,000ft (7,600m).
Weights:	Empty 12,264lb (5,563kg); gross 15,900lb (7,210kg).
Dimensions:	As previous models.
Performance:	Maximum speed 395mph (636km/h) at 25,000ft (7,620m); time to climb to 20,000ft (6,000m) 8.8min; range with 300US gal (1,136ltr) 425 miles (684km) at 305mph (490km/h).

P-38G

Engine changes were often signified by a new block number, and Allison V-1710-51/55s were installed in the 708 P-38Gs, though rated horsepower remained the same as before at 1,325hp (988kW) for take-off. Other changes brought about six production blocks: the eighty P-38G-LOs were similar to the P-38F-15 apart from the new engines, improved oxygen equipment and radios; the twelve P-38G-3s were fitted with B-13 turbosuperchargers, and the sixty-eight P-38G-5s had yet more revisions to the instrumentation and radio, the SCR-247N type being fitted on this model.

In an interesting experiment at Orlando, Florida, P-38G-3 42-12791 was used to test the feasibility of towing gliders. The test aircraft was fitted with pick-up gear attached to the tailplane stubs outboard of the fins. This enabled the aircraft to tow a Waco CG-4A, and it was proposed that a single P-38 could haul up to three troop-carrying gliders in 'trains', using a Lockheed yoke-type tow system. Several experimental flights were apparently made before the Lightning was completely wrecked in a crash. The idea was not adopted for operational use.

The largest block of the G series comprised 548 P-38G-10s, which incorporated the improvements of the two earlier sub-variants as well as winterization equipment and provision to carry a greater offensive load. The maximum permissible weight of bombs carried on the wing racks was raised to 1,600lb (725kg), and two attachment points were located on each side of the central nacelle to take a 4.5in M-10 triple-tube rocket launcher. In overload condition the P-38G was stressed to carry an additional two triple-tube rocket launchers under each wing outboard of the nacelles, as well as two on the fuselage and a pair of drop tanks below the centre section. This configuration is not known to have been used in combat, and even the fuselage-mounted M-10 launchers saw only limited action.

The RAF Lightning Mk II allocation made up the balance of the P-38G total, with 174 P-38G-13s (equivalent to the P-38G-3) and 200 P-38G-15s, which were similar to the P-38G-5. Total P-38G production was 1,462 aircraft.

One P-38G-5, 42-12866, served as a test bed for the proposed XP-49's armament of two 20mm cannon and four 0.50in machine-guns. Machine-gun positioning was as for a standard P-38, but the central location of the cannon was revised in favour of two short-barrelled weapons set diagonally. Further stress tests revealed that the stronger wing of the P-38G could accommodate a pair of 250lb bombs on a twin-'shoe' pylon outboard of each engine nacelle. The installation was apparently tested by the 82nd FG in the Mediterranean Theatre of Operations (MTO), but few details of operational use, if any, are known.

This P-38H-5 was part of the final production batch of Lightnings with the original 'sweptback' engine cowling configuration. Completed in mid-1943, the H-5s were the first to have 'bars to the star' with a red outline. *Lockheed*

Specification – P-38G (Lockheed Model 222)

Powerplant:	One Allison V-1710-51 (port) and one V-1710-55 (starboard), each providing 1,150hp (860kW) at 25,000ft (7,600m).
Weights:	Empty 12,000lb (5,530kg); gross 15,800lb (7,170kg).
Dimensions:	As previous models.
Performance:	Maximum speed 400mph (644km/h) at 25,000ft (7,620m); time to climb to 20,000ft (6,000m) 8.5min; range 300 miles (560km) at 310mph (500km/h).

P-38H

The last model of Lightning to retain the original radiator fitting and sharply raked lower engine cowlings, the P-38H was further refined over earlier models. The engines were Allison V-1710-89/91s providing 1,425hp (1,060kW) for take-off. Fitted with B-33 turbochargers and automatic oil-radiator flaps to help solve engine over-heating, these Allisons enabled military power settings above 25,000ft (7,620m) to be increased from 1,150hp to 1,240hp (860kW to 925kW).

There were 226 P-38H-1s, which were otherwise identical to the P-38G-10. Production then switched to a second batch consisting of 375 P-38H-5s. These had few changes apart from B-33 turbochargers instead of the B-13 type as before, and an AN/M2C 20mm cannon replacing the earlier M1.

In performance terms the P-38H had an impressive enough service ceiling of around 40,000ft (12,000m) and, even though the engines of the early machines remained very susceptible to extreme cold, the aircraft set and briefly held an unoffical world altitude record of 44,940ft (13,700m). This flight, which took place on 30 April 1943 with Joe Towle at the controls, was the more remarkable because he had a passenger, Col Ralph Lovelace, chief of the USAAF's aeromedical laboratory at Wright Field, in the piggyback seat.

By the time Lockheed had begun building the P-38H, the civilian airlines had been contracted to act as modification centres to relieve the pressure on the

Production at Burbank gradually picked up during 1941–42, Lockheed completing P-38s at a steadily increasing rate. IWM

Specification – P-38H (Lockheed Model 222)	
Powerplant:	One Allison V-1710-89 (port) and one V-1710-91 (starboard), rated at 1,240hp (925kW) each at 27,000ft (8,200m).
Weights:	Empty 12,380lb (5,616kg); gross 16,300lb (7,390kg).
Dimensions:	As previous models.
Performance:	Maximum speed 402mph (647km/h) at 25,000ft (7,600m); time to climb to 25,000ft (7,620m) 9.7min; range (normal) 300 miles (480km).

manufacturers. With excellent maintenance facilities, the airlines were able to incorporate the latest technical changes, taking new aircraft straight off the line and modifying them before delivery to depots and combat units. Delta Air Lines' plant at Atlanta was one of several centres that worked on P-38s.

P-38J

At about the mid-point of its wartime fighter production programme, Lockheed initiated the first major technical change the shallow engine contours of proceeding models by sandwiching the intercooler air intake between deeper 'chin' oil radiators to create the primary external recognition feature of the P-38J and subsequent models. The engines remained the same V-1710-89 (left) and -91 (right) as fitted in the P-38H.

By removing the turbocharger intercoolers from the wing leading edge, Lockheed was able to offer the pilot much-improved control of supercharger operation and to fit a 62US gal (235ltr) fuel tank into each wing leading edge. Not all P-38Js had the

removal of the manual gun charger-selector previously operated by the pilot, this work now being done on the ground. Many fuzes were replaced by circuit breakers, enabling the pilot to operate the electrical system more efficiently.

Production of the J model ran to five blocks, beginning with ten P-38J-1-LOs assembled in the experimental shops at Burbank under contract W535 AC 21217, which also covered the P-38K-1 and F-5A-1 and -3 models. All of the J-1s and J-5s had the early-style windscreen, the optically flat, bullet-proof redesign not appearing until the J-10.

The P-38J's powerplant was the same V-1710-89/91 as fitted to the H model, with a similar output for take-off, though a more efficient installation brought a further increase in military power, from 1,240 to 1,425hp (925 to 1,060kW) at 27,000ft (8,230m). At that altitude the war emergency power (WEP) rating was raised to 1,600hp (1,190kW).

There were 210 P-38J-5s with provision for two 55US gal (208ltr) tanks in the

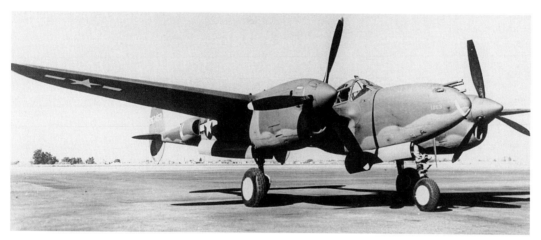

Lockheed P-38J-10 42-67452 represents one of the last steps towards the ultimate Lightning, the P-38L. MAP

to the P-38 in the J-LO model. Much research was carried out into the effects of drag and its reduction, and data obtained in full-scale tests with a YP-38 in the NACA windtunnel at Moffet Field, California, suggested that over half of the airframe drag was caused by the coolant radiators. NACA recommended that the P-38's radiators be built into the wing leading edge, as was done with the de Havilland Mosquito, but Lockheed felt that this major engineering change would cause problems, not the least of which was the risk of upsetting the aircraft's c.g. Having redesigned the air-intake system, the company revised

extra tanks; those that did were marked with a small black cross painted on the fuselage adjacent to the data block to confirm the fact. The characteristic Prestone coolant scoops on each side of both booms were also redesigned and slightly enlarged.

Other minor drawbacks of earlier Lightning models were rectified on the P-38J. One was the fact that ground crews had to remove a large section of armour plate to gain access to the radio equipment behind the pilot's seat. In the P-38J the introduction of Dzus fasteners enabled work in this area to be carried out much more easily. Concurrent improvements included

wing-leading-edge space previously occupied by the intercoolers. This change finally restored the original P-38 internal fuel capacity of 410US gal (1,550ltr).

Other improvements incorporated on the J model included further revision to the cockpit controls and instrumentation. Most noticeable was the replacement of the original half-wheel control yoke by a neater 'spectacle' hand grip incorporating gun firing and ordnance release controls. The P-38J-10 also introduced the Lynn L-3 reflector gunsight, as fitted to all subsequent models as standard, though Lightnings later acquired the K-14 gyroscopic computing

Specification – P-38J (Lockheed Model 422)

Powerplant:	Allison V-1710-89 (port) and V-1710-91 (starboard) providing 1,425hp (1,060kW) each for take-off and 1,600hp (1,200kW) each at 27,000ft (8,250m).
Weights:	Empty 12,780lb (5,797kg); gross 17,500lb (7,940kg).
Dimensions	Height 9ft 10in (3.0m).
Performance:	Maximum speed 414mph (666km/h) at 25,000ft (7,600m); time to climb to 20,000ft (6,000m) 7min; service ceiling 44,000ft (13,400m).

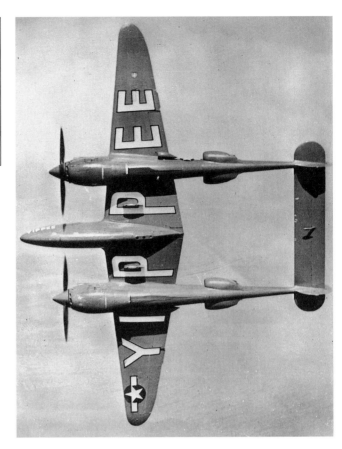

sight, in common with other US fighters. Attached directly to the windscreen glass by three mounting studs, the Lynn sight was set high enough to be directly in the pilot's line of sight, well above the cockpit coaming, which in the P-38J was protected by a section of armour plate.

Production of the early model P-38Js (up to the J-10) took the number of Lightnings built to 1,010, of which 790 were J-10s.

Few further changes were made on the 1,400 P-38J-15s apart from a revised electrical system, these aircraft being otherwise similar to the J-10. The Ames Research Center received J-15 43-28519 on 30 August 1944 and retained it for a lengthy programme of various NACA-sponsored tests lasting until 15 November 1946. NACA took delivery of a second P-38J in October 1944, when the Lewis Research Center conducted a study into icing effects on the aircraft's induction system that continued until July 1945.

There were 350 P-38J-20s, which had some modification of the turbo regulators, and the 210 P-38J-25s were fitted with power-boosted ailerons and electrically-operated dive or 'combat' flaps below the wings, outboard of the engine nacelles. These small double areas of sheet metal bestowed further manoeuvrability, and had the added benefit of staving off the worst effects of compressibility. Deploying the flaps quickly brought the aircraft out of a steep dive by breaking up the airflow pressure or compressibility load on the wing. Operated by a button on the control yoke, the flaps offered a huge improvement in this respect. Pilots had confidence that it was now easier to prevent the Lightning from entering a hitherto unknown but dangerous regime, and dive flaps were fitted to all subsequent production P-38s.

The P-38J-20 44-23296 became the 5,000th Lightning completed, and Lockheed celebrated this by giving it an overall bright red colour scheme and painting the word 'Yippee' in large white letters under

Celebrating Lockheed's increased production rate, P-38J-20 44-23296 became number 5,000 off the line. A suitable red paint scheme and wording gave a clue! Lockheed

the wing, filling almost the full chord. With two more 'Yippees' along each side of the nose, the aircraft was well photographed, usually with Milo Burcham at the controls, and became a useful advertisement for the company.

Late-production P-38J-25s, of which 210 were completed, were externally identical to the following P-38L, as the circular landing light of the former was removed from the underside of the port wing (from aircraft 44-23559) and replaced by a 'square' type set into the leading edge on the same side. This made the final P-38J-25s externally indistinguishable from the P-38L and almost impossible to identify without reference to the serial number and a full list of block-number changes.

P-38K

Another 'one-off' Lightning, the P-38K was a P-38E airframe, 41-1983, used primarily as a test bed for the revised radiator configuration of the P-38J and L. It was powered by the 1,425hp (1,060kW) Allison V-1710-75/77 engines fitted to the J model, with the deeper radiator intakes, and had broad-chord propeller blades.

P-38L

Further refinement of the P-38J led to the outwardly similar P-38L-1, which, along with combat flaps, had statically- and dynamically-balanced differential ailerons with hydraulic boosters to reduce the load on the control stick. As a result the load was approximately one-sixth of what it was previously, thus improving manoeuvrability and greatly reducing pilot fatigue.

The accumulated technical updates made to the P-38L as a result of combat experience produced the most effective Lightning model of the war. Powered by 1,475hp (1,100kW) Allison V-1710-111/ 113 engines with a 1,600hp (1,190kW) WEP at 27,700ft (8,440m) and a military rating of 1,475hp (1,100kW) at 30,000ft (9,145m), the 1,290 P-38L-LOs were otherwise similar to the P-38J-25.

The late-production P-38Js and the P-38L arrived in time to replace numerous older models in all war theatres, a process that was completed quite rapidly, as they were that much more capable than their forebears. Few Lightnings other than Js and Ls remained in front-line USAAF service at the war's end.

An in-flight study of a P-38L-5 of the penultimate production batch. It is no accident that the wing leading edges look exceptionally smooth, as the aluminium-enamel paint had a distinctive matt finish. *Lockheed*

BELOW LEFT: The starboard dive recovery flap of a preserved P-38J. This simple device helped turn the late -J and -L models into outstanding fighters. *Aeroplane*

BELOW: The yoke of the P-38J and L was noticeably different. Gone was the dive-limitation chart, replaced by the dive-flap control on the left arm of the yoke. This is a 'modern' P-38J, though it is true to a wartime aircraft. *Aeroplane*

In common with other models it was possible, by removing the SCR-522 VHF radio set, to fit a jump seat for a second occupant. These two-seaters, or 'piggy-back ships', as they were commonly known to the Americans, were officially designated TP-38Ls.

One P-38L-1, 44-23880, was used as a 'proof-of-concept' vehicle for a 'pathfinder' version. Fitted with an elongated nose to accommodate an H2X-derived (APS-15) ground-mapping radar set, the aircraft also had observation windows and space for a radar operator's seat. Flown on operational trials in England to take night-scope photographs of potential bombing targets, it was the forerunner of twelve conversions carried out on behalf of the US Eighth Air Force in July 1944. The Lightning conversion proved to be less versatile than a similar radar installation in heavy bombers, as the lack of available space meant that the scanner could sweep through only 210 degrees, rather than the full 360 degrees required. The programme was discontinued on 13 February 1945, and there is some doubt as to whether all conversions were delivered to the Eighth AF. At least one, 44-23878, was used by the 107th Tactical Reconnaissance Squadron of the 67th Tactical Reconnaissance Group, US Ninth Air Force.

One example of the last production model of Lightning, the P-38L-1, 44-23601, was fitted with three 0.60in machine-guns with extended barrels. This installation, carried out at Wright Field, was not a success, mainly because the guns proved structurally weak, and during flight testing at Eglin Army Air Base the shell links failed under both positive and negative acceleration.

A further experiment, aimed at producing a specialized ground-strafing version, saw the installation of eight 0.50in machine-guns in the nose of P-38L-1 44-24649, which additionally carried two further Brownings in a pair of pods slung under each wing, outboard of the nacelles. Sixteen guns would have made the Lightning a potent strafer, but this particular idea was not proceeded with. Gun pods were also tested on unarmed P-38s, with a view to providing the F-5 with some teeth, but the idea was not carried over to front-line operations.

In an effort to adapt the P-38L to carry 'zero-length' launchers for high-velocity aircraft rockets (HVARs), Lockheed attached fourteen rounds under each wing of L-1 44-2490. The first installation

A rear view of the triple-tube 'Bazooka'-type 3in-rocket launchers used on the P-38J. The degree of suspension required is noteworthy, and clearly something with less drag was preferable. P. Jarrett

The P-38L was tested with fourteen HVARs on the zero-length launchers that were standard on other fighters, but the necessary wing modifications proved too complex. Lockheed

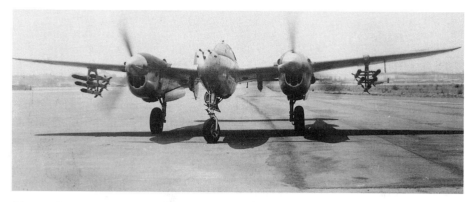

A better solution was the HVAR 'Christmas tree', two of which held ten rocket rounds. The installation proved itself in action. Lockheed

actually comprised two sets of launchers with the aft row angled back towards the flying surfaces, presumably to ensure clearance when the rockets were fired. This arrangement and its associated wiring proved to be quite complex, entailing some structural modification to the wing. Extra space had to be left between the third and fourth set of launchers under the port wing (reading outwards from the nacelle) to allow the missiles to clear the pitot mast, and similar spacing was made on the starboard side for continuity.

The Lightning appears not to have taken too kindly to this weighty burden, as no such HVAR arrangement was fitted to front-line aircraft. Lockheed clearly played it safe, deciding that wing efficiency and performance should not be compromised in combat by such a load. Instead, a 'tree' grouping of five rocket rounds attached to horizontal 'branches' was devised. This arrangement placed five rounds of either the 4in or 5in HVAR well below the wing surface. The aircraft used to prove the rocket-tree installation for service use included P-38L-5 44-25413.

The 'Christmas tree', as nicknamed by pilots, or 'cast rocket cluster' to quote the parts manual, was factory-fitted from P-38L-5 44-26784, and worked well enough, though the end of the war was fast approaching as the kits were being produced and there were few opportunities for the P-38 to use rockets in anger. One unit that did was the 49th FG, which flew enough sorties in the last stages of the Pacific war to impress the pilots with the accuracy of the rockets. Sighted by the standard gunsight, the missiles were found to have an effective range up to 500yd (460m). To save weight when the trees

were fitted, no 20mm ammunition was carried, at least by aircraft of the 49th.

By 1944–45 single-seaters were increasingly performing in the fighter-bomber role, which invariably demanded extra weaponry. In common with many other USAAF fighters, Lightnings were modified in the field using armament kits. In addition to issuing 998 kits of M-10* triple-tube launchers compatible with the P-38J, 1,000 sets of ten-round rocket trees (two trees of five rounds per aircraft comprising one complete kit) were produced for retrofitting to late-production Lightnings, including the P-38M.

P-38L-5

There were 2,250 examples of the P-38L-5, the final production model in terms of 'new build' airframes. Few further changes were made over the previous model, although the location of the fuel pumps was changed. Four booster pumps were fitted as standard below the wing, two located

inboard near the fuselage nacelle and two outboard of the booms.

Pilots flying the P-38L-5 also found that at last the Lightning's notorious lack of adequate cockpit heating and the associated windscreen condensation/misting problem had been overcome by an effective defrosting system. It was widely reckoned that, even in the bone-numbing cold air of the Aleutian Islands, the L-5 was a 'shirt-sleeve' aircraft.

Reservations that some pilots had about the early P-38s lessened significantly when the L model came into service. There had been a degree of fierce loyalty for the twin-engine fighter in several war theatres and, equally, there were those who mistrusted it on several counts. But the above modifications, plus the fact that the leading edge fuel tanks bestowed a maximum range of 1,000 miles (1,600km) or more, helped persuade the sceptics that the P-38L was a fighter to be reckoned with.

Human endurance, rather than technical drawbacks, was often the singular critical factor in extreme-range missions. Understandably, pilots did not take too kindly to sitting in a one-man cockpit for the 8 or 9hr the P-38L was able to stay aloft. Such discomforts had to be endured on occasion, but a comfortable pilot was naturally more alert than one who was suffering from cramp and backache, even if he no longer had reason to complain of being cold.

One of the late-war refinements for USAAF fighters was tail warning radar. An unknown number of P-38Js and Ls received the AN/APS-13 set, the receiver aerials of which were located on the lower vertical tail surfaces on the right side only. This adaptation of the P-38's communications equipment was a complete lightweight radar

Specification – P-38L (Lockheed Model 422)	
Powerplant:	One Allison V-1710-111 (port) and one V-1710-113 (starboard), providing 1,425hp (1,060kW) each for take-off, 1,425hp (1,060kW) at 26,500ft (8,100m), and 1,600hp (1,195kW) WEP at 28,700ft (8,750m).
Weights:	Empty 12,800lb (5,810kg); gross 17,500lb (7,940kg); maximum take-off 21,600lb (9,800kg).
Dimensions:	Span 53ft (15.85m), length 37ft 10in (11.53m); height 9ft 10in (3.00m); wing area 327sq ft (30.4sq m).
Performance:	Maximum speed 414mph (666km/h) at 25,000ft (7,600m); time to 20,000ft (6,100m) 7min; service ceiling 44,000ft (13,400m); range with 3,200lb (1,450kg) of bombs 450 miles (720km); ferry range 2,600 miles (4,180km).
Armament:	One 20mm M2 cannon with 150 rounds, four 0.50in machine-guns with 500 rounds each, ten 5in HVAR, two 1,600lb bombs.

system, though there was no cockpit scope. Instead, the presence and/or approach of enemy aircraft was triggered by the transmitter aerials radiating energy in a given range cone. The receiver aerials converted the signal to illuminate a red warning light adjacent to the gunsight and actuate an audible warning bell.

With the P-38L representing a high point in technical reliability and combat capability, the USAAF confirmed that Lockheed's existing production plant should be supplemented by output from the Consolidated-Vultee factory in Nashville, Tennessee. A contract was awarded in June 1944 for the manufacture of 2,000 P-38L-5-VNs, which were identical to Lockheed-built examples. However, there was some delay in plant start-up, and by August 1945 only 113 aircraft had been completed, the first being 43-50226. Then the end of the war overtook

the plan. The contract was cancelled soon after VJ-Day, 1,887 aircraft short. In addition, Lockheed had 1,380 P-38L-5s cancelled at that time.

P-38M

With the data accumulated from the early single-seat P-38 nightfighter sorties, Lockheed was able to offer the USAAF a custom-built variant of the P-38 that could perform this demanding task more efficiently. To save time the new nightfighter was created by providing the single-seat P-38L with a second seat for a radar operator. This requirement had been one of the most fundamental to emerge from combat experience, as flying a fighter and tracking an enemy aircraft in the dark was a demanding task for a lone pilot. The job was made that much easier if a radar operator was

there to concentrate fully on the electronic equipment and guide the pilot into a favourable attack position. With two-seat P-38s in existence in the form of 'piggyback' conversions, Lockheed had weight and balance data to hand, and relatively few structural modifications were required to create the 'Night Lightning'.

The most urgent requirement was to give the second-seat occupant more headroom and the means to see out. Even if the latter facility was largely psychological in a nightfighter, it was deemed important enough, and by designing a clear Perspex 'bubble' and inserting it into the aft section of the cockpit canopy immediately behind the pilot's seat, Lockheed overcame the main drawback. The radar operator now had a set of instruments and a distinctive domed cockpit cover to provide an excellent view, even if his position was still cramped for a

The dramatically different P-38M was just too late to influence the course of the night war. This aircraft was the eleventh conversion from a P-38L, all of the M series originating in this manner. Lockheed

tall person. Directly in front of his seat were the electronic consoles surmounted by the central scope of the US Navy AN/APS-4 or -6 radar set.

After earlier tests with a wing-mounted radar, the P-38M's radar scanner was housed in a streamlined pod located underneath the extreme nose. This 'suspended' arrangement for the radar used a modified bomb pylon as a carrier 'shoe' and was similar in size and shape to the air-sea-search (ASH) type developed for the US Navy and carried as a wing mounting on the Grumman TBM Avenger and other types. Small enough to be tucked away below the nose, the pod had no undue effect on the P-38's performance and did not compromise the nose gun battery, though the

cannon was removed to save weight. Flash suppressors were fitted to the machine-guns to minimize any disruption of the pilot's night vision. Experiments were conducted with a view to damping the turbocharger exhaust, which became so hot that it glowed in the dark. It therefore seemed pointless to concentrate on shielding the actual efflux, and nothing was done in terms of flame damping on the P-38M.

Even if it was something of a compromise, the P-38M Night Lightning offered several advantages over single-seat nightfighters, and the USAAF contracted Lockheed for eighty P-38L-5 conversions in late October 1944. Not surprisingly the aircraft proved faster than the larger and heavier Northrop P-61A Black Widow,

the Night Lightning having a top speed of 406mph (653km/h) at 15,000ft (4,600m), compared with the Black Widow's 369mph (594km/h) at 20,000ft (6,000m). The P-38M's initial climb rate was 3,075ft/min (935m/min), and it could reach 20,000ft (6,000m) in 8.7min.

After P-38L-5 44-25237 had been converted to nightfighter configuration it was moved to Hammer Field near Fresno, California, for USAAF testing. Retaining its natural-metal finish throughout, it completed six flight trials of the extra equipment before it was lost in a crash. The first 'production' example of the P-38M-6-LO, 42-6831, was flown for the first time on 5 January 1945.

By that time the need for such an aircraft had diminished. With the P-61 Black Widow giving satisfactory service, the USAAF had little need for another nocturnal type, and certainly not one powered by reciprocating engines with the new turbojet age looming. Lockheed nevertheless continued to convert late-production P-38Ls with a view to completing the nightfighter contract, but there is some doubt whether all eighty conversions were delivered. All conversion work on the P-38M was carried out at the Dallas Modification Center.

When the last P-38 had been completed, Lockheed at Burbank and Vultee at Nashville had produced a grand total of 10,036 P-38s for the USAAF and Allied air forces. When the war ended there were eight combat groups still flying P-38s, one in the European Theatre of Operations (ETO), three in the MTO and four in the Pacific. This was a good enough record, considering that several fighters designed before the conflict had been phased out.

A close-up of a P-38M, showing the radar pod tucked neatly below the nose, and the flash suppressors on the guns. P. Jarrett

Specification – P-38M (Lockheed Model 422)

Type:	Two-seat nightfighter.
Powerplant:	One Allison V-1710-111 (port) and one V-1710-113 (starboard), providing 1,475hp (1,100kW) for take-off and 1,600 (1,195kW) WEP at 28,700ft (8,750m).
Weights:	Gross 17,646lb (8,000kg).
Dimensions:	As for P-38L, but height 10ft 10in (11.52m).
Performance:	Maximum speed 391mph (629km/h) at 27,000ft (8,440m); service ceiling 44,000ft (13,410m).
Armament:	Four 0.50in machine-guns, ten 5in HVAR.
Radar:	AN/APS-4.

P-38 Production Timescale

P-38D deliveries from	August 1941
P-38E deliveries from	October1941
P-322 delivery from (AE478)	February 1942
P-38F deliveries from	March 1942
P-38G deliveries from	September 1942
P-38H deliveries from	April 1943
P-38J deliveries from	August 1943
P-38J-25 deliveries from	June 1944
P-38L-1 deliveries from	June 1944
P-38L-5 final deliveries	June 1945

CHAPTER THREE

Islands of Fire

Early Service

The Lockheed Lightning entered service with the USAAF (the USAAC became the USAAF on 20 June 1941) in the summer of 1941, when the 1st Pursuit Group (PG) (Fighter) partly re-equipped with P-38-LOs at Selfridge Field in Michigan. Pilots of the Group had flown the YP-38s in evaluation tests at Wright Field, and equipping the 1st PG was a natural progression of that process. Initially there were only enough aircraft to equip the 27th and 94th Pursuit Squadrons (PS) with the twenty-nine examples of the first production model P-38, the more recently formed 71st Sqn continuing to fly obsolete Republic P-43s and Seversky P-35s for the time being. The first deliveries of P-38Ds took place in August, but by the autumn the Group was still operating a mix of the older single-engine types, including several Curtiss P-40s.

The years 1941–42 saw a massive expansion in the number of new pursuit (fighter) groups in the US Army, a process spurred by the declaration of war with Japan right in the middle of the period. This event found the USA not only ill-prepared for hostilities with anybody, but barely strong enough militarily to fulfil the nation's defence commitments. One way to offset the shortage of aircraft and trained personnel was to bleed off cadres of experienced men to form the nucleus of new groups. In line with this policy, concurrent with the 1st PG receiving P-38s and enough trained air and ground crew, the unit was obliged to assist new units destined to fly fighters, though not necessarily the P-38. In their turn these new units 'fathered' others. By this expedient, Lightning Groups such as the 20th PG were created, which then provided personnel to get the 35th PG up and running. This unit, in turn, eventually assisted the formation of the 55th PG in January 1941.

A similar process had to be adopted to raise several units 'in theatre', a prime example being the 475th FG, which had no previous existence in the USA.

The 1st PG also had a hand in the formation of units such as the 49th and 51st PGs, which otherwise flew Curtiss P-36s and P-40s. The latter's 26th PS (at least) was operating P-38Ds from March Field, California, by the autumn of 1941, these probably being loaned only for the duration of the Pearl Harbor crisis.

Having been activated on 15 January that year, the 51st PG was actively engaged in the defence of the US West Coast following the Japanese attack, before leaving for the Far East in January 1942. Typically, the unit continued to fly a variety of older fighter types before the outbreak of war, while deliveries of newer aircraft, particularly the P-38, remained slow. When it did move overseas, no P-38s went with the P-40-equipped group, although the 449th

A flight of P-38Fs with the red-centred 1940–41 national insignia, seen over Californian mountains. IWM

Fittingly, the 1st Pursuit Group was among the initial recipients of the P-38, though the first production models were not reckoned to be combat-worthy. US Navy

PS later re-equipped with P-38H and J-model Lightnings in the China-Burma-India Theater (CBI).

Like the 51st, the 14th FG was activated at Hamilton Field, California, on 15 January 1941. Having taken delivery of enough P-38s for its squadrons (the 48th, 49th and 50th) the group moved to March Field on or about 10 June. From 7 February to 16 July 1942 the Group was stationed at Hamilton, before moving to England on 18 August.

In November 1941 the 1st PG took its P-38Ds to South Carolina to participate in the USAAF manoeuvres, the Lightnings ostensibly being distributed between White and Red Forces and respectively sporting large recognition crosses in appropriate colours on their camouflaged wings and noses. Various bases were used by the 1st during the manoeuvres, including Randolph Field in Texas.

According to some of the participants chaos ensued, the pilots having little idea what to do, where to go or who was supposed to be giving them orders. Some individuals simply took their fighters aloft, working on the basis that there is no such thing as too much practice, but as a dress rehearsal for war the games were all but worthless.

When the USA was really at war the flow of P-38s to front-line units remained a trickle. Two days after Pearl Harbor the 1st PG was posted to the West Coast to fly patrols from San Diego Naval Air Station (NAS). It remained there for some weeks, in case of a second carrier strike by the Japanese. This possibility, which preoccupied the US military for weeks, never materialized despite numerous rumours to the contrary. Instead, in an atmosphere of unreality and doubt, the would-be defensive force searched for any sign of the Japanese. Pilots flying the P-38 gained much practice in intercepting ships, enforcing discipline in the air, working out formations, honing radio procedures and generally overcoming the problems experienced with a new combat aircraft.

With an illustrious history dating back to the First World War the 1st PG considered itself the US Army's premier fighter unit, but it took time to organize itself into a useful P-38 fighting unit. The situation was not helped by the departure of the relatively few key experienced personnel to form the

The 51st Pursuit Group operated the P-38 for only a short period during the chaotic weeks after Pearl Harbor. P. Jarrett

A gathering of Lightnings at the Muroc gunnery range in 1942, including, on the right, P-38F 41-7538. The small number 125 and triangular device on the boom are noteworthy. Edwards AFB via P. Jarrett

nucleus of other outfits, including the 82nd FG, which was activated on 9 February 1942 with a full complement of P-38s. In its turn the 1st FG moved to Los Angeles on 1 February 1942 and remained there until May, when it prepared for deployment overseas to England on 10 June.

The outbreak of war in the Pacific resulted in considerable reshuffling of units and revised aircraft inventories. As the P-38D was not then considered suitable for combat there was an understandable tendency for the USAAF planners to fall back on the only fighter that was, the P-40. All P-38s therefore remained Stateside until well into 1942, the War Department planners awaiting delivery of the combat-capable P-38Fs in sufficient numbers to equip all three squadrons of a Group (ideally). This did not always prove possible; hence the deployment of squadrons rather than full Groups to the Lightning's initial combat theatres, Alaska and the Aleutians. Other units had to operate two or more aircraft types for their initial period of combat. This was particularly true of Groups assigned to the Pacific Theatre, which was given a lower priority in line with the 'Germany first' war plan for the US air forces.

Operation *Bolero*

An urgent requirement by the War Deprtment was to get enough combat aircraft to England to build up the new Eighth Air Force. Bombers could be flown across the U-boat-infested North Atlantic, but fighters posed a different challenge. If they were not to be lost in great numbers when the freighters transporting them were sunk, they too would have to be flown over. That meant that only twin-engine fighters could undertake the crossing by the most direct route.

Lockheed had carried out much valuable research into external, jettisonable fuel tanks for the P-38, and knew that combat-capable aircraft could boost their range by using this additional fuel capacity. The problem with having the tanks fitted was an earlier ruling enforced in the USA, that external fuel tanks were by definition dangerous, and that led to a prohibition order. It took USAAF commanding general Hap Arnold to rescind it and order Ben Kelsey to organize the first of the Operation *Bolero* flights to comply with Roosevelt's desire to 'get into this war' by flying P-38Fs specially adapted to carry 300 US gal (1,140ltr) drop-tanks across the Atlantic.

All subsequent Lightnings were built with provision to carry drop tanks, which became a very great asset to aircraft likely to deploy to Europe. If overseas movement had to be by sea, increasing German U-boat activity in the North Atlantic posed a grave risk. It was felt that an aircraft that could fly across the Atlantic stood that much better a chance of reaching England safely, notwithstanding the hazards of bad weather and the risk of pilots losing their way if they became separated from their formations. Heavy bombers were invariably deployed as part of the fighter formations, the crew undertaking the navigation and en-route radio beacon checkpoints for the occupants of the single-seaters. Each P-38 also had its VH radios changed to the VHF type to be compatible with British sets. The whole operation could be completed in a matter of days, much faster than an Atlantic crossing by sea, and a northern ferry route was established with various waypoints. It began in Maine and went via Goose Bay in Labrador, Bluie West One in Greenland, Reykjavik in Iceland and, finally, Prestwick in Scotland. The 3,000-mile (4,800km) route was established, improved in terms of facilities and communications and maintained throughout the war, having been proved by the first P-38s (and Boeing B-17s) to use it, beginning in June 1942. Although many hundreds of US combat aircraft were to be ferried during the war, the vast majority were bombers and transports, rather than fighters.

Bolero initially involved the P-38Fs of the 1st and 14th FGs, plus the B-17Es of the 97th Bomb Group (BG), which departed the USA on 27 June. Almost immediately the flight was temporarily delayed by adverse weather conditions and four of the ten 'navigator' B-17s were forced to crash-land or ditch, with few crew injuries.

The flights then resumed, and the first B-17 touched down at Prestwick on 1 July 1942. Nine P-38Fs, the first of their type in USAAF service to arrive in the British Isles, landed in Scotland on 9 July. Between then and 27 July two-thirds of the 1st FG arrived in England, the 27th FS having remained behind in Iceland to offer some air defence of the region, an interlude that lasted until 28 August. The Lightnings of the 14th FG departed the USA on 22 July, also flying the northern ferry route, but these machines did not immediately proceed further than Iceland. The aircraft were required to meet an urgent need for some air defence in that region.

On 15 August the 'left-behind' 27th FS participated in a scramble when 2nd Lt Elza E. Shahan of the 27th, in company with a P-40 flown by J. K. Shaffer of the 33rd FS, intercepted and shot down a Focke-Wulf Fw 200C-3 *Condor* off the Icelandic coast. This was recorded as the first German aircraft destroyed by a USAAF pilot in the new ETO.

The 14th FG's 48th and 49th Sqns touched down in England during the last two weeks of August, the Group also having left its 50th FS behind in Iceland. This unit replaced the 27th, which duly departed for England to rejoin its parent 1st FG, the squadron having been reduced in number when seven P-38s were forced to land on the icecap and had to be abandoned. All of the fighter pilots plus two bomber crews were rescued from the frigid wasteland, but their aircraft were left to the forces of nature. The subsequent saga surrounding the rediscovery of several of the 27th FS Lightnings is recounted in a later chapter.

When *Bolero* was completed, 178 P-38s and 40 B-17s had arrived in England by air; but a further 656 P-38s had been despatched by sea. While the later North American P-51 was certainly capable of flying from the USA to the UK, and even short-range Spitfires (with extra fuel tanks) had made the Atlantic crossing in the opposite direction, the P-38 remained the only fighter type to be ferried across in substantial numbers.

By late 1943–1944, as the situation in the Atlantic improved, Lightnings were

also shipped across as deck cargo on tankers and freighters. Although this was a slower method of transportation there was no risk of pilot losses en route. Economics also impinged on the *Bolero* plan, as it was far less costly to ship fighter aircraft than to fly them across.

A similar method of getting aircraft to far-flung combat areas extended to the Pacific and CBI theatres, where depots located respectively in Australia and India handled the reassembly, ground running and flight test of partially stripped-down Lightning airframes despatched from the USA by sea.

Debut in Alaska

Following the US entry into the war following Pearl Harbor, the country faced the dilemma of providing defence against further Japanese air strikes on its territory and also supplying enough aircraft to the primary war theatre in Europe. Forces were spread very thin in the early months of 1942, but an effort was made to cover the most important danger areas and consequently a small number of P-38Ds were despatched north to Fairbanks and Anchorage in Alaska. The P-38s staged through British Colombia en route to Longview Airfield on Adak Island.

Despite joining Alaska Defense Command, these P-38Ds were not considered ready for combat. Lockheed made an effort to redress that situation, and the early aircraft were quickly replaced by P-38Es, initially equipping the 'independent' 54th FS. This unit had been detached from the 55th FG before it was sent to England, and its aircraft had been hurriedly brought up

to more-or-less P-38F-1 standard under Project *Snowman*, the modifications for which included the capability to carry the essential drop tanks.

As an outgrowth of the Alaskan Air Force, which had been activated on 15 January 1942, the Eleventh Air Force was formed the following month, with its main base at Elmendorf, Alaska. Although it comprised fighter and bomber commands in line with other USAAF air forces, the Eleventh was tiny by comparison, with few air assets in the beginning. However, by 'borrowing' units such as the 54th FS, a riposte to Japanese plans to occupy land areas in the Northern Pacific region could be made. Destined never to rejoin the 55th FG in England, the 54th FS was attached to Eleventh Fighter Command from 31 May to 11 September 1942, and thereafter became part of the 343rd FG in the Aleutians for the duration of the war.

During the earlier of these assignments, pilots of the 54th FS were among the first to confront the Japanese, for in June 1942, concurrently with their clash with the US fleet at Midway, the enemy invaded the Aleutian island of Kiska.

By thus creating a new, isolated – and ultimately worthless – Northern Pacific war front, the Japanese Army nevertheless attempted to hold on to this latest possession in their war against the Western Allies. If for no other reason than propaganda, a Japanese presence in 'America's back yard' was an irritation that could not be tolerated. More threatening was the fact that the US base at Dutch Harbour was within range of Japanese bombers.

Consequently, USAAF counterattacks included fighter sorties from Fort Glenn on Umnak Island by the 54th FS's P-38Es,

First seeing combat in the Aleutians, the P-38 was one of several USAAF types that held the Japanese at bay. The P-38s were joined by F-5s to keep the enemy under surveillance while C-47s brought much-needed supplies to Amchitka on 23 December 1943. IWM

sorties that began to emphasize the lost cause that the Aleutian invasion would ultimately represent to the enemy. To underscore this, Lts K. Ambrose and Stan A. Long intercepted and shot down a Kawanishi H6K 'Mavis' flying boat on 4 August. This victory was the first for the P-38 in the Northern Pacific war theatre.

Subsequently able to mount a limited number of fighter sweeps, the P-38s literally weathered the appalling flying conditions that regularly made life miserable for all personnel based in the Aleutians. As a result of these operations, combined with medium- and long-range bombing by North American B-25s, Martin B-26s, Boeing B-17s and Consolidated B-24s accompanied by P-40s and P-39s, it was not long before command of the air passed decisively to the Americans. This despite the USA's 'fair-weather' aviators; trained to fly in the generally clear skies of the USA, young, inexperienced pilots found themselves penetrating fog, rain and snow immediately after taking off in conditions that would have given Stateside instructors apoplexy.

As the first of the Pacific war fronts to involve US forces, the Aleutians campaign took an almost superhuman effort to sustain. Many USAAF missions were more of a harassing nature, owing to the small number of aircraft available.

For their part the Japanese were quite astute in their Aleutians operations in not trying to operate landplanes from inadequate airfields that would have been vulnerable to attack. Instead, the Imperial Japanese Navy (IJN) made extensive use of floatplanes, and it was these, particularly the Nakajima A6M2-N 'Rufe', a 'Zeke' derivative, that became important in the theatre.

The main unit deployed by the IJN was the 452 Kukutai, which had arrived on Kiska on 15 June, equipped with six A6M2s. The 2nd Air Fleet's 5 Koku Kantai had additional floatplanes and H6K4 'Mavis' long-range flying boats. However, floatplanes could not easily be hidden; nor could they avoid becoming a primary target for US fighter sweeps and heavy-bomber sorties.

American Response

On 30 August 1942 US ground forces landed without opposition on Adak Island, the main purpose being to establish an advance airfield from which Japanese forces on Kiska could be attacked. Terrible (or usual) weather disrupted air operations for several days,

but the occupation of Adak was completed by 1 September. Two days later five P-38s of the 54th FS and six B-24s took off from Fort Glenn airfield to attack Kiska, initiating the longest non-stop overwater mission of the war to date, a 1,260-mile (2,030km) round trip. Although three P-38s and five Liberators were forced to abort the mission owing to bad weather, the rest pressed home an attack on moored IJN floatplanes, claiming four destroyed before the small force returned safely to base.

A 343rd FG headquarters was formally activated at Elmendorf on 11 September 1942 to take over direction of the 11th, 18th and 54th FSs. Although the 343rd was to have been an all-Lightning Group, supply of the aircraft was such that only the 54th FS was so equipped, the other two units retaining P-40s.

Most Aleutian fighter missions were on a modest scale, with as few as two aircraft active on some days, but the USA's determination not to cede the area to the enemy was emphasized by the completion of the advanced airfield on Adak, also on 11 September. This base was 250 miles (400km) closer to the IJN base at Kiska, a fact greatly appreciated by the crews. A pair of P-38s strafed a seaplane tender and ground target on Kiska on 13 September, one P-38 pilot downing a single A6M2-N. This turned out to be the last occasion

when aircraft from Umnak flew a direct mission to Kiska, as the Adak Island base proved more convenient to use. To ram this home, an operation on the 14th saw 54th FS P-38 pilots and P-39s of the 42nd FS shoot down four 'Rufe' floatplanes. Strafing and bombing by US pilots caused additional damage on Kiska, the cost being two P-38s, which collided with the loss of both pilots. Mid-air collision was to dog the P-38 throughout its existence. An analysis of accident reports cited the common problem of temporary loss of vision by the pilot when the aircraft entered certain manoeuvres and his view became obscured by one of the engines.

Anti-Submarine Strikes

Searching for enemy submarines was a chore assigned to thousands of pilots during the war, the Aleutians being no different to any other theatre in this respect. These operations continued sporadically in deference to typical bad weather, which included winds so strong that someone suggested that a 500lb bomb would make a useful windsock!

An actual anti-submarine strike was an unusual duty performed by two 54th FS P-38s on 23 September. The Lightnings were over Amchitka Island to escort a

Freighters and tankers ferried P-38s to the distant Pacific battlefields, as this deck view of five lashed and masked aircraft being docked in the Solomons shows. IWM

Cranes hoisted each P-38 off the ship and on to dockside transporters, as seen here with an early J model in the Solomons. IWM

Consolidated PBY landing a survey party to determine the island's suitability as a base. It proved unsuitable, and the P-38s bombed a radio shack and claimed to have sunk a submarine before departing. The IJN operated a number of small I-Class submarines in Aleutian waters, several of which were abandoned when Kiska was evacuated and captured by US forces.

Japanese surface traffic was also attacked off the islands, the participating bombers usually being escorted by both P-38s and single-engine fighters. A 54th FS Lightning pilot claimed a Mitsubishi A6M Reisen (Zero or 'Zeke') destroyed on 28 September.

On 3 October the 343rd's P-38s and P-39s were again successful over Kiska harbour, five IJN floatplanes being shot up on the water. In succeeding days Kiska was repeatedly attacked, as were IJN naval units at sea. Sorties sometimes brought inconclusive results and flak damage to some of the aircraft involved, though there were relatively few losses. Storms raged in late October, 80mph (130km/h) winds being recorded along with torrential rains that flooded the main runway at Adak. Surface water was a hazard with which USAAF aircraft could usually cope, provided the pilots took extreme care.

Take-offs and landings during this period were often spectacular. Some were filmed by noted film director John Ford, who captured, among other enduring images, P-38s ploughing along runways that had become lakes of water, and creating waves more associated with PT boat operations than aviation.

To circumvent the weather hazard, a secondary airstrip was commissioned early in November, but the severe weather connived to ground XI Fighter Command for most of the rest of November and a large part of December. There was some activity by the P-38s, but little success against shipping targets could be recorded. Patrols and attack sorties alike were despatched,

Manpower was needed to ensure that each Lightning was secured to a crane. P-38G-10 41-13187 was shipped to India, where it was unloaded on 22 February 1944. IWM

Nosing upwards, '187 shows how Lightnings retained their drop tanks and were secured to trestles until their wheels could be lowered on dry land. IWM

only to fail to penetrate low cloud, fog and rain squalls and locate the objective.

Nine P-38s escorted six Liberators to Kiska on 26 December while a second P-38/B-24 force attacked targets on Attu, where one P-38 was lost. Lightnings escorting B-25s to Kiska later in the day failed to find the target and aborted.

The enemy on Kiska showed his teeth on 30 December, when P-38s were part of a low-level attack force sent against shipping in the harbour. The USAAF aircraft were attacked by four 'Rufes' at 11.45hr. A P-38 shot down one floatplane, but two Lightnings and a B-25 were lost. The Lightnings exacted small revenge on the 31st, when nine 343rd Group aircraft were again sent against Kiska harbour shipping. Hits on two ships were claimed, and the destruction of an A6M2-N was shared by two P-38 pilots at 14.30hr.

A week into January 1943 saw P-38s escorting B-25s and B-24s to Kiska, but only the Liberators were able to find their target on the 7th, and then only after circling for 2hr to find a break in the cloud! Six P-38s and nine B-25s, B-26s and B-24s were airborne from Adak on the 18th to attack two ships reported at Kiska. No hits were scored, and a returning B-24 crashed into two P-38s, writing off all three aircraft.

Bad weather continued to disrupt US operations, and it was 4 February before a fighter and bomber strike could again be mounted on the IJN submarine base at Kiska. Four P-38s participated, and a new IJN fighter strip was reported by US pilots. Similar attacks took place on the 10th and 13th, P-38s shooting down three A6M2-Ns over Kiska at midday on the latter occasion. The IJN had previously mounted retaliatory attacks against Amchitka aerodrome, the penultimate sorties taking place on 15 February. The following day the last such IJN strike was little more than a nuisance raid before a force of P-40s moved in. The Warhawks dealt with further incursions while the P-38s and the bombers continued to take the war to Kiska.

On 7 March the 54th FS moved forward to Amchitka aerodrome, positioning the P-38s better for their war of attrition against Kiska. On 10 March a solitary F-5 photographed Japanese installations on Kiska, shortly followed by a fighter and bomber strike. Lockheed P-38s conducted a strafing attack on Kiska on 13 March, two days before a 'maximum effort', by Aleutian standards, was launched. The operation included thirty-two P-38s of the 343rd FG, which bombed and strafed installations. The same number of P-38s was sent on another mission to the same area the following day.

The Lightning fighters operated from Amchitka and Adak during this period, while the allocation of F-5 PR aircraft to the theatre increased. Fifty-two P-38/F-5 sorties were made on 21 March, the number of available aircraft now allowing attacks on Kiska to be mounted in waves. Such raids were spread over several days in early April, five separate missions being achieved on the 10th.

Winding Down

As a result of the Aleutian Campaign the Japanese abandoned their bases on Kiska, all resistance having effectively ended by 30 May, the date of the US landings. By mid-1943 US and Canadian troops were firmly in control of the island chain including Kiska.

In successfully wrapping-up operations in the Aleutians, the USAAF was instrumental in safeguarding a remote area from Japanese control. It was undoubtedly a wartime backwater, but clearly could not have been left in the hands of the enemy. It was also the only area of North American soil to experience combat during the war.

With the Japanese threat lifted, the Joint Chiefs of Staff gave some thought to using the Aleutian Island chain as a springboard for an invasion of the Home Islands, but this idea was shelved, primarily because of the hostile conditions. The

Most of the P-38s that saw combat in the Solomons arrived via Australia, as this mid-1943 photo shows. Although each aircraft was supposed to be repainted after all sealing was removed, this was not always done, giving a worn appearance. IWM

Aleutians were within range of the Kurile Islands, which contained a Japanese naval anchorage and were built up late in the war. Several US air strikes were made against these bases before the end.

Fatigue Study

The hostile conditions led indirectly to a study of operational fatigue among P-38 pilots flying in the Aleutians. It differentiated between combat fatigue in a dangerous, highly-charged area such as the ETO and the area where the Eleventh Air Force pilots often faced long missions from Adak, Shemya and Amchitka. A survey of the operational records of thirteen pilots who flew seventy missions over two months on short-duration sorties and those lasting more than 6hr found that Japanese aircraft contacts totalled just four. The study revealed that, on long missions, a pilot could remain fully alert for the first 30 to 45min and partially alert for the next 3 to 4hr, but would eventually become so fatigued that he was unable to search the sky properly, even though he knew his life might depend on it. The threat of bad weather caused tension and anxiety. This was a very real fear, as five pilots were killed by flying in adverse weather conditions

over a three-month period. There was a strange counter to this condition when pilots were forced to get deep under low hanging cloud and fly just above the water. No sign of anoxia and little effect from cold was apparent, as the docile Lightning could be trimmed to fly hands-off. However, the cockpit became very uncomfortable after 6hr because there was no room to stretch the legs or body, and sitting in one position for so long led to soreness of the buttocks or 'parachute ass', as the Americans termed it. Tall pilots bumped their heads on the canopy roof, and seven of the men participating in the study said they found difficulty in urinating in flight.

A sense of loneliness, helplessness and futility, always greatly exaggerated on single-aircraft flights, was noted by all participants. In the Aleutians, conditions on the ground offered little in the way of light relief, a problem that was compared in the study with other theatres particularly the South West Pacific, with its opposite extreme of climate. Hot, humid conditions and primitive bases forced men to live in tents amidst dust or mud and eat monotonous, low-nutrition canned food which led to a loss of weight, and clothes were invariably damp most of the time. In addition there was the all-pervading insect life in the jungles surrounding most airstrips.

Yet, for all the deprivations of its operational area, the 343rd FG acquitted itself well, maybe too well in the opinion of the pilots and ground crews, for they were destined to stay in the Aleutians. Only three of the Group's four squadrons had P-38s, the early models being replaced as newer versions became available. The 343rd was credited with twenty-seven aerial victories, combat over the northern reaches of the Pacific trailing off until the Japanese became a distant memory. After the Group logged its final combat mission, in October 1943, the attached squadrons flew routine patrols and reconnaissance sorties until the war's end. The final act was to dispose of the remaining Lightnings, among them P-38Js, which were broken up and dumped on Shemya when hostilities ceased.

The 342nd Composite Group, which had a relatively short war in Alaska, had two squadrons partially equipped with P-38s before it was disbanded on 18 March 1944. In that time the dearth of enemy aircraft activity resulted in a group total of just 4.5 victories.

Combat in the South Seas

Having established a vital forward air base in the South West Pacific Area (SWPA)

Guadalcanal was the final destination for many P-38s. This shark-mouthed example of the 80th FS had arrived on the island by April 1943. US Navy/IWM

BELOW: 'Headhunters' P-38Hs escort an 'Air Apaches' B-25D over the Solomons, *circa* November 1943. Aircraft 'A' was probably the mount of ace Ed Cragg; the identity of the pilot who flew 'V' is uncertain. USAF

on Guadalcanal in the Solomon Islands in August 1942, the USAAF was able to develop airfields and launch offensive sorties against the Japanese with commendable speed. All of the early fighter combat had been in the hands of the famous 'Cactus Air Force', mainly comprising Army P-40s and P-39s and Marine Corps Grumman F4F Wildcats, P-38s not arriving until November. In the meantime the Thirteenth Air Force had been formed to direct USAAF operations throughout the Solomons area.

The first twelve Lightnings had been shipped to Noumea in New Caledonia, assembled, and then flown by ferry pilots to Guadalcanal. With few aircraft, the pilots assigned to the 70th FS of the 347th FG were integrated with those of the 339th.

The P-38G was the preferred type to fly, though others had to be content with the P-39. As it was the only Lightning outfit in the entire SWPA, it was fortunate that most of the 347th's pilots were experienced flyers, and small items of procedure, such as learning the location of the propeller feathering buttons, could be undertaken along the way. One pilot swore it took him ten missions to locate those buttons, which could have saved his life if an engine had quit in flight.

Tactics also had to be figured out as they went along, pilots making due allowance for the limitations of the P-38 against the agile Japanese single-engined fighters, particularly the IJN's Mitsubishi A6M. However, the Lightning's excellent dive and zoom capability, coupled with its manoeuvring

flaps that enabled sustained turns to be made, were attributes that stood USAAF pilots in good stead in combat. And nobody forgot that it was now possible for an Army fighter to return to base with an engine out. Hitherto, engine failure had often meant a dunking in the ocean at the very least, with the pilot fervently hoping that a nice fat PBY 'Dumbo' had been quickly alerted and was on the way to him with all speed.

On 18 November the 339th FS took its P-38s into action from Henderson Field for the first time. Its mission was to escort B-17s and tackle any Japanese fighters that attempted to attack the bombers. Three enemy aircraft were claimed shot down.

By that time the direct threat to the Solomons from Japanese air and surface attack had faded. Having all but abandoned the islands, which had badly drained their resources, Japanese surface units withdrew to Truk while the IJN's air force consolidated at its three main air bases at Rabaul on New Britain, which lay over 500 miles (800km) from the main US base on Guadalcanal. In addition the Japanese maintained bases in the Shortlands and Bougainville, but something of a stalemate persisted in 1943 as both sides marked time and built up their base facilities and forces in the South West Pacific. Meanwhile, each side mounted a series of air strikes designed to reduce enemy effectiveness and prevent reinforcements and supplies getting through.

Although the 347th's 339th FS was the only P-38 unit in the Solomons for some months, the F4U Corsairs of VMF-124 arrived in February 1943. With regard to the Lightning, the exception to the dearth of long-range fighters was a brief period the previous November, when the Fifth Air Force had deployed the 39th FS of the 35th FG for a mere nine-day stay. As there were other US Army fighters on Guadalcanal, a plan to deal with Japanese bombing raids was activated. When an alert was sounded, all the fighters were scrambled, each climbing to its best operational height. Thus the P-38s zoomed up to 30,000ft (9,000m), the Marine Corsairs orbited at 25,000ft (7,600m) and the F4F Wildcats, P-39 Airacobras and Curtiss P-40s guarded the airspace at 12,000ft (3,600m). With the approaches covered, American fighters could deliver a nasty shock to IJN bomber raids from Rabaul, and victory claims by the Cactus Air Force rose accordingly.

Any Japanese tactical plan that would succeed in ousting the Americans from Guadalcanal seemed increasingly less feasible. Combat operations recorded markedly more success for the Americans than the Japanese, who were soon to suffer a significant loss directly attributable to the P-38.

Continuing to base much of their Pacific strategy on winning major surface engagements with the American fleet, the Japanese had been forced to defend their island outposts against burgeoning US airpower, which threatened all their operations. In their turn the Americans had been buoyed by several successful air operations, ably supported by the Royal Australian Air Force (RAAF). Bringing long-range fighters into the SWPA could only help the strategy of isolating the Japanese and preventing them from threatening Allied supply lines during

a gradual build-up for future operations into the Central Pacific.

Anti-Shipping Strikes

Keeping the Japanese off the backs of the US forces meant that fighters were occasionally sent out after ships. These were interesting attempts to sink enemy shipping, as ingenuity was required if the fighters were to inflict more than superficial damage with their fixed guns. Even freighters proved tough nuts to crack, and something more lethal was required. A trio of 347th FG pilots, Tom Lanphier, Douglas Canning and Delton Goerke, decided to try. Having made three strafing runs on a small vessel they found off Vella Lavella on 2 April, the pilots saw few visible signs of damage. As they were still carrying their extra fuel tanks, they decided to drop these and ignite them with gunfire. Lanphier went in first, then Canning and Goerke. The pilots spread fuel all over the ship and started fires with their guns. Plenty of flames resulted, but the freighter remained afloat. Disgusted, the trio returned to base, as their fuel was then running short, but they were not denied their kill. A PBY was sent to the area to report back, and the 339th FS pilots heard that the ship later blew up and sank.

Increased activity from 2 April heralded the start of the IJN's ambitious Operation *I-Go*, a renewed air offensive entailing numerous sorties against Allied installations and bases throughout the South West Pacific, particular attention being paid to the Solomons. The coast watchers and the forward airfield radio operators confirmed much increased activity as enemy bombers and their fighter escorts flew down 'The Slot' to reach their objectives. Usually they did so, but at considerable cost, so much so that the overall results of *I-Go* were far less than the hoped-for major success. But to save face the operation was trumpeted as having achieved all of its aims, a fabrication that was indirectly to seal the fate of the IJN's most able commander.

Get Yamamoto!

In April 1943, having cracked the IJN's secret radio code shortly after the attack on Pearl Harbor, the Americans were ideally placed to counter many potentially dangerous enemy moves in subsequent

months. One of the greatest coups of the Pacific war took place on 18 April 1943, when Allied Intelligence learned the itinerary of Adm Isoroku Yamamoto, Commander-in-Chief of the IJN, several days before he was due to fly to Buin and Bougainville to visit front-line personnel. If Yamamoto's aerial entourage could be intercepted and the admiral incapacitated or killed, the IJN would be thrown into disarray. Even if this situation was only temporary, it was estimated that Yamamoto's replacement would invariably be a lesser individual in terms of tactical skills and planning foresight. The Thirteenth Air Force made the calculations and estimated that a small force of P-38s based on Guadalcanal could do the job, even at the limit of their range.

It was as a result of the Japanese telling Yamamoto what he wanted to hear, rather than the truth, that he was in the area at all. At the conclusion of Operation *I-Go* the admiral had been informed that great damage had been wrought by a combined Japanese Navy Air Force and Japanese Army Air Force (JNAF/JAAF) air offensive. He therefore decided to visit forward bases and offer his congratulations to the fliers concerned. Unaware of the actual results of *I-Go*, Yamamoto and his staff duly took off from Rabaul, flying in a Mitsubishi G4M 'Betty' piloted by Flying Chief Petty Officer Takashi Kotani. A second 'Betty' had Flying Petty Officer 2nd Class Hiroshi Hayashi at the controls, and both bombers and their fighter escort flew west, destination Ballale, a tiny island base in the Shortlands, lying off the southern tip of Bougainville.

On Guadalcanal, pilots drawn from the 12th, 70th and 339th FSs made up a eighteen-ship force to fly the 435miles (700km) to rendezvous with their target just as the Japanese arrived off the coast of Bougainville. Fortunately in April the 12th FS had received enough P-38Gs to replace (temporarily, as it transpired) the unit's P-39s, which would have been hard-pressed to perform the mission. The 70th FS continued to fly the Airacobra, although two pilots were seconded to the Yamamoto interception force to fly that important mission, codenamed *Dillinger*. Major John Mitchell planned the operation down to the minutest detail, and all credit for its successful outcome was due to him.

The Lightnings took off from Henderson Field at 07.30hr on 18 April, each carrying a pair of 310 US gal (1,170ltr) external

Pilot Roster, Yamamoto Mission, 18 April 1943

Name and rank	Squadron
Ames, 1st Lt Roger J.	12th
Anglin, Ist Lt Everett H.	12th
Barber, 1st Lt Rex T.	339th
Canning, 1st Lt Douglas S.	339th
Goerke, 1st Lt Delton C.	339th
Graebner, 1st Lt Lawrence A.	12th
Hine, 1st Lt Raymond K.***	339th
Holmes, 1st Lt Besby T.	339th
Jacobsen, 1st Lt Julius	339th
Kittel, Maj Louis R.	70th
Lanphier, Capt Thomas G.	70th
Long, 1st Lt Albert R.	12th
McLanahan, 1st Lt James D.	339th
Mitchell, Maj John W.	339th
Moore, 1st Lt Joseph F.	339th
Smith, 1st Lt William E.	12th
Stratton, 1st Lt Eldon E.*	12th
Whittaker, 2nd Lt Gordon**	12th

* KIA 30 August 1943
** MIA 29 April 1943
*** MIA 18 April 1943

tanks. Two aircraft were obliged to abort the mission almost immediately, following the circuitous route chosen for them to avoid being detected. En route the aircraft dropped down to as low as 10–15ft (3–5m) to avoid detection, fuel sloshing around in drop tanks that lacked any internal baffles to prevent it, and tending to throw the aircraft out of trim.

Radio silence was observed for most of the flight, though, as the American pilots sighted their quarry some two hours after take-off, Lt Doug Canning warned the others of the presence of 'Zekes' above them.

Given all the possibilities of Yamamoto and his party being delayed, even by a few vital minutes, the on-time rendezvous achieved by the Lightnings was an admirable feat of timing and navigation. As the two 'Bettys' and their escort of 'Zekes' were identified, the P-38s went into action without further delay. Lanphier and Barber broke away after one of the G4Ms, Besby Holmes and Ray Hine going after the other.

Strikingly-marked 80th FS P-38H-1 42-66506 was flown by Ed Cragg, whose score peaked at fifteen victories, fourteen having been scored by 22 December 1942. Cragg, nicknamed 'Porky', went MIA that month. IWM

But tumbling auxiliary fuel tanks warned the American pilots that the escort was alert to their intention, and Lanphier zoomed up to cut off the leader of the fighter flight. A long burst from his guns crossed with fire from the 'Zeke', but it was the Japanese aircraft that fell away. Meanwhile, Barber had engaged two 'Zekes', giving Lanphier a clear line to the bombers. He dived, cutting his throttles to prevent overshooting his targets. In their turn two 'Zekes' overshot the skidding P-38 and dived at the G4Ms from Lanphier's right side, intending to prevent him from firing at the bombers. All five aircraft were on a collision course, and Lanphier took his chance. A long deflection shot across a 'Betty's' nose did the trick. Its right engine and wing caught fire and it began to nose down, too low for anyone to survive if they baled out.

Rex Barber shot down a 'Zeke' to clear his path to the second 'Betty', which carried a very startled but otherwise calm Vice-Admiral Matome Ugaki. The P-38's fire killed several members of his 'Betty's' crew before it was put down in the sea. Ugaki saw Yamamoto's G4M plough into the coastal jungle as his own aircraft prepared to ditch. The vice-admiral was badly injured but survived the crash.

The Lightnings flew off to claim three 'Zekes' downed in addition to both 'Bettys'. Only Ray Hine, wingman to Besby Holmes, failed to return. Holmes himself made a late return after diverting to Sunshine Island, low on fuel.

Low Profile

Because of its location the Thirteenth Air Force in the Solomons remained small, the war gradually moving beyond the range of single-engine fighters, though the P-38 continued to hit the furthest targets. Despite the dramatic conclusion of the Yamamoto mission there was no immediate increase in the number of P-38 squadrons. The men who had flown one of the most important fighter interceptions of the war were even denied the satisfaction of seeing their story in the newspapers. No details of *Dillinger* were published for months, for fear that the Japanese would guess that their radio code had been compromised. Some compensation came in the form of a visit by Generals Douglas MacArthur and Dene Strother to congratulate all the pilots who flew the historic mission and present medals to Lanphier and Barber.

To this day the identity of the pilot who fired the fatal burst at Yamamoto's G4M remains in some doubt, opinions of the participants differing as to whether Lanphier or Barber was responsible. Suffice it to say that this remarkable long-range interception was one of the most famous combat flights made by the P-38 (or any other fighter) during the Second World War, and the loss to the Japanese of a very capable commander had a far-reaching, detrimental effect on subsequent IJN operations.

Build-Up of the Fifth

Gen George Kenney had taken over the Fifth Air Force on 2 August 1942, and shouldered the enormous responsibility of preventing further Japanese expansion in New Guinea and thwarting any threat of an invasion of Australia. With precious few resources, Kenney began to lobby Washington for more long-range fighters, and eventually his tenacity brought results, more of the Lockheed fighters being earmarked for his Fifth Air Force. However, P-38 production was still steady rather then record-breaking, and shortfalls continued to occur. At first only single squadrons of the allocated fighter groups could be equipped with Lightnings, the 39th FS of the 35th FG being the first in the Fifth Air Force to receive them, trading its P-39s for P-38Fs in October 1942.

Twenty-five P-38s arrived in Brisbane, Australia, that month, and sixteen were flown to Port Moresby without delay. When they reached New Guinea the fighters were found to have leaks in their wing-leading-edge intercoolers, which kept the aircraft on the ground until the problem was solved.

As the leaks necessitated almost a complete rebuild of the wing, no P-38 sorties could be undertaken until the latter part of November. Aircraft were flown as they were repaired, and although the Japanese could rarely be coaxed into action, there was some contact for the 39th.

At that time the enemy was still ensconsed on the coast of New Guinea, and the Allied air forces were preoccupied with preventing any further build-up of the Imperial Army that could threaten friendly troops fighting in the interior of the country.

Pilots found some light relief in the fact that the enemy base at Lae was on the same radio frequency that they used, but much taunting over the airwaves failed to lure the Japanese into combat.

November/December 1942

Not until 27 December did the 39th FS record a memorable day's action. On that day twelve P-38s were sent to intercept a Japanese force comprising bombers with fighter escort, en route to Dobodura, a major base on the north coast of New Guinea. Led by Capt Thomas J. Lynch and with Richard I. Bong and Kenneth Sparks in the van, the Lightnings circled 'Dobo', awaiting the incoming formation. About twenty-five enemy aircraft hove into view, and the Americans split into three separate Flights before attacking.

The ensuing massacre was something of an acid test for the P-38 in the SWPA, formerly the stamping ground of the reliable but limited old P-40. The 39th FS's pilots felt that they needed some convincing that the larger Lockheed fighter was the equal of the nimble Japanese interceptors. This encounter proved that it was. Fifteen enemy aircraft were claimed destroyed with no P-38 losses, and, although the American pilots knew their tactics left something to be desired, these were early days. Lynch, Sparks and Bong claimed two kills apiece, and the squadron's morale went sky-high.

Deliveries of Lightnings to the SWPA remained modest, but by January 1943 Kenney had received enough to re-equip the 9th FS of the 49th FG. Several 39th FS pilots, including Dick Bong, transferred to pass on the benefit of their experience. Again, a few P-38 test hops were enough to convince a P-40 outfit that this was a suitable replacement for their war-weary Warhawks.

February 1943

In February 1943 the 80th FS of the 8th FG converted from P-39s to P-38Fs, but an unexpected event forced the group to pull out of New Guinea during the month. A malaria epidemic struck down so many pilots and ground crew that rest and recuperation in Australia was the only sensible course. While there, the group embarked upon two months of conversion training before returning to the war in March.

Early results achieved by squadrons of the 8th and 49th FGs confirmed that the Pacific Ocean Area was tailor-made for a fighter with the built-in safety factor of two engines.

But with Lockheed output still not matching the demands of three different war theatres, both Pacific Groups were obliged to operate a mix of Lightnings and Republic P-47 Thunderbolts, there being sufficient P-38s for only a single squadron in each Group. This situation prevailed for some months, and while the 8th achieved this integration well enough, not all the pilots believed that the P-47 was the right aircraft for the theatre. Air combat scores tended to reflect this view.

March 1943

Although their early victories had secured them a number of outposts throughout the south-west Pacific, the Japanese had no air resupply capability to speak of. This left the garrisons increasingly isolated if seaborne supplies could not get through the Allied blockade. The fact that the Fifth Air Force and RAAF could continue to direct most of their efforts without undue disruption from the enemy was an indication of how the Allies gradually gained the upper hand in the SWPA during the rest of 1943.

In March the IJN made one last major attempt to get a supply convoy through to the coastal airstrip at Lae. The resulting Battle of the Bismark Sea saw the USAAF and RAAF pounding the troopships during two solid days of unrelenting operations. Above the ships, enemy fighters tried in vain to ward off marauding Australian Bristol Beaufighters and Beauforts and American B-25s and Douglas A-20s, with P-38s, P-39s and P-40s giving good cover and shooting them out of the sky. With their ships in dire straits the Japanese flew numerous retaliatory sorties, but the Allied fighter pilots knew how important the outcome of the battle was for their bases in New Guinea.

Lightning pilots of the 39th and 9th FSs waded into the enemy fighters, claiming totals of seventy-seven and fifty-six victories respectively by 20 March. Some kills were shared with other units, but the real carnage took place on the surface of the sea when aircrews were ordered to strafe Japanese troops trying to swim ashore from crippled freighters. There was no alternative but to kill as many as possible before they reached dry land and posed a threat.

Overall, the results of the battle were impressive enough, adding weight to Kenney's request to have more aircraft and, in particular, a full P-38 Group in the Pacific as soon as possible. Hap Arnold had promised Kenney as much, and he raised the matter again during a visit to Washington in late March.

May 1943

When he returned to the Pacific in mid-May, Kenney scrounged as many men and supplies as he could to equip a new fighter group in-theatre and from scratch, which he had offered to undertake even without a nucleus of Stateside personnel to staff it. This new Group, the 475th FG, was much scorned by other units when their best pilots were poached on the specific orders of the commanding general. Kenney transferred Maj George Prentice from the 39th FS to head the 475th and prepare it for combat. By August the new Lightning group was ready for the fray. Kenney would not be disappointed with its performance.

June 1943

Mid-1943 saw the P-38 becoming firmly established as the leading fighter in the Pacific, with several pilots emerging as top flight leaders and individuals such as Tommy Lynch of the 39th FS being assigned to the 475th FG. Having secured the necessary firm bedrock of experience, the 431st and 432nd FSs were operating from Twelve Mile Strip (this, and other airfield names, denoting their distance from Port Moresby) and Ward's Drome, near Moresby, by 11 August. The 433rd FS, which completed the strength of the 475th FG, moved up to Jackson Drome on the 16th.

As in other theatres, the P-38s based in the south-west Pacific flew a variety of missions, including bomber escorts. These were often heavy-firepower missions, with the Lightnings covering B-25 and A-20 strafers, but on 21 June the bombers carried supplies; 'biscuits' rather than bombs. While flying escort on one of many such missions, the 80th FS got a call that about thirty Japanese fighters and bombers were in the air shortly after the supplies were on the way to a garrison at Guadagasel. With its four-ship Flights spread out, the 80th went after the enemy fighters. The American score rose to thirteen, 'Corky' Smith heading the list with three A6Ms. Three other pilots notched up double victories, including George Welch, who had scored some of the first aerial victories of the Pacific war over Pearl Harbor.

July 1943

The mid-year weeks of 1943 rolled on with the Fifth's Lightning pilots steadily adding to their toll of enemy aircraft. During the latter half of July the 39th and 80th FSs were in the thick of several actions in a single week. On the 21st both squadrons were escorting a B-25 strike to Bogajim Roads when up to thirty enemy fighters came on the scene. The P-38 pilots reacted well, knocking down eleven of them, and Jay Robbins of the 80th FS claimed three. Eventually top ace of the squadron, Robbins finished the war with an impressive twenty-two victories.

The victories on the 21st were well spread among the two squadrons, three pilots of the 80th FS and two from the 39th being credited with doubles. Ten others each scored single victories. Twelve more enemy aircraft succumbed to the guns of the P-38 squadrons two days later.

The 9th FS of the 49th FG took centre stage on 26 July, when the opposing sides clashed over the Markham Valley. Dick Bong, who had been scoring steadily, had a field day, wading into about twenty Nakajima Ki-43 'Oscars' and Kawasaki Ki-61 'Tonys'. Two of the fighters at which Bong fired went down in flames, and two disintegrated under his fire. Next day Bong added an 'Oscar' to bring his personal total to sixteen.

The 35th FG continued to operate only one squadron of Lightnings throughout most of the year, and the 39th FS with its P-38Hs, moved to a new base at Tsili-Tsili in late July, ready for operations on the 26th.

As a result of the pounding of Lae and Salamanua, the Japanese had been forced to abandon these important bases and concentrate much of their airpower on Wewak and distant Rabaul. Allied reconnaissance kept a close watch on the former base, which was reinforced during August 1943. Hitting Wewak was the debut effort of the 475th FG, in a period when it met with some success. From the 16th until the end of the month the new Group claimed fifty-three enemy aircraft, mostly over Wewak. It was a score that would have been the envy of more experienced P-38 Groups in other theatres, but the 475th was no ordinary outfit. Inspired and aggressively led, it had been formed around some of the best pilots in the Fifth Air Force, and was to carve out an unsurpassed reputation for skill and discipline in the air that was to make it the most famous P-38 unit in the Pacific.

September 1943

Lae, Salamaua and Nadzab were in Allied hands by September 1943, with the result that much of the northern coast of New Guinea was free of Japanese air and land bases. The entire lower Markham Valley became a gigantic air base for the Fifth Air Force to range out as far as Rabaul to give the enemy a bloody nose. More territory gave Kenney a welcome boost to his freedom of action in supporting ground forces in pushing the enemy further back up the vast, jungle-covered land mass.

With Wewak effectively neutralized as a Japanese base, the focus in the SWPA turned on Rabaul. This major enemy stronghold was repeatedly attacked to prevent any sizeable build-up of forces, and the P-38's long range really came into its own when Fifth Fighter Command added its weight to the neutralizing of the New Britain base. Rather than supporting a potentially costly invasion, the Joint Chiefs had decided to leave Rabaul to 'wither on the vine', as MacArthur put it.

December 1943

It was decided, however, that a foothold elsewhere on New Britain was in Allied interests, and troops went ashore at Cape Gloucester on 26 December. The P-38s of the 475th FG, plus the 80th FS, undertook much of the air support for the operation. The Japanese deployed dive bombers in an attempt to sink Allied invasion shipping, and on the 27th Capt Tommy McGuire was leading the 431st FS on a patrol over the cape. A force of Aichi D3A 'Vals' twenty to thirty strong was reported about to dive bomb. McGuire led his troops in and made contact just as the 'Vals' were beginning their dives. The intervention of the Lightnings unnerved the Japanese pilots, who promptly jettisoned their bombs from much too high an altitude for them to be effective. From 8,000 to 10,000ft (2,500 to 3,000m) below, Allied sailors witnessed this display in amazement. Only one ship, a destroyer, was hit in the attack, sinking as the P-38s chased off the offending enemy aircraft. Towards the end of the combat McGuire joined up with P-47s from the 36th FS, and together they blasted a fifth 'Val' from the sky. McGuire was credited with four 'Vals' to add to the 475th's forty-six victories for the month.

Despite the great success of the P-38 in the Fifth Air Force, one of the problems that had plagued the aircraft in Europe was not entirely unknown in the Pacific. Aircraft were not returning because they had been lost through simply running out of fuel. Although the problem was sometimes weather-related, George Kenney could not afford to lose valuable pilots and aircraft in accidents not attributable to enemy action. The common problem was the habit of young pilots to run their engines in high blower to maintain maximum revolutions, even when they were not in a combat area.

Such actions ate up fuel, and had always proved detrimental to aero engines, which had a short enough life under hostile combat conditions, but instilling a 'feeling for the machinery' was far from easy. Unfortunately, heavy-handiness claimed lives. Trying to undo the doctrine of training seemed possible only if a highly respected pilot demonstrated how it should be done, preferably in the same aircraft and under operating conditions similar to those the Fifth Air Force pilots faced almost daily. Help was on the way.

In November the 49th FG found to its horror that its 9th FS had to convert to the P-47D. Despite exhortations and impressive demonstrations by leading Pacific Thunderbolt exponent Neel Kearby of the 348th FG, the men of the Flying Knights felt that their squadron nickname was grimly inappropriate. To say that they felt shortchanged would be an understatement.

There were, of course, those who accepted the inescapable fact that Kenney's command lay at the end of a very long supply line, and that there were not yet enough aircraft of the right type to equip all of the units that needed them. Those individuals adapted to the Republic monster with alacrity. Others could only wait until sanity prevailed in higher echelons and replacement P-38s arrived. The wait lasted five months, after which the 9th FS received P-38Js and its scoring rate against enemy aircraft picked up almost immediately, compared with the 'victory doldrums' that had marked the P-47 period.

The arguments for and against one versus two engines in fighters implied no slur on the capability of the P-47 as a combat aircraft, but there was no denying that it was single-engined, heavy and thirsty. To those in any position to compare it with the P-38 there was simply no contest. The detractors (and there were a few) could similarly criticize the Lightning for being heavy and thirsty, but they could never accuse it of going out with only one engine.

Not that the Lightning always had things its own way in Pacific combat. There was ample evidence that Japanese fighters could indeed outmanoeuvre the P-38, as enough American fighter pilots reported at the time. And it was not unusual for pilots to note enemy flyers executing aerobatics for no apparent reason other than supreme confidence in their aircraft and their own ability.

Precautionary instructions were posted in USAAF briefing tents as the handling characteristics of the different Japanese fighters gradually became known, so that dangerous situations could be avoided whenever possible. The adage 'never dogfight with a Zero' was taken to heart by every newcomer, but the opposition was not always the A6M. Despite dozens of American combat reports seeming to confirm that the IJN's best fighter had been engaged, the Mitsubishi fighter was often mistaken for the Ki-43 'Oscar' and other types. The fact that the Zeke or Zero gradually lost its edge was another factor, though legends tend to die hard. Japanese pilot quality also declined markedly, but there were always individual pilots who were the exception to any general rule. Nobody could afford to be too complacent. Fortunately for the P-38 Groups, many fighter-versus-fighter engagements took place below 10,000ft (3,000m), where the Lockheed fighter's manoeuvrability, particularly its outstanding zoom and climb capability, could be used to advantage.

Safety Waiver

What often made the difference in combat was the enemy's foolhardy and large-scale skimping of such essentials to survival as parachutes and armour-plate protection for the pilots and/or crews, the fuel tanks and the engine(s) of most warplanes. A short burst from the concentrated firepower of the P-38's guns was often enough to 'flame' a Japanese aircraft that might have survived to fight another day had it been adequately protected. This factor alone lost the Japanese far more aircraft than necessary.

Another factor that gave American fighter pilots their edge and kept losses to a minimum was air discipline. It was stressed time and again that an aerial engagement was no place for a pilot to be flying alone. If he lost his wingman a pilot was advised to make every effort to join up with another P-38 so that the flexibility of the two-ship element could be maintained. For their part, the Japanese habitually foreswore any noticeable formation or cohesive teamwork, the US pilots reporting aircraft coming at them in seemingly undisciplined swarms or gaggles; a whole bunch of individualists in an arena where teamwork was vital for survival.

The enemy also used the highly dangerous practice of sending a single fighter aloft, if only for ferry flights. On occasion these singletons achieved spectacular results if they surprised Allied aircraft, the pilots of which could not always be certain that a second Japanese fighter was not lurking above, waiting to pounce. In short, if their tactics had been as good as their fighters, the toll of Allied aircraft could have been greater.

Those Nicknames

There is, curiously enough, some evidence to suggest that Japanese fighter pilots did not rate the P-38 very highly. Quite apart from the sometimes grossly exaggerated aerial victory claims made against it by various individuals, there appeared to be a general conviction that a twin-engine fighter was inherently cumbersome and therefore unable to dogfight IJN or JAAF single-seaters on equal terms, despite overwhelming evidence to the contrary.

It is on record that the Japanese even went as far as coining contemptuous nicknames for the Lightning, calling it *Perohachi*. This was a word-play on a Japanese term for something easy to destroy and *hachi*, meaning eight, the last digit of the P-38's designation – the implication was that the Lightning was easy to damage or destroy, which in the light of events was highly questionable! Then there was the simple 'two aeroplanes with one pilot' and 'Mezashi' or 'dried sardine', a term

that apparently stemmed from the way these small fish were packed in Japan, with a piece of bamboo running through their gills, representing the P-38's wing. In New Guinea Allied pilots were entertained by the Pidgin English term used by the natives to describe the Lightning 'One belly – double ass fella – he smellum out Japan man'; no translation needed here.

Whether these terms were widely used or even known on the Allied side is not clear. The sayings may well be apocryphal, as indeed appears to be the case with the oft-quoted German term 'der Gabelschwanz Teufel' (fork-tailed devil). Former Luftwaffe pilots are reportedly at a loss to recall this nickname, despite it being quoted in most P-38 references. Such nicknames often stemmed simply from colourful journalese, and that bestowed on the Lightning had the right ring to it and has persisted to the present day. It beats dried sardines by some margin.

An Escort of P-38s

War demands a lot of waiting and wondering, as shown by these 1st FG ground crews sprawled on Goxhill's grass. The P-38F-1 flew in the Press flight demonstration on 29 July 1942, during which the following five photographs were taken. **IWM**

By early 1942 a burgeoning USAAF training organization was working hard to prepare dozens of combat groups for overseas duty, and it was inevitable that less-capable production models of first-line combat aircraft became transitional training types. This was normal practice insofar as fighter groups would usually be issued with P-39s or P-40s to prepare for combat in later model P-40s, P-47s or P-51s. But if they had trained on the P-38, with its entirely different characteristics, air and ground crews alike found it something of a shock to be confronted with single-engine aircraft in their assigned war theatre. It did not happen often enough to create insurmountable operational problems, but there

were howls of protest in some quarters when pilots (and ground crew) were convinced that the brass had made an error.

This was the experience of the 78th FG. Assigned to England and the Eighth Air Force after several weeks of flying the P-38G Stateside, pilots found that they were to fly not Lightnings in combat but the P-47. Such a transition could be time-consuming, not to mention counter-productive, as everyone connected with aircraft operation had to go back to school, if only for a short period. The Thunderbolt period was actually left to newer pilots in the 78th, as it was mainly the 'old hands' who were posted to North Africa to be reunited with the Lightning, so there were few problems.

Earlier, a similar situation arose when the unit that became the most famous exponent of the P-47 in the ETO was to have received P-38s instead. The 56th FG just missed this change when P-38s were allocated elsewhere, such was the ever-changing nature of USAAC plans to provide enough combat groups for duty overseas. And just when one war plan seemed to have been finalized, shifting military priorities enforced yet another change in the deployment of fighter groups.

A similar mix-up occurred with theatre assignments (or so it seemed to the personnel involved), though with everything in a state of flux after Pearl Harbor, the mother of necessity had to be appeased.

Therefore, when the 1st, 14th and 82nd FGs arrived in England in the summer of 1942, there was initially every intention of absorbing their nine component squadrons into the Eighth Air Force. This would have given the heavy-bomber Groups a useful long-range escort fighter early on, and might (in hindsight) have enabled deep-penetration raids from England to have begun soon after VIII Bomber Command's debut mission, on 17 August 1942. Had such operations had the benefit of a P-38 escort, the 'bad-weather woes' experienced by the Lockheed fighter might well have been solved during the winter months of 1942–43, instead of a year later.

Assuming that all three P-38 Groups would have suffered losses to weather-related causes similar to those later suffered by the assigned Eighth Air Force Lightning Groups, there could still have been considerably more penetration of German airspace by American fighter cover by the summer of 1943 than there actually was. Furthermore, the greater time available for remedial work would probably have revealed the adverse effects of England's weather on Allison engines pushed to the limits of their capability, enabling the problem to be solved sooner.

In the event, an early chance to prove the Lightning's suitability in the escort role never came about. In their wisdom, USAAF chiefs decreed that all P-38 groups already in England in 1942 would become part of the Twelfth Air Force in North Africa, the air support for Operation *Torch*.

No Lightnings would be available to the Eighth for another eleven months, and not even the handful of photographic reconnaissance F-5s based in England escaped the exodus to North Africa.

This situation was seen as extremely grave in some circles, as the P-38 was believed to be the only fighter in the USAAF inventory capable of protecting the Eighth's heavies right into German airspace. Therefore, although the appearance of the P-38 in England had been brief, there was every intention that the Lightning would become an integral part of the Eighth as soon as possible.

Depot Support

To handle the erecting of Lightnings shipped to the UK, oversee the supply of spares and carry out any necessary modifications to its aircraft in the ETO, Lockheed established a depot at Langford Lodge in Northern Ireland. This complemented the company's main depot at Speke in Lancashire, which worked in conjunction with the Eighth Air Force's operational engineering base at Bovingdon in Hertfordshire.

To ensure that the interests of Lockheed were well supported, the company appointed Cunliffe Owen as its UK 'shadow'. This became standard procedure for all the major US manufacturers supplying aircraft and associated equipment to the UK during the war. The British companies acted as troubleshooters to help untangle red tape,

provide technical support and assist with numerous small details that in general only became apparent after US aircraft arrived in the country. The technical changes varied depending on the aircraft type and, to some extent, the military equipment requirements in vogue at the time it arrived.

Over by Sea

Despite the general success of Operation *Bolero* over the North Atlantic ferry route, the P-38s that had to be left in Greenland highlighted the hazards facing single-seat aircraft flying over such a distance. It was therefore decided not to extend *Bolero*-type airborne ferrying for fighters, but henceforth to rely on seaborne transport. This held its own hazards, but no pilots would be lost if enemy action happened to sink the temporary aircraft carriers. The number of P-38s that could be moved in this way varied according to the size of the vessel and its other cargo, but up to six could be accommodated by a Liberty-ship-size freighter.

Lockheed found that each P-38 need only be partly disassembled before being lifted on to a freighter deck by crane and secured against the rolling and pitching of the vessel. The most obvious aid to convenient stowage (and to minimizing damage) was to reduce the amount of space normally taken by an aircraft with a 52ft (15.85m) wingspan. This was achieved by removing the wing panels outboard of the nacelles. Each undercarriage oleo was fully retracted

There was little to give away the unit identity of the early P-38F-1s that equipped the 1st FG at Goxhill in mid-1942. IWM

and the doors closed and sealed. Protective Cosmolene covering was applied to the cockpit canopy and any vulnerable areas such as hatches and small air scoops. All armament was removed, and fuel and oil was completely drained off.

Upon the aircrafts' arrival in England, Lockheed technical representatives supervised the depot staff who prepared each one for flight. The first priority was to put each aircraft back on to its wheels so that it could be towed easily. In Liverpool and Belfast the

sight of P-38s rolling from the dockside and being towed out through the port gates and into the city streets became commonplace. Moved to a depot, each aircraft was inspected before its outer wing panels were attached. Any protective material and/or adhesive applied to the airframe to minimize the effects of salt water was removed, and the airframe thoroughly cleaned by hosing down using high-pressure steam.

The receiver airfields became hives of activity as tractors towed wingless P-38s to

dispersals for final assembly and inspection before they were fuelled and despatched to training or operational bases. Depending on the period of war, Lightnings were alternatively sent to 'holding' airfields for short- or long-term storage or modification.

Personnel stationed at airfields local to each depot and disembarkation port served as reception teams for American aircraft. As the presence of the Eighth Air Force in the UK increased, base air depots (BADs) such as Burtonwood in Lancashire were

TOP: Several Lightnings were demonstrated at the Goxhill Press facility, among them P-38F-1 41-7580, ticking over here as a fellow pilot gives his Lightning the gun. IWM

ABOVE: A P-38F of the 1st FG gets airborne at Goxhill. Although they were convinced they were in England to stay, as part of the Eighth Air Force, the 1st FG's pilots were soon in North Africa. IWM

RIGHT: 'A hell of a way to get into an airplane!' When the pressmen requested a demonstration, 2nd Lt James A. Force of Denver, a member of the 71st FS, 1st FG, showed how it was done. IWM

Lieutenant Force in the cockpit, demonstrating how the top section of the canopy was opened and closed with the aid of that stout handle. IWM

ground troops into action as early as possible was paramount, taking precedence over almost any other consideration. Therefore Operation *Torch* was boosted in terms of air assets to the detriment of the Eighth Air Force at a crucial time, but USAAF chiefs had little choice. There were too few trained fighter or bomber groups available in the autumn of 1942 and, to a degree, what experience there was had to be spread very thinly. It was also true that, at that time, the fallacy of the unescorted bomber formation operating in daylight had not been fully appreciated.

To the pilots of the Lightning Groups the chance to take on the fighters of the Luftwaffe, widely reckoned to be the enemy's best, was a challenge few would have turned down. Most individuals had put the exciting but demanding flight to England behind them, and there was ample evidence that the young pilots were more than eager to prove the P-38 in action. They had been demonstrably 'sold' on the Lockheed fighter's qualities, and the small matter of actually proving how it would fare in a tough war theatre appeared not to worry them in the slightest.

July 1942

On 26 July 1942, as the first USAAF fighter operation of the Eighth Air Force (by Spitfires) took place, so the P-38Fs of the 1st FG were arriving. Coming in to Goxhill, Lincolnshire, the unit was commanded by Col John Stone, with none other than Lockheed test pilot Ben Kelsey as a member of his Group. Now a colonel in the USAAF, Kelsey was to remain in the UK and join the Eighth's air technical organization along with such able officers as Maj Cass Hough.

In common with most other American aircraft arriving in England, all P-38s had to remain on the ground until their HF radio sets were changed to conform to RAF VHF standards. Without such 'tweaking' of the radios, pilots would have been unable to use the emergency channels in the event of technical malfunction, becoming disoriented over unfamiliar terrain or having to ditch in the sea.

This work took several weeks to complete on every single P-38, but on 29 August the 1st FG was able to send up four aircraft to 'intercept enemy raiders' presumably detected heading for Goxhill. No action materialized, however, and no enemy aircraft were seen.

developed to repair aircraft. Many hundreds of P-38s were to pass through the doors of the BADs, where the USAAF took advantage of the engineering skills and efforts of a local labour force to prevent any serious shortfalls in the number of aircraft available to combat units.

The seaborne freighting of P-38s as deck cargo extended to other theatres of war, and Lockheed depots were established in Australia to serve the SWPA. Such facilities developed from modest beginnings into vast maintenance, staging and storage areas. A great deal of US materiel was also moved into India to supply units in the

CBI, P-38s coming into the picture during 1943, when they were assigned to serve with the Tenth Air Force in Burma. To transit the vast ocean distances involved, escort carriers were often loaded with fighters as deck cargo, it being common for the US Navy to ship both its own aircraft and those of the USAAF in this way.

Primary Goal

If the bombing of Axis targets from England was seen as a key element in the US war effort, the importance of getting American

September 1942

On 1 September the 1st FG put up thirty-two P-38s for an equally uneventful practice fighter sweep along the French coast. In responding to various alerts over the next few days, the Lightning gradually became a familiar sight over England. The sizes of the formations sent aloft by the 1st FG during this period ranged from two to two dozen aircraft, but on 26 September the ground crews were alerted to ready thirty-six P-38s for an initial heavy-bomber escort mission. In the event this did not take place, and the Group was ordered to return to base. Heavy cloud had ruined the mission and the heavies were recalled, bringing their bombs home. Bad weather set in for several days, restricting air activity, and it was not until 2 October that the 1st FG was able to make its true operational debut.

On that day, part of three B-17 Groups attacked St Omer and Longuenesse aerodromes and plant at Meaulte in France, with Bostons bombing a ship in Le Havre docks. Of the thirty-one Lightnings despatched to cover the B-17s bound for Meaulte, nineteen were effective, reaching the target area and releasing their bombs. In addition the bombers were escorted by twenty-three Spitfires of the 4th FG, which claimed the only aerial victories for the day. None of the P-38 pilots reported any action in the role they had come overseas to perform. Nor did they do so on 9 October, when the 1st FG flew what turned out to be its final mission from England with the Eighth Air Force.

Few of the participating pilots could escape the feeling that the Group was not exactly being unleashed against the Luftwaffe. The rumour mill started to suggest that the unit was about to move, but where to was anyone's guess. The word spread quickly enough; the US Army was going to war in North Africa, and its air support would be coming from England.

Operation *Torch*

When the first two P-38 Groups assigned to the new Twelfth Air Force prepared for action in a new theatre, they too were confident enough in their aircraft. The 1st and 14th FGs were part of the air umbrella in a theatre of war that had seen Allied and Axis success and failure for nearly three years before American involvement. The *Torch* force was to prove decisive in eliminating the threat of German and Italian domination in North Africa by linking up with the British 8th Army.

Refuelling under way in the care of Pte Otis Neely, Cpl Wallace Gilliard, Cpl B. F. Prann and Tech Sgt F. Holleman. By 29 November 1942, the date of this photo, this P-38F was about to depart for North Africa.
IWM

November 1942

Of the three Eighth Air Force P-38 Groups, the 82nd had arrived in the UK to await its aircraft, which were flown to England via the southern ferry route. The Group had seen no operational flying with the Eighth, remaining at Eglington in Northern Ireland on training duties, which although tedious, probably stood the unit in good stead. It lodged briefly at Ibsley before moving to Tunisia to join the Twelfth. To reach their new operational area the P-38s were to fly non-stop to Oran, 1,500 miles (2,400km) from England, with Gibraltar as an emergency stopping point at 1,200 miles (1,900km) if any of the pilots experienced problems.

Ilfrey's Incident

Even before the P-38s had made their Mediterranean combat debut in terms of actually shooting at anything, the 94th FS caused a diplomatic incident. On 9 November, having been ordered to North Africa, and led by Col John N. Stone, squadron pilot Jack Ilfrey took off from Ibsley.

Each section of eight aircraft carried external tanks, and every drop of fuel the P-38F could carry had been pumped in. The route taken was over the Bay of Biscay, across the coast of Spain or Portugal, through the Straits of Gibraltar and thence to the coast of Spanish Morocco and, finally, Oran.

Ilfrey and his squadron colleague, Jim Harmon, experienced trouble. Ilfrey noticed the loss of one external tank when his starboard engine stopped. Although it fired up again when he switched tanks, it was clear that the P-38 was flying on 150 US gal (575ltr) less than when it left England. There was nothing for it but to seek an airfield. Conflicting thoughts of the 'bale-out, ditching, return to England or get to Gibraltar' variety went through Jack Ilfrey's mind, but he soon had fewer options than this. After flying over the sea for some time he turned south, hoping to make landfall on the coast of Spain or Portugal. It turned out to be the latter, and the P-38 was soon flying inland, following the course of the Tagus River towards Lisbon, burning up precious fuel.

Remembering that the squadron briefing officer had said little about what pilots should do if they had to land in Portugal, other than the fact that the natives were probably more friendly than the Spanish, Ilfrey looked for a place to put down. An airport just outside Lisbon (actually Portela de Sacavem) looked beautiful to the lone American, with wide runways, buildings and hangers and, no doubt, ample aviation fuel.

Although he fully realized that he would be interned and his aircraft impounded 'for the duration', Ilfrey had little choice. He landed without mishap and agreed to his P-38 being refuelled with 87- rather than 100-octane fuel (there was no other grade available). Surrounded by assorted officials, German airline crews and mounted Portuguese soldiers, he was wondering what to do next when Jim Harmon's Lighting came in to land on one engine. As his aircraft had by then been refuelled, Ilfrey was in the process of explaining the controls to a local pilot, who he assumed was intending to fly the Lightning to a military base after his 'conversion course'. At that point Ilfrey decided on another course of action. With the crowd temporarily distracted by the arrival of the second P-38, he saw his chance. Starting the port Allison, he threw all the necessary switches and the big fighter began to move. The unfortunate Portuguese pilot was forced to abandon ship in the slipstream, and Ilfrey was taxying on to the runway before anyone could stop him.

Heading for Gibraltar by the most direct route, Ilfrey eventually landed and was

Apart from the Pacific, the main war zone for the P-38 in early 1943 was North Africa. Here, Bernard Mouldoon of the 49th FS, 14th FG, has pilots synchronize their watches outside the HQ tent before a mission.
USAF

among friends – other 1st FG pilots who had had to divert from the ferry trip to Oran. The incident went all the way to Washington, via a very irate colonel in charge of US operations on The Rock, and to Eisenhower. Nobody took any action against Jack Ilfrey, despite a suggestion (several, in fact) that he and his P-38F would be returned for internment if the Portuguese insisted. Mercifully, 1st Lt Ilfrey was left to get on with the war and his eventual attainment of acedom flying P-38s and Mustangs with the 1st and 20th FGs. The Portuguese ended up with Capt Harmon's P-38F-1, though he too was able to return after agreeing to leave his aircraft in Portugal.

Combat Debut

The 14th FG's 48th FS undertook the first P-38 sorties in the MTO, taking off from Tafaraoui on 11 November, the day their aircraft arrived. Other group echelons, including the ground crews, arrived over succeeding days, the bulk of the 49th FS coming in on the 18th.

Three days after making the transition from the UK, one squadron of the 97th BG carried out a 'second-debut' mission when six B-17s bombed Sidi Ahmed Aerodrome at Bizerte. The 97th, now part of the Twelfth Air Force, had flown the first mission for the Eighth Air Force the previous August. The Bizerte raid meant that the P-38 squadrons were in the escort business.

Meanwhile, the 1st FG had occupied its first North African airfield at Tafaraoui in Algeria by 15 November. It moved to a second Algerian airfield, at Nouvion, one week later, and to a third, Youks-les-Bains, on 28 November.

Both P-38 units were the unintended victims of Gen Dwight Eisenhower's perceived misuse of tactical airpower. Spreading the combat units thinly along a 600-mile (960km) front rendered them vulnerable to being caught on their airfields by Axis bombing raids, as the 48th FS found to its cost.

By managing to field twelve Lightnings for a Douglas C-47 escort mission on the 18th, the 48th FS at least completed its first combat mission.

The 1st FG was joined in Algeria on 19 November by the 14th FG's squadrons, but after they had moved into Maison Blanche on 20 November the Germans dive-bombed and strafed the airfield that night, damaging hangars and seven P-38s. Two

P-38s were so badly damaged that they had to be written off, a sobering introduction to combat. Both squadrons of the 14th moved to Youks-les-Bains the following day. The 1st FG, which was not yet operational, had already relocated to Youks.

First Victory

On 21 November 1942 the 48th FS encountered the Luftwaffe in the air for the first time. During a B-17 escort the Lightnings chased off four Bf 109s that were threatening the bombers. Lieutenant Carl Williams gave chase and shot down one enemy fighter that had characteristically attempted to dive away, thus claiming the first MTO victory for the Lightning.

Early sorties for the P-38 units in the new MTO consisted almost exclusively of escorting heavy and B-25 and B-26 medium bombers to targets in Tunisia. These were relatively short-range missions for the Lockheed fighters, though operations were hardly trouble-free in terms of living conditions and support on the ground. Having traded the cold and damp conditions of English airfields in winter for warmer climes, the 1st and 14th FGs came to terms with their primitive surroundings; tented accommodation, scant facilities for adequate undercover servicing, and poor food were just a few of the deprivations. And if the North African weather was warmer during daylight hours, it held new hazards. It was freezing cold at night, and abrasive, all-pervading sand plagued men and machines alike. Expecting precision-engineered aeroplanes to function well under such conditions was, at the very least, optimistic.

Airfield facilities were poor or non-existent, and most servicing was carried out in the open or under canvas. Desert weather conditions did little for the temperamental Allison engines, and enemy ground fire and pilot inexperience in powerplant management and navigation resulted in an unacceptable number of forced landings. With fluid front lines beneath them, several pilots were lost when they had to put down in enemy territory hitherto declared to be in friendly hands. Featureless landscape in some areas added to the problems of pilots unable to call for assistance for fear of attracting the wrong sort of attention to themselves.

Luftwaffe aircraft based in Sardinia occasionally put in an appearance and destroyed US aircraft on the ground, but

these raids were never on a sufficient scale to wreck Allied plans. On escort missions the guns of a growing number of B-17s offered a crippled P-38 a degree of protection, and more than one fighter pilot was grateful for this service. Conversely, the bomber boys were more than happy to see a friendly fighter riding along with them.

Simply moving to forward airfields in Algeria to be nearer to the front line held hidden hazards, as the 14th found in a minor disaster of 21 November. Flying into Youks, six P-38s were wrecked attempting to land after dark, but the Group managed to mount two strafing missions the following day to help relieve the pressure on an American ground force fighting in the town of Gafsa.

Air operations on 24 November recorded two engagements for the 14th FG, when the P-38s came upon Italian transports and downed eleven of them between Gabes and Sfax. There were two separate air actions, but two pilots of the 49th FS, Lts Virgil M. Lusk and James E. Butler, shared all the enemy aircraft. Lusk claimed five, which would have made him the USAAF's first ace against the Axis and the first 'ace in a day' in the theatre. He was denied both honours, however, being credited with only four transports, though some doubt remained. In another two missions on the 26th, seven enemy transport aircraft were destroyed by the 14th. In a run of successes to the end of November the 1st and 14th shot down six more enemy aircraft.

December 1942

On the 1 December the P-38s were sent to attack enemy tanks located near Djedeida, with unknown results, but the Lightnings' 20mm cannon would have been very useful in what is believed to have been the first such action. What were officially termed 'aggressive sweeps' by the P-38 units resulted in nine enemy fighters shot down on 2 December, and three more Bf 109s were despatched on the 3rd. These sweeps continued for several days and brought further positive results, the ground-attack missions being interspersed with escort sorties by the P-38s. Such bomber targets as the port facilities at Bizerte, Sfax and Tunis appeared regularly on mission schedules to keep the Lightning Groups busy. On 12 December the Twelfth Air Force was able to announce its first P-38 ace when Lt Virgil H. Smith

Outdoor servicing was the order of the day for the ground crews attached to the 1st, 14th and 82nd FGs in North Africa. This was a typical scene surrounding a P-38F landing ground in Tunisia. IWM

shot down an Fw 190 over Gabes Aerodrome in the afternoon.

By the end of 1942, forced by a period of bad weather, the North African ground fighting had at least stabilized in preparation for a British Eighth Army drive to clear the Axis out of Libya. Much hard fighting lay ahead, with the air forces offering all the support they could. The principal combat area for the time being was to be Tunisia, and the Twelfth Air Force was built up accordingly.

The P-38s escorted medium and heavy bombers to various targets, the 14th FG having a particularly busy December. The Group's Lightnings provided high cover to medium bombers, flew reconnaissance sorties, laid on double missions on single days and escorted an increasingly strong heavy bomber force. When the Luftwaffe reacted it succeeded in picking off both bombers and escorting fighters in small numbers. Several P-38 pilots and aircraft were lost in air combat; three on 3 December alone. Flak was also a hazard at some targets, the Axis defending its airfields and ports with vigour. But the bomber crews were encouraged to see their P-38 escort on most missions, and their presence undoubtedly helped to keep losses to a minimum.

Virgil Smith of the 14th FG was shot down during an operation in the Gabes area on 30 December. Twelve P-38s of the 48th FS had been escorting a dozen Bostons bombing troop concentrations on the edge of the town when II./JG 53's Bf 109s attacked American aircraft exiting the target area. One of the Messerschmitts picked off the Lightning flown by Smith, and two

others fell to a second Bf 109. This was a bad day for the Group, as it had lost another pilot, of the 49th FS, during a sea-search mission that morning.

Christmas Debut

When it was finally able to settle at Oran on Christmas Day 1942 and plan operations, the 82nd FG was handed an anti-submarine patrol. Based initially at Tafaraoui, the unit's pilots had claimed at least one victory and one damaged while in combat with Junkers Ju 88s over the Bay of Biscay on the way over from England. The most likely Luftwaffe unit to have clashed with P-38s over the bay at that time were those of V./KG 40, the Luftwaffe's seasoned anti-shipping unit. One Ju 88 of this unit was indeed reported lost on 23 December.

The 82nd FG moved to the grass airfield at Telergma in Algeria and from 3 January 1943 began flying long-range fighter sweeps, medium-bomber escorts and anti-shipping strikes. For the last-named missions the P-38s used the tried and tested method of skip bombing against enemy shipping.

With some misgivings the 82nd was almost immediately obliged to hand on twenty-four Lightnings to the battered 1st and 14th FGs to make good combat attrition. In addition, the pilots, most of whom had no engineering training, had to maintain their own aircraft until their delayed ground crews arrived soon after the move to Telergma. This location offered the

aircrews spartan facilities, extremely cold nights and only the barest minimum of accommodation.

However, anticipation as to how the Group would fare in combat was positive. In common with the two Groups already in the theatre, the 82nd's pilots believed that the P-38 would have the edge on any enemy aircraft encountered in combat. Such was the confidence of youth. But reality struck the 82nd as forcefully as it had hit its colleagues and rivals.

For its first mission, on 3 January 1943, the 82nd put up eight P-38s to escort eight to twelve medium bombers at altitudes of 10,000 to 12,000ft (3,000 to 3,700m). This meant that most pilots could stay off oxygen and avoid any detrimental effects that the equipment might have if the pilot was forgetful about operating it in the heat of combat. Introduction to the opposition was not long in coming, and in those days the Axis air forces were strong enough to put up scores of fighters to intercept a single bombing raid. Encounters with up to fifty Bf 109s were not uncommon.

As well as targeting tanks and aerodromes, the P-38s had had some success in attacking Axis rail traffic, which was increasingly vital in moving supplies from docks to depots along the coastal strip of North Africa. The battering the ports were receiving from Allied airpower made rapid movement by road and rail imperative if freshly unloaded supplies were not to go up in flames following a hazardous sea voyage from Europe.

In the MTO the first heavy bomber raids were flown at altitudes that were comfortable for both the bomber crews and their P-38 escort. At heights of 10,000ft (3,000m) or thereabouts the then-current P-38F and G Lightnings did not experience as much cold air and resultant engine trouble as they would later over Europe.

With a stalemate on the ground, air support became increasingly important, and with the front lines a considerable distance from the RAF/USAAF desert landing grounds, the P-38 was the only fighter in the Allies' inventory with sufficient endurance to carry out lengthy patrols.

January 1943

Not every Lightning had left the UK in 1942. There were enough on hand partly to equip the 346th and 347th FSs of the 350th FG, which had been activated in England on 1 October 1942. This move was made under a special authority granted to the Eighth Air Force, with the 350th's component squadrons departing for North Africa during January-February 1943. The Group, which flew P-39s and P-40s as well as P-38s, generally undertook a ground-attack role in the MTO.

All three P-38 Groups, plus the 33rd (P-40s) and 52nd (Spitfires), claimed four enemy fighters in combat on 8 January while escorting several different bombing missions. Familiar targets such as Sfax, Tripoli and Gabes were repeatedly bombed. These missions were flown in conjunction with anti-shipping and anti-tank strikes by P-38s, often in the form of bomber support sorties to divert hostile attention from the medium and heavy bombers. Skies could get pretty crowded in certain sectors, causing considerable confusion to the airmen concerned when it came to reporting exactly what happened. Such a mission took place on 21 January, when the Lightning pilots of the 82nd escorted 319th BG B-26s in an attack on an Axis convoy en route from Sicily to Tunisia. A running fight developed after one freighter was sunk, enemy aircraft intervening to drive off the Allied fighters and bombers. They hardly succeeded, as the Lightnings fought back and claimed seven German and Italian fighters in return for two of their own pilots and aircraft. Claims were often optimistic on both sides owing to inexperience and other factors, such as the Americans habitually failing to distinguish Italian fighters from German, similar mistakes also being made by the 'other side'. Aircraft

falling away trailing smoke would be assumed to be fatally damaged in the heat of battle, but this was often not the case. In fact the Axis aircraft lost on the 21st were two Savoia Marchetti SM.84 transports and three Bf 109s – or Macchi MC.202s. German pilots claimed to have shot down two P-38s, while the Italians claimed one.

Strafing was an effective part of the offensive against an increasingly hard-pressed Afrika Korps now trying to extricate itself from Tripoli, and on that busy 21 January the 1st FG found the Gabes–Medenine–Ben Gardane road clogged with Axis transport. Twenty-four P-38s swept in and claimed sixty-five vehicles destroyed by their fire, plus a pair of Bf 109s that unwisely made an appearance. The aircraft claims had a touch of fantasy about them, as the two Bf 109s were apparently JG 77 machines flown by Lt Bar and his wingman, both of whom returned to report combat with twenty P-38s and claimed two shot down. In fact, all aircraft on both sides returned safely.

It appeared that Lady Luck rode with the Lightning pilots only temporarily, as every success seemed to be achieved at the price of a couple of P-38s on the same day or the day after. Four more P-38 pilots were officially posted as 'missing in action' (MIA) in the following few days. Accidents and pilot injuries had to be added to operational attrition as a direct result of combat, and this slow sapping of strength began to have a very detrimental effect. On 28 January the 14th FG was withdrawn from combat and its aircraft handed over to the 82nd. Some new pilots were also transferred. The 14th FG's 48th FS had experienced a particularly gruelling period of combat since 18 November, having lost thirteen pilots and some twenty P-38s in that short time. Six aircraft went down on 23 January, which was something of a last straw in terms of morale. The Group was ordered to Mediouna Aerodrome near Casablanca for rest and retraining, and remained off operations until May.

Back in England the as yet non-operational 78th FG had fifty-eight P-38Gs on strength by January. But in February the word came down that the unit's pilots and aircraft were to leave for North Africa without delay, to serve as replacements. The Group's ground echelon remained in England to await re-equipping with the P-47, much to the displeasure of many personnel.

February/March 1943

If the early experiences of the P-38 groups assigned to the Twelfth Air Force were much the same – universally depressing and morale-denting – they did improve gradually. It was obvious in the early days that the largely inexperienced Lightning pilots were up against some of the Luftwaffe's best and, if anyone doubted this, the 'Axis Sally' radio broadcasts constantly reminded them that it was so.

In time, things began to shape up as the RAF and USAAF deployed an increasing number of fighter squadrons in a manner that suited the performance of the aircraft flown by the units. International co-operation helped, as did an improved command structure to direct a vast number of air operations over considerable distances.

For the P-38 Groups that had overcome extreme difficulties in hostile conditions, the spring of 1943 brought enough air combat success to justify their continuing as an integral part of the Twelfth Air Force. On 20 March the 82nd FG was escorting B-25s attacking seaborne targets when both German and Italian fighters jumped the bombers. The P-38s dived through a thin cloud layer to counterattack. The bounce worked well, and eleven enemy aircraft – eight Bf 109s, one Macchi and two Ju 88s – were claimed shot down.

By then US tactics had adapted to the demands of the theatre. In the early stages P-38 units had adopted a line-abreast formation, which, although it offered a good cross-over and enabled the P-38s to match the speed of the bombers they were escorting, put them at a disadvantage when attacked. From cruising speed the big US fighters could not accelerate quickly enough when the more agile Axis single-seaters waded in. There was a positive outcome to this poor formation, as the pilots had also used a 'scissors' manoeuvre to stay with the bombers. This exploited the Lightning's good turning and climbing capability, which was highly effective when used intelligently.

On 22 March the 82nd again did well when twenty-three P-38s of the 97th FS were despatched to escort 17th BG Marauders. When the formation was jumped out of the sun north of Cape Serrat, one P-38 went down before the rest could react. Such hit-and-run tactics often served the Axis fighters well, but on this occasion the tables were later turned when an estimated twenty Bf 109s attacked.

Two P-38s were lost, but the group claimed seven Bf 109s destroyed.

Transport Prey

Time was running out for the Axis in North Africa, and increasingly risky attempts to beat the Allied air and sea blockade were made. Allied pilots saw scores of Junkers Ju 52s ferrying troops and equipment from Sicily via Cape Bon in April. The 1st and 82nd FGs took part in the destruction of the German transports, caught at low level in daylight with minimal fighter protection. The 1st FG claimed eleven Ju 52s and five fighters, and the 82nd seven Ju 52s and eight fighters, at the cost of five P-38s.

On 10 April the 1st FG's Lightnings came upon more transports and shot down ten, plus seven Italian fighters. Later that day the 82nd destroyed another ten Ju 52s and a Ju 88. So complete was Allied domination of the battle arena that several B-25 gunners were able to join in the carnage without due risk to themselves.

With a revised and more cohesive command structure running the broadening air war in the Mediterranean, the P-38 Groups (temporarily down to two) continued to 'ride shotgun' for the bombers. On 20 March an 82nd FG escort to B-25s on a sea search off Cap Bon was attacked by fifty Axis fighters. The Lightning pilots reacted well and claimed eleven destroyed, two unconfirmed and two damaged without loss to themselves, a rare result and one to be celebrated.

Boeing B-17s began bombing Sicily on 22 March, the month in which more shipping strikes by the P-38s were recorded. Five vessels were claimed as destroyed by P-38s of the 82nd FG. At the end of the month the Mareth Line was in British hands, a move that also secured the port town of Gabes. Periodic bad weather reduced air operations at this time, but the 82nd was able to claim a Ju 88 and a Bf 109 on a late afternoon patrol on the 31st.

April 1943

On 5 April Operation *Flax* was launched. This was an Allied drive to cut off the flow of Axis reinforcements and supplies coming from Italy by air. While mounting an escort to B-25s at 08.00hr, twenty-six 1st FG pilots ran across enemy fighters escorting some seventy transports over the Straits

of Sicily north of Cap Bon. The P-38s waded in and pilots claimed seventeen enemy aircraft destroyed, eleven of them transports. The combats also cost four Lightnings, but Capt Darrell G. Welch of the 27th FS became an ace when he was credited with three Ju 52s.

Twenty minutes or so after the 1st FG's combat the 82nd was escorting B-25s on a shipping strike when another large formation of Axis transports was seen in the same area. As the Mitchells selected their seaborne targets, the Lightnings divided their force to engage the enemy fighter escort while simultaneously going after the transports. Nine of the latter were claimed destroyed, along with five other German aircraft of various types and three Bf 109s. Two more Bf 109s were claimed by the 82nd later that day.

German resistance in North Africa was waning fast, and by 10 April Sfax was in the hands of the Eighth Army. The Germans maintained the dangerous air route north of Cap Bon to reach Sicily, a typically large formation of about fifty Ju 52s being reported by 1st FG pilots at 06.20hr that day. There were actually twenty transports, Italian SM.82s and SM.75s, escorted by at least six Macchi 200s. The Lightnings shot down ten transports (eighteen were claimed), the results often being visually spectacular as most of the enemy aircraft were carrying fuel. Top honours went to pilots of the 71st FS, but the day was not yet over. At 10.45hr the 82nd was flying a B-25 escort when some thirty enemy aircraft were observed. These were mainly Ju 52s heading for Tunis via Cap Bon, a location fast becoming infamous as an aircraft graveyard. The 1st FG's claims later had to be downgraded to five Ju 52s and three Me 323s.

Victory claims made in the heat of combat were seemingly inflated in proportion to the number of aircraft in the sky at the time; an understandable problem. Totals were often reduced after subsequent investigation, but that day's announcement that USAAF P-38 pilots had shot down thirty-nine transports and twelve escorts did nothing but good for morale. However, it was badly affected by events as the 1st FG headed back to base, unaware that it was being shadowed by fifteen Bf 109s that had taken off from Bizerte. The German pilots waited until the P-38 formation was over Cap Rosa at 13.10hr before opening fire. They shot down one P-38 and damaged three others before making good their escape.

Flying another sweep over the Sicilian Strait after taking off at 06.15hr, the 85th FS Lightnings found twenty more Ju 52s at 08.00hr. They dived to get good firing positions as the enemy aircraft flew slowly at zero feet, hoping that their escort of four Ju 88s and four Bf 110s, plus a higher cover of seven Bf 109s, could keep the P-38s at bay. The escort failed to do so, and the Lightnings shot down the entire formation, plus several of the escorts, for the loss of three of their own number.

One flight of twenty 82nd FG P-38s on a sweep at 07.30hr came upon yet more Ju 52s and destroyed five. It might have been more had the four flights of the 96th FS not missed their heading and flown off in the wrong direction. Again there was a price to pay, Lt W. B. Rawson failing to return after possibly falling victim to a Bf 110 of III./ZG 76.

Return of the 14th FG – May 1943

On 13 May 1943 the pattern of the war in the Mediterranean changed dramatically with the surrender of 270,000 German and Italian troops who were trapped on the north coast of Tunisia and simply had nowhere to go. In the meantime the 14th FG, with new P-38s and an additional squadron, the 37th, added to its strength, returned to combat duty. It boasted ninety Lightnings for the forthcoming round of operations. A normal three-squadron USAAF group compliment was standardized on seventy aircraft, so the 14th now had some leeway in terms of strength.

By May the 82nd FG had also suffered sobering losses. Since entering combat in December 1942 it had lost sixty-four P-38s in return for claims of 199 enemy aircraft destroyed, 329 unconfirmed and 47 damaged. In human terms that translated into 60 of the 120 assigned pilots in its first ninety days in the MTO. Unlike the 14th it was not pulled back, but stayed in the line to undertaken forthcoming missions against Pantelleria, Sicily and Italy. Likewise, the 1st stayed the course in the MTO, but its combat figures offered little comfort to USAAF planners. At least sixty P-38s had gone down, their pilots having been lost to the Group in three main categories: killed, missing or prisoner of war. This total included those injured in crashes or accidents and, in some cases, returned to the Group later to complete their interrupted tours. But, in terms of P-38s totally or temporarily lost to strength, the drain on replacement aircraft was heavy.

During May the 350th FG, which flew P-39 Airacobras as part of Northwest African Coastal Air Force, acquired six P-38Gs and distributed two to each to its three squadrons. Their main purpose was to track and attempt to intercept high-altitude German reconnaissance aircraft, a move that met with some success, as four Ju 88s were shot down between 19 June and 8 July. The Lightnings operated under radar control in an experiment that lasted until 1 October.

End in Tunisia

At the close of the Tunisian campaign the USAAF in the MTO had turned the corner as far as P-38 operations were concerned. The campaign had been less than encouraging in some respects, but the period of combat ended with the following pilots of the 1st FG emerging as aces: Meldrum F. Sears (7); Jack Ilfrey (5½), Newell O. Roberts (5½); Jack A. Owens, Jr, Darrell G. Welch, Lee V. Wiseman and John L. Wolford had five victories each.

The 14th FG's leading aces at that time were Virgil H. Smith with six and Virgil W. Lusk with five. The 82nd's leader in terms of aerial victories was Claude R. Kinsey, Jr, with seven, followed by Thomas A. White and Charles J. Zubarek with six each. Five more pilots had scored the baseline five to become aces.

Once the technical difficulties of the P-38 had been overcome, the MTO proved to be a happier hunting ground for all the P-38 Groups compared to the ETO. The 1st FG eventually produced eleven aces with a score above the baseline five, the 14th five and the 82nd sixteen.

Eight more pilots of the 1st FG became aces when the P-38 Groups were transferred to the 15th Air Force, with the 14th adding another eleven and the 82nd five. Two pilots, Willian J. Sloan of the 82nd and Michael Brezas of the 14th, shared the top place among P-38 aces in the MTO, with twelve victories each. Sloan obtained all his victories in 1943 as part of the Twelfth Air Force, while Brezas ran his score up in 1944 with the Fifteenth.

The above figures resulted in the MTO becoming the second most successful theatre in terms of aerial kills by P-38 pilots, behind the Fifth Air Force. In addition, several pilots destroyed enemy aircraft on the ground, but in common with most other USAAF air forces the Twelfth did not count these as part of the overall score credited to individual pilots.

Sicily

The reduction of the island of Pantelleria was achieved purely by Allied airpower, which, despite delivering more than 6,000 tons (6,090 tonnes) of bombs, caused relatively light damage but induced the Italian garrison to capitulate without need of an invasion.

With Axis resistance in Tunisia ended, Operation *Husky*, the invasion of Sicily, went ahead on 3 July. The Allies made good progress, enjoying excellent air support, and by the end of the month the liberation of the island from German control was not in doubt.

Air cover for the ground troops was improved the nearer fighter bombers were based to the front lines, and with the P-38 Groups based in Sicily such support could be extended and refined. The Lightning squadrons were not unique in giving themselves nicknames to assist identity and retain anonymity over air–ground radio channels, and to reflect *esprit de corps*. There were instances of both radio call-signs and nicknames being in vogue at the same time, an example being the 27th FS of the 1st FG. This unit was known as the 'Petdog Squadron' or the 'Desert Rats', these being respectively the unit's regular radio call-sign and the self-explanatory description of the primitive living conditions and constant moves that had been necessary to keep up with the ground advances of the North African war.

The other two squadrons of the 1st were identified as Craigmore and Springcap, and so common did these names become that they were occasionally used in lieu of other, more racy nicknames as a matter of convenience by several squadrons in different theatres of war. Radio call signs were also useful to the press, the members of which could freely quote the call signs without too much risk of identifying the unit in question.

For the P-38 pilots, combat over Sicily posed similar challenges to those of the North African conflict, the difference being that by mid-1943 fundamental problems could be more easily overcome by experience. For example, the aircraft was found to be unsuited to fast, sudden manoeuvres. A pilot on the receiving end of enemy fire was surprised to realize that shoving the Lightning's control wheel hard over produced precisely nothing. For a few terrifying seconds the P-38 would maintain course before the bank came on. After banking 5 or 10 degrees the aircraft went over quickly, but by that time the pilot might have had more pressing things on his mind.

Another problem with the P-38 was what one pilot described as 'queer ailerons'. Until power boost was introduced, the aircraft was unable to roll into a dive fast enough to catch German fighters diving away after a characteristic split-S. Even with power boost the ailerons required muscle power to make them effective, particularly at low airspeeds. The Lightning's ability to maintain a turn and tighten it up helped redress the situation, however, and some pilots reckoned that a well-flown P-38 could stay with almost any opposing fighter in a turn because it had the reserve power to prevent any dangerous loss of speed or altitude.

Diving the P-38 was exhilarating, as the aircraft lost height very rapidly. It could also be looped without restriction, and there was no difficulty in executing Immelmann turns and Cuban eights. The Lightning was particularly adept at manoeuvres in the vertical plane, and had excellent zoom and climb characteristics, superior to those of most single-engine fighters.

Despite a spiralling attrition rate the MTO P-38 groups soldiered on. Replacement pilots and aircraft were absorbed, but the general availability of the Lockheed twin remained limited. This was one reason why the MTO had priority and no new Groups could be sent to the Eighth Air Force until the autumn of 1943.

Intelligence confirmed that Rommel was attempting to save as many of his troops as possible by a risky airlift of men and materiel from Sicily to Italy, the clock moving towards the surrender of the country in September.

In marked contrast to their colleagues in the Eighth Air Force, the bomber crews of the Twelfth enjoyed complete out-and-back fighter escort for most of their missions, right from the word go. The fact that the North African-based bomb groups were flying against relatively short-range targets did not alter the fact that fighter cover was a huge boost to the morale of the bomber men.

While the early combat experiences of the 1st and 14th FGs had much in common, there were numerous detail contrasts.

Having suffered a few gruelling months in conditions that were not very conducive to smooth air operations, the trio of 12th Air Force P-38 Groups had gradually weathered the storm and emerged to become a formidable force. Heavy and medium bomber operations in the MTO enjoyed 'an escort of P-38s', which was always highly appreciated. And it was nearly always possible not only to provide an escort, but for the fighters to take the bombers right through to their targets and back. There was no question that an escort of P-38s continued to be highly appreciated by the bomber crews.

October 1943 – Slaughter of the Stukas

On 4 October 1943 the USAAF was called in to help its British allies fighting a rearguard action in the Dodecanese Islands. This operation had met with unexpectedly heavy German resistance, and troops were forced to withdraw by sea. Convoys plying the Aegean needed protection from the Luftwaffe, and the P-38s of the 1st and 14th FGs were despatched. On the 5th the 1st FG departed Mateur to head for Gambut III in Libya, an airfield that had seen plenty of action but had been abandoned after Rommel's Afrika Corps had been forced into headlong retreat. Each P-38G was carrying two 165 US gal (624ltr) drop tanks, and every pilot, familiar with desert conditions and the general lack of facilities on primitive landing grounds, had crammed his cockpit and any other available space with rations, bedding and extra clothing.

The Group's thirty-six aircraft flew east over Tunis, Sfax, Gabes, Tripoli, Benghazi and Tobruk. A turn at Tobruk took the Lightnings south to what the pilots thought was Gambut. Spotting an abandoned airfield littered with wrecks, the 1st landed shortly before night closed in. The pilots tumbled out to check their exact location, but before they could do so the sound of the P-38s of the 14th FG became audible. It was then dark, so the 1st FG pilots turned on their landing lights to guide the newcomers safely down. This was accomplished by all but one P-38, which overran and crashed through an Arab tent, killing an unfortunate slave girl.

More lights appeared in the sky, and soon the Lightnings were joined by a group of C-47s. The airfield was filling up fast, but to their distress the Americans learned

that Gambut actually lay some 15 miles (25km) further east. There were no facilities at the present base, but the pilots had no choice but to bed down for the night and sleep next to their fighters.

On the morning of 9 October a search aircraft took off and its pilot duly reported the error, plus the fact that the 1st FG's ground crews had landed at Gambut. The P-38s moved to the right base, and from there took off for the convoy cover mission.

The squadrons of the Group patrolled the convoy in relays, Petdog and Craigmore aircraft thus covering the ships in the morning, with the 14th FG due to take the 'afternoon shift'. Petdog Squadron then spotted four Junkers Ju 87s with two Bf 109Es as escort at 7,000ft (2,100m), and hit the German formation before it could launch an attack on the ships. Apparently unnoticed by the enemy fliers, the P-38s achieved surprise and sent two Stukas down while the other pair attempted to drop their bombs. These too were shot down by the fast-diving P-38s, the Messerschmitts having sought cloud cover rather than action.

With the arrival of Springcap Squadron the 1st FG was at full strength, well able to provide shipping escort for another two hours before returning to Gambut. Another hour passed before Craigmore Squadron finally left the area, handing over patrol duty to one of the 14th FG's squadrons.

The Germans had apparently monitored all this activity on their radars at Athens and on Crete, but the operators failed to notice that when the 1st FG aircraft had left, the 14th FG had immediately taken its place. Signals were sent to Luftwaffe airfields, ordering attacks on the ships, which were now believed to have no air cover. By the time the Germans had hurriedly launched thirty Ju 87s and Ju 88s the 14th FG was in place. Like the Lightnings of the 1st FG before them, those of the 14th had flown out to the ships' position at wave-top height, avoiding radar detection.

Shortly after midday Maj William Leverette, leading the 37th FS, the first squadron of the 14th to arrive on the scene, called in a row of dots on the horizon as the unsuspecting Germans headed for the British ships. Suddenly they were set upon by a pack of twin-tailed wolves. The P-38s carved into the slow dive-bombers with devastating effect and they fell like 'leaves in the wind'. Seventeen enemy aircraft, sixteen Ju 87s and one Ju 88, were claimed shot down by the Americans.

The Germans abandoned the shipping strike and the remnants limped away, some of the Ju 87s trailing smoke.

In his first-ever encounter with enemy aircraft, Bill Leverette became an 'ace in a day' by claiming nine in the heat of battle. He was allowed a still highly respectable seven Stukas, destroyed in less than ten minutes of hectic combat. This was to stand as a record score for a USAAF pilot in a single engagement during the war. For his feat Leverette was awarded the Distinguished Service Cross. Element leader Lt Harry 'Troy' Hanna also became an ace in a day, being officially credited with five destroyed and one damaged.

Naturally enough, all this success by their rivals did not sit too well with the pilots of the 1st FG, who, but for a few hours, had missed their chance under the unforgiving 'fortunes of war'. For the 14th such a banner day of action helped wipe out the memory of the initial weeks of combat in the MTO, which had been sobering, to say the least.

The Desert Aces

It was almost inevitable that the second air war of the twentieth century would be compared with the first in terms of the number of fighter pilots who scored five or more aerial victories and warranted the term 'ace'. The accolade was good for morale and a personal stamp of approval of individual skills, and the USAAF forces in all of the war theatres were able to announce their aces, sooner or later. For the P-38 squadrons such pinnacles may appear to have been harder to achieve, compared with the pilots of other units flying other aircraft types, and, on the face of it, the European-based units did not do so well in this respect. But this narrow comparison should be avoided, as the 'numbers game' cannot tell the full story. The USAAF's fighter pilots were not simply flying missions to knock down enemy aircraft. If 'protection by presence' was enough on many P-38 bomber-escort missions, who cared if the would-be interceptors were destroyed by Warhawks, US-manned Spitfires or any other fighter, come to that? Certainly not the bomber crews. To them, what mattered was to get their bombs on target and get home safely, and if their fighter escort had little to do but simply be there, few had cause for complaint. Red-blooded fighters knew that, but shooting down a few more '109s would have been good.

CHAPTER FIVE

Weathering the Storms

When, in the summer of 1943, the Eighth Air Force was finally assigned several squadrons of P-38s that were not going to be whisked away to serve elsewhere, USAAF bomber chiefs breathed a collective sigh of relief. Here, they still believed, was the one fighter in the inventory that could reduce bomber losses by escorting them all the way to their most distant targets. By that time such an asset was long overdue, despite the continuing stubborn insistence in some quarters that bombers armed with a dozen machine-guns apiece could take care of themselves. Stark evidence to the contrary could have been provided by every bomber base in England. The view from Washington was remote in more than physical terms, and somewhat clouded by figures showing percentage losses versus achievements. It was easy to be blinded by the mounting bomber effort comparing

unfavourably with German loss of production, not to mention the spiralling cost in B-17 and B-24 crews.

For escort missions over Europe the P-38 equipped with two 75 US gal (280ltr) drop tanks boasted a range of 520 miles (840km), about 100 miles (160km) more than the P-47D needed to fly to Berlin. That was still not enough to shepherd the B-17s and B-24s to the far corners of eastern Europe, but it was the best that was then available. By February 1944, when drop tanks of 108 US gal (388ltr) capacity were available in quantity, the P-38 could reach 585 miles (940km) from base, which took it as far as Berlin.

Europe was, however, the one war front where the Lightning encountered natural and political conditions to the extent that it came to be both lauded and derided. Yet in England the P-38 found a powerful friend,

well placed to fight its corner if need be. Colonel Cass H. Hough, head of the Eighth Air Force's technical department, fell for the aircraft immediately and acquired a P-38F-1 (41-7552) for his own personal use. Hough soon started wondering what other roles the P-38 might perform to assist the Eighth Air Force, and began to tinker. His ideas were later turned into hardware, as recorded elsewhere.

Hough always maintained that both Lockheed and Wright Field had placed too many restrictions on the Lightning, rendering it less than effective in the hands of inexperienced pilots. He also said that one of the aircraft's main defects was that the engine induction system had been made too small and that powerplant problems were often caused by inappropriate pilot action.

In July 1944 Cass Hough was himself the victim of an unfortunate press release

Burbank stepped up production of P-38Fs, Gs and Hs, aided by the Californian weather, which permitted a good deal of final assembly work to be done out of doors. IWM

As part of the mechanized assembly of P-38s, Lockheed built a chain conveyor which moved at a minimum speed of 4in/min to enable near-complete aircraft to be worked on without the line actually halting. IWM

TOP: Meanwhile, in England, the first of four Lightning Groups allocated to the Eighth Air Force got itself organized for the important long-range escort duty, for which 150-gal drop tanks were vital. IWM

ABOVE: Bicycles were important items of base equipment on airfields in Britain, as were workstands to enable servicing crews to reach a P-38's propeller hub. IWM

about the P-38, one that dogged him for years afterwards. The story, naturally picked up by the press, told the world that Hough had: 'been awarded the American DFC for "independent flight research". Diving both a Lightning and a Thunderbolt, he attained a speed in excess of 780mph [1,255km/h]. The actual speeds are military secrets.' Despite such a feat being technically and physically impossible with a piston-engine aircraft, people believed it. For his part, Hough spent the next few decades trying to live down something he had not done, and had never claimed to have done.

No Sweat

The first unit of the second Lightning force that arrived in the UK to join VIII Fighter Command was the 55th FG, based at Nuthampstead, Hertfordshire. By the time it arrived, in September 1943, the Eighth Air Force's bombers were being badly mauled when they flew beyond effective US fighter escort range, and much was expected of the 55th, a Group with the potential to redress the situation. Unfortunately the generally positive 'official' reputation gained by the P-38 (enhanced by some good combat results elsewhere, not to

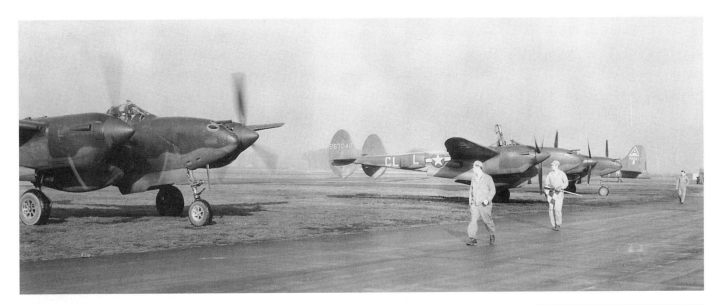

TOP: The scene at Bassingbourn on 12 December 1943 as P-38Hs, including 42-67042/CL-L of the 338th FS, 55th FG, prepare to fly an escort mission to their host B-17s of the 91st BG. USAF

ABOVE: The Eighth Air Force's dynamic technical officer, Cass Hough, acquired P-38F-1 41-7552 for his personal use, and had a skunk painted on the nose to match the small toy skunk he carried as a mascot. Here he is flanked by S/Sgts Eliseo Borrego (*left*) and Karl R. Olson. The latter was responsible for maintaining the Lightning, while Borrego looked after Hough's P-47D. Author's collection

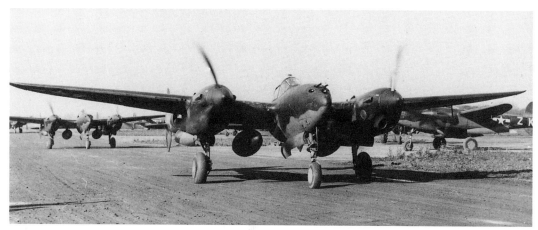

The 20th FG taxies out at King's Cliffe, Northants, for an escort mission. RAF Museum

mention company publicity) tended to cloud what lay ahead for a largely untried group of pilots. Irrespective of the problems encountered by the Lightning Groups on the southern front, this was England, the ETO, the big league. If better airfields, transportation and ground facilities were any yardstick of success, then this was the place to be. Group CO Lt Col Frank B. James had every confidence that the P-38Hs equipping his three squadrons, the 38th, 338th and 343rd, would take the war to the enemy in a big way.

Any reputation-denting feedback from Groups flying the same aircraft on different fronts did not always read across, because operating conditions, leadership experience, the strength of the opposition and so forth, were often fundamentally different. So if the early experiences of the three Groups in the MTO did not exactly engender over-confidence in their Eighth Air Force colleagues, the conditions hardly compared. Given that fact, however, a deeper probing into the reports should have emphasized that, in many combat situations, the P-38 was at times found to be no match for a well-flown Focke-Wulf Fw 190 or Messerschmitt Bf 109.

Anyone criticizing the P-38 by comparing it with contemporary single-seaters had it pointed out, often quite forcibly, that the American fighter had the undeniable advantage of two engines. It was also docile and easy to fly, handling like 'a Link trainer between two P-40s', very well armed and fast. Such undeniable attributes appeared to silence the doubters. But few had thoroughly examined the implications of one engine failing, and the resulting strain imposed upon the remaining Allison during a flight home of a few hundred miles. That the failure could be

caused by atmospheric conditions, with no enemy action whatsoever, was also overlooked. Malfunction of vital items of equipment while in German airspace could also lead to disaster, and all too many P-38 pilots were to find out that the hostile conditions prevailing in the skies over continental Europe cared nothing for reputations.

October 1943

Weather and technical problems delayed the combat debut of the 55th FG until 15 October 1943, when thirty-six aircraft were despatched on an initial fighter sweep over the Dutch islands that proved uneventful, as shakedown missions were supposed to be. The Group recorded its early combat sorties in a somewhat sobering atmosphere, for the memory of the previous day's terrible loss of sixty B-17s on the second of the notorious Schweinfurt missions was far too fresh in everyone's mind. Fervent hopes were voiced that the P-38H-5s of the 55th FG would be the first of the saviours of the Eighth Air Force bombers, and prove instrumental in preventing another, similar occurrence. As it happened, the 'second Schweinfurt' mission was the last of the heavy-loss raids of 1943, though as far as solid protection from 'all-the-way' fighter escort went, hopes were largely dashed. As the 55th's pilots and ground crews came to grips with the severity of an English winter and the bitter, damp cold over north-western Europe, things began to go awry. Having to service many of the Group's aircraft in the open air did little for the morale of the men on the ground, who nevertheless performed their duties as best as they could. The pilots, flying their P-38s at altitudes of

40,000ft (12,300m), literally froze, despite being swathed in fleece-lined flying suits. All too frequently pilots and aircraft were posted as missing in action due to technical problems, but at the time the reasons for the growing list of MIAs were in many cases unknown, which made the situation that much worse.

Solutions were urgently sought, but more than one ill dogged the P-38. Daniel Whitney, 'father' of the Allison V-1710 engine, later analysed some of the problems:

- Many pilots had too little experience before arriving in England;
- Stateside conversion training on the P-38 had stressed the wrong power settings for the engines; high rpm and low engine manifold pressure during cruising flight. This put a great strain on the engines, and such procedures were not recommended in Allison or Lockheed technical directives;
- Additives such at tetraethyl lead (TEL) in the fuel, used in England, were believed to have caused condensation in induction manifolds, leading to detonation. This destructive explosion of fuel mixture, rather than controlled burning, often had catastrophic results.

One solution that occupied numerous individuals at the time was the possibility of substituting Rolls-Royce Merlin engines for the P-38's Allisons. Although the engine problem took some time to bite, a change for the Lockheed twin became seemingly more feasible when Packard began tooling-up to produce the British engine in the USA for the revised P-51 Mustang. The Merlin might have done as much for the P-38 as it did for the Mustang, but we shall never know, as the idea was vetoed for reasons unknown. One obvious factor was Allison's reputation as a leading supplier of engines to the USAAF. Had a second fighter had its Allisons replaced by Packard Merlins, the implication that the American product was inferior would have been hard to answer. Time was also against such a change, as the re-engined aircraft could hardly have flown in the numbers required before the P-38's role as a high-altitude escort fighter in Europe had been all but eclipsed by the P-51 in 1944.

November 1943

In common with the earlier models, the P-38Js also needed radio modifications, and in the case of the 20th FG these delayed the combat debut until 11 November 1943, when the Group provided enough P-38Hs to form a support squadron to the main force of fifty-nine 55th FG aircraft. What was planned as a 'maximum-effort' attack by VIII Bomber Command heavies on marshalling yards at Munster and Wesel was aborted owing to adverse weather conditions.

The group's H-model P-38s were soon replaced by J-5s and J-10s, the latter being the most numerous model flown during the Lightning period, though J-15s were taken on strength by all three squadrons before the change to the P-51.

On 13 November the 55th sent forty-five Lightnings to cover bombers attacking targets in the Bremen area, and lost seven aircraft for claims of seven enemy aircraft destroyed, three unconfirmed and five damaged. It could hardly have been a worse time for the Group to enter combat, for although military operations cannot be seriously delayed by weather, adverse conditions over wartime England wrecked scores of carefully planned operations by the air forces. The P-38 squadrons were far from alone in this respect.

The autumnal weather still intervened, adversely affecting the heavies as well as the fighters, and low-key bomber operations continued for several more weeks. Raids were launched but recalled because visual bombing conditions over Germany were doubtful or non-existent. The escorts also attempted to reach the Reich, and for the fighters bad weather sometimes proved to be even worse than it was for the bombers. The 55th lost seven P-38s on 29 November, its pilots being able to claim but two enemy aircraft.

December 1943

To these woes already experienced by the P-38H with its 1,425hp (1,060kW) power setting was added the challenge of a new model with higher settings. In December 1943 the first P-38J-5s arrived in England. Although this model incorporated several improvements as a combat aircraft, the 1,500hp (1,120kW) Allisons in the J model required a higher standard of maintenance. There was evidence that this was not always possible, although individual aircraft with conscientious ground crews (and pilots with a 'feel' for the machinery) experienced less trouble operationally.

The all-pervading dampness in the English air in the autumn and winter months could not be kept entirely at bay, but, as their experience built up, the ground crews could at least sign off their charges, confident that if they were handled with care they would be able to complete the mission and return. All too often they were disappointed. And in any event it was probably unrealistic to expect young pilots to fly combat missions in a state of apprehension, waiting for the dreaded sound of a rough engine just as the Luftwaffe interceptors were spotted. Psychologically, this fear of technical failure put the Americans at a disadvantage.

It was true that the P-38J had improved supercharger intercoolers that greatly reduced manifold temperatures, but this encouraged TEL condensation in the manifolds during cruising flight and increased spark-plug fouling. Water injection might have improved the performance of the P-38's engines, as it did with the P-47 and P-51, but it was not made available.

Three more Lightning Groups, the 20th, 364th and 479th, joined the Eighth Air Force. All were to record similar experiences to those of the 55th, depending on the number of missions they flew and, to some extent, the time of year in which they made their combat debut. Ground crews, having had more exposure to the challenges the P-38 faced in the ETO, were arguably better equipped to come to grips with malfunctions in the spring of 1944 than the 'pioneers' of the 55th the previous winter.

The 55th could not be faulted for lack of intent to knock down enemy fighters threatening the bombers, for it fielded a high proportion of its strength during these difficult months, when for a time it was the sole unit operating the Lightning in the ETO. There must have been some relief when the 20th FG, with the 55th, 77th and 79th FSs, became operational, for there was at least another Group of pilots to share common experiences. Moreover, it was in the nature of things that a second unit flying the same aircraft under similar conditions bred a healthy rivalry and spurred a desire to beat the odds and be seen as the better performer. But if the heavy bombers turned back, the

Colonel Jack Jenkins and his much-photographed personal P-38H-5, 42-67074/CG-J, soon after arrival in the UK in October 1943. Jenkins was the executive officer of the 55th FG. IWM

fighters had little to do, as the Luftwaffe was equally hampered and did not put in an appearance if pilots could not find their targets.

This situation was galling for all concerned, but particularly for the 55th, as it was seemingly all too easy to lose aircraft to technical malfunction without any combat taking place. Such had also been the lot of the pioneering P-47 groups in England, but they had not arrived with the baggage of a 'wonder weapon' that could do everything asked of it and more.

On 28 December the 20th FG at King's Cliffe in Northamptonshire was able to operate at full strength for the first time. Thirty-six P-38s flew an uneventful fighter sweep along the Dutch coast, making no claims and suffering no losses. By then numerous pilots had gained operational experience by flying with the 55th as a fourth squadron. The mission of 31 December was a little more productive, as the heavies bombed targets in France. After an abortive 30 December, when the 20th and 55th FGs operated together for the first time, this short-range penetration of enemy airspace brought up the Luftwaffe, and the P-38s of the 55th claimed three of them shot down for the loss of one aircraft. One 20th FG pilot put down safely on the Isle of Wight.

Jack Jenkins flew several P-38s apart from the one here, its nose artwork having been rendered by an accomplished artist. The camera gun was moved from its nose location to a drop-tank pylon to cure vibration. USAF

January 1944 – Circle over Kiel

Drawing the enemy away from the bombers was part of the job of protecting them, and on 5 January 1944 the 20th and 55th FGs achieved this well on an escort to Kiel. The Lightning Groups despatched a total of seventy aircraft, and during the mission a group of twenty-three P-38s was attacked from above by a gaggle of Bf 109s and swung into a Lufbery circle. From the pilot's perspective this defensive manoeuvre has the advantage in that, with all your own aircraft flying in a circle, anyone who gets on your tail will almost certainly have one of yours on his tail. This also means that, to shoot you down, the enemy will be at roughly the same altitude, thereby throwing away nearly all of his height advantage.

On the Kiel mission the P-38s adopted a double Lufbery, the second group orbiting anticlockwise 500ft (150m) above the first, thus enabling head-on attacks to be made on any enemy machines attempting to dive into the first circle. The forming of a second circle was designed to prevent an astute enemy pilot from flying the wrong direction inside a single Lufbery and shooting at everyone who came around. Occupying a mile or so of airspace, the double Lufbery was not the easiest manoeuvre to maintain, but when it worked it offered distinct advantages.

On escort missions P-38s also formed Lufberys to keep all participating aircraft together and prevent them being split up and driven to the deck in individual dogfights. The Luftwaffe fighters soon realized that escorted US heavies could be shot down more easily if their protecting fighters were drawn away first. The USAAF recognized the purpose of these tactics, and took appropriate steps to counter them.

On the Keil mission the P-38s also had to contend with another enemy ploy; the positioning of Messerschmitt Me 410 decoys, armed with rockets and orbiting well out of range. Allied pilots learned to ignore these decoys unless they actually ventured within range of the bombers. However, Bf 109s did enter the circle, and at the height of the engagement American pilots reported about a dozen turning with them, but six were shot down and the rest fled after making one or two turns. Unfortunately the day's hard flying and fighting brought its share of P-38 casualties. The 20th reported three aircraft missing, and the 55th four. All their pilots were also listed as MIA. There seemed no way to improve the attrition rate.

One Hundred Plus

Depending on serviceability, both P-38 Groups were able to put up between fifty and seventy aircraft, although, on 14 January 1944, this total was increased to ninety-eight and, on the 24th, to a combined 101.

Low-key results for the Eighth Air Force continued into February, little being achieved by bomber or fighter units in deference to the winter weather. Single-figure claims by P-38 pilots during this period were offset by an equally consistent number of aircraft being reported missing, but the more-or-less even balance of the 'profit and loss' account was disturbed on 4 March, when the 20th lost three aircraft and the 55th one while escorting bombers attacking oil industry targets in Germany. No claims for enemy aircraft could be made.

The technical problems in the air and on the ground might have been easier to bear had the Lightning racked up an impressive air-combat record against the Luftwaffe fighter force, but this bonus was largely denied to the ETO Groups. It was forcibly brought home to the pilots that a large twin-engine aircraft was invariably at a distinct disadvantage when pitted against highly manoeuvrable single-seaters. Just in case the P-38 did prove to be extraordinarily capable, Bf 109 and Fw 190 pilots developed special tactics to neutralize any such advantage. They were generally able to recognize the Lightning's distinctive twin-boom configuration miles from the point of contact, which put the Americans at another disadvantage.

The third P-38 Group assigned to the Eighth Air Force was the 364th, which made its combat debut over Europe on 2 March 1944 by fielding thirty-three aircraft for an escort to Germany. There was little action on the Group's first five missions, though two enemy aircraft were claimed on 6 March for one P-38 down. That same day Eighth Fighter Command laid on a second mission, to targets in France, the 364th accompanying the 20th for a short-range escort to Chartres Aerodrome.

March 1944

All three P-38 units contributed to a force of eighty-nine aircraft on 3 March for another disappointing mission. Owing to bad weather the bombers had a much-reduced total of effective sorties raiding Wilhelmshaven and targets of opportunity,

Jack Jenkins confers with Lt Russell F. Gustke before a mission in October 1943, with the aid of essential fighter-pilot 'hand talk'. Gustke had then flown 46 operations, mainly in the MTO, and held the DFC. IWM

and lost eleven aircraft to flak and fighter attack. The massive USAAF fighter force (730-strong) found itself faced with heavy broken cloud cover which favoured the Luftwaffe more than the Americans, and groups became widely separated as a result. But the 55th FG came home with a record in which it understandably took pride; it had become the first VIII Fighter Command group to fly over Berlin. Among the participating P-38 pilots, Col Jack S. Jenkins, flying his personal P-38H, *Texas Ranger*, was as surprised as anyone. He had more to think about on the mission than pinpointing his historic position over the German capital, as he was frustrated by a malfunctioning engine. Having nursed the aircraft home, Jenkins was barely able to acknowledge the accolades, as it took time to overcome the exhaustion of a long flight.

One 20th Group Lightning came down in the Channel but there was a little more to show for the day's massive effort with eight victories being claimed – and nobody could deny the P-38 its 'First over Berlin' record.

Fighter sorties to Berlin continued on 4 March and brought about the early return of three P-38s. When Lts Charles Hallberg and Edgar Malchow of the 20th Group experienced engine trouble, 2nd Lt Joe Ford was despatched to escort the two cripples as they turned away from the bombers and set course back to England. At the Dutch coast the good engines in both Hallberg and Malchow's Lightnings seemed to be holding up despite being low on fuel, and all three flew out over the Channel, Ford fearing that any moment the damaged Allisons in the other two P-38s would give up the ghost. A brief scare from coastal flak and Focke-Wulfs behind him, Ford called ASR for a homing and the trio eventually landed safely. Joe Ford received the DFC for his cool handling of a tricky situation on this his first combat mission in the ETO.

The P-38 engine malfunction jinx struck the 55th particularly hard on 6 March and forced the entire group to turn back.

On 8 March the P-38s came home from a mission to Berlin with better combat figures of 9-2-5 enemy aircraft in return for

three aircraft missing. Somewhat ironically (and doubtless teeth-gnashingly in some quarters) all the honours went not to the two 'veteran' groups but the newcomer 364th. The 55th lost one aircraft and the 364th two from a total of 104 P-38s on the three-group escort mission to 'Big B'.

Succeeding March days were tedious, with little to show for the efforts of the bomber and fighter groups but in the latter part of the month something new was tried with the Lightning. Maj Tom Gates was given command of a small Eighth Air Force detachment to investigate the feasibility of night intruder operations with 100 (Bomber Support) Group, RAF. The American detachment consisted of two P-38Js and two P-51Bs. Several sorties were flown, enough to apparently show that neither fighter type was suitable for the work and the unit was withdrawn.

The weather improved only gradually as March 1944 came to an end and the small percentage of victories and damaged enemy aircraft accruing to the P-38 groups remained almost unchanged, as did the number of aircraft that went missing. For the enormous effort involved on the part of the pilots, ground crews, admin staff, transport and the rest of the army of personnel necessary even to launch a single fighter squadron, a lack of something big to celebrate made the ETO a far from happy theatre.

April 1944

An increasing number of P-51s was now available for escort duty, but even these were having a thin time in terms of destroying the Luftwaffe. Most of April brought more of the same for all of the Eighth's fighter units. At this time the bomber force was also enjoying relatively light losses but, on the other hand, it was often unable to strike at the most important strategic targets, as had been anticipated.

All P-38 Groups in the Eighth participated (probably with some enthusiasm, considering the difficulties inherent in high-altitude escort) in damaging the Luftwaffe on the ground. Fighters returning from escort missions were given *carte blanche* to drop down and strafe anything useful to the enemy anywhere in occupied Europe. Despite the hazards of attacking defended ground targets, particularly airfields, the P-38 had few peers if the man at the controls knew his business. Bringing his heavy weaponry to bear in a concentrated stream of shells and bullets (the 'buzz-saw' effect), he could usually devastate anything at which he fired. This policy definitely paid dividends in the months leading up to D-Day, as it succeeded in wrecking German plans to offer any cohesive air support to counter the invasion when and where it came.

May 1944

By the spring of 1944 the invasion of the Continent had entered the advanced planning stage, and VIII Fighter Command achieved its planned complement of fifteen operational Fighter Groups. The Eighth Air Force could also draw on extra escort help from the IX Fighter Command Groups, and on 6 May the P-38-equipped 474th FG made up the entire Lightning element (fifty-seven aircraft) of the escort when the bombers were sent to various 'No-ball' targets (V1 flying-bomb launch sites) in the Pas de Calais and Siracourt. There was no enemy air action, but the experience was useful for the tactical pilots, who gained a different perspective on the air war in Europe at that stage of the war.

On 11 May IX Fighter Command supplied ninety-nine P-38s for a sweep that involved other tactical groups of P-47s and P-51s as well as the fighters of the Eighth. There was some action for a few of the 471 pilots involved when the Jagdwaffe was engaged and lost eleven of its number for four US fighters.

When the P-38-equipped 479th, the last Fighter Group assigned to the Eighth Air Force, flew its first shakedown sweep to the Dutch coast on 26 May it set a record by becoming operational faster than any other Group before it. Since arriving at Wattisham, Cambridgeshire, on the 15th it had taken just eleven days to organize, plan and execute its combat debut. Two groups of P-38s, thirty and fifty strong, were despatched on a day when there was low-key activity elsewhere in the theatre.

Ground attacks on a long list of enemy targets in north-western Europe was now the order of the day, in line with Allied policy of neutralizing the Luftwaffe before *Overlord*. Many of the sorties flown were aimed at wrecking the French transport system and denying the Germans the means to move troops, fuel and supplies, and at destroying as many enemy aircraft as possible in the air and on the ground, in line with the USAAF directive to that effect. It was vital that total air superiority be achieved before a single Allied soldier stepped ashore on the French coast.

A new P-38J receives a high-pressure steam bath after arrival in the UK. Airframes had to have all traces of corrosive salt removed following an Atlantic sea crossing. IWM

Ground strafing brought its own hazards and challenges for Allied fighter pilots, and the 364th was not alone in having learned the hard way the best method of attack at least cost. On 15 April the Group lost eight P-38s in a wild strafing attack on various German airfields, finding little but small-arms fire to greet it at Wenzendorf.

Attacking this base resulted in the loss of four P-38s, due, it was believed, to planning flaws, a major one being that the airfield was not properly scanned for the presence of worthwhile targets. Most of the casualties were the result of flak. Group commander Col Roy W. Osborn ordered his pilots to ignore airfields where no enemy

aircraft were clearly visible. Such places were often flak traps, and there was no gain whatsoever in losing pilots and aircraft by giving German gunners target practice.

May 1944

On the 364th's mission No 46, on 13 May, Tom Lanphier, one of the pilots instrumental in Admiral Yamomoto's demise, joined the 383rd FS for one of several ETO indoctrination missions. The skies over Europe must have seemed incredibly crowded to one used to seeing little but jungle and ocean below his P-38 for hours on end. On 24 May a similar reaction might even have been felt by Ben Kelsey, who had some ETO combat experience when he joined the 383rd FS for several missions. The Lockheed test pilot would have been more used to the presence of aircraft than Lanphier, though they were hardly any threat. Kelsey flew on George F. Ceuleers' wing on that occasion, and was Red Leader on the 27 May withdrawal support mission to Mannheim and Ludwigshafen. Ceuleers subsequently became the 364th's top ace, with 10½ victories, though only one Fw 190 was confirmed while he was flying the P-38.

ABOVE: **By February 1944 P-38Js were beginning to come into the UK in unpainted natural aluminium finish, the state in which most US aircraft would see out the war. Here, Lightnings are being towed away to have their wings fitted at an unidentified base.** IWM

RIGHT: **Well-trained USAAF ground crews handled major repairs to P-38s on open-air dispersal points in England, such as this one at Nuthampstead, home of the 38th FS, 55th FG.** IWM

The 364th and 479th FGs were part of a 170-strong P-38 escort force on 27 May, the bombers striking a number of German targets. By now not only was the Eighth Air Force target list taking in pre-invasion tactical targets, but the daily figures for fighter operations included the results of ground attacks by the Lightning Groups of the Ninth Air Force. There were therefore seven groups of P-38s in England before Operation *Overlord* went ahead.

Part of the USAAF's fighter deployment before the invasion entailed the destruction of any European railways that might enable the rapid movement of supplies if they were left intact. The Eighth therefore instigated 'Chattanooga' sweeps, designed to cripple as many locomotives as possible throughout the extensive French rail system. All groups participated, the P-38Js of the 364th flying their first train-busting mission on 21 May and claiming twenty locomotives destroyed.

Three for the Ninth

At the end of 1943 the USAAF had re-established the old Ninth Air Force after service in North Africa as a new tactical formation in England, principally to support American ground forces during the forthcoming invasion of Europe. For this purpose the new organization's IX Air Support Command was allocated fifteen Fighter Groups, three of them, the 367th, 370th and 474th, flying P-38Js. These Groups, along with the P-47 units, embarked on a pre-invasion softening-up of the French coast lasting several weeks.

The Ninth Air Force's P-38 units arrived in England in the first half of 1944; the 370th in February, the 474th in March and the 367th in April.

Colonel Howard F. Nichols commanded the 370th, based at Aldermaston, Berkshire, with its component 401st, 402nd and 403rd FSs. One of Nichols's primary tasks was to get his pilots proficient on the Lightning, as the Group had trained on P-47s at home. There were the inevitable mishaps as the theatre training period proceeded, several Lightnings being written off in crashes. Among the host of tactical procedures the unit had to come to grips with in the busy ETO was dive bombing. The 370th was to use this form of attack against selected targets, including radar stations and flak towers, during its first weeks on operations, which began on 1 May.

At Warmwell in Dorset Col Clinton C. Wasem's 474th FG, comprising the 428th, 429th and 430th FSs, made its combat debut remarkably quickly, on 25 March. A routine patrol over the French coast was the calm before the storm, for the unit was soon pitched into a hectic round of activity, mainly over northern France.

Stoney Cross, Hampshire, was the home of the 367th FG, comprising the 392nd, 393rd and 394th FSs and commanded by Col Charles M. Young. Lockheed P-38s were issued to the squadrons upon arrival in the UK, the pilots having trained on P-39s in the USA. Conversion training had its exciting moments, but all was ready when the Group was declared operational on 9 May. Its initial area of operation was the western part of France, which contained a multitude of pre-invasion targets. The P-38s also escorted bombers to their targets in the same region.

The hazardous business of ground-attack saw the P-38 undertaking a role to which it was eminently suited. In the warmer air at low altitude the Allison engines functioned much more smoothly than they did up high, and the concentrated firepower available to each pilot could be quite devastating against a wide range of aircraft, vehicles and installations. The use of bombs to boost its offensive capability brought the Lightning a high degree of pre-invasion success.

Overlord

On 6 June VIII Bomber Command despatched more than 1,150 heavy bomber sorties to plaster enemy positions behind the invasion beaches. Meanwhile, 2,000-plus fighters, including 555 from all eight P-38 units of the Eighth and Ninth Air Forces as well as P-47s and P-51s, maintained a pattern of continuous patrols throughout the day. Concurrent with *Overlord*, Operation *Neptune* was the fighter shield that kept the Luftwaffe from interfering with the invasion. The Lightning's configuration was such that, when additionally bedecked with black-and-white 'invasion stripes', it was the most recognizable Allied aircraft in the sky, and for once it was in great demand. This asset appears to have been borne out by the claim by several of the Groups of twenty-six enemy aircraft destroyed and eight damaged. No losses among the VIII Fighter Command groups were reported. Ben

Victory Issue

As the number of German aircraft destroyed on the ground rose, such kills were given equal credit with aerial victories by VIII Fighter Command headquarters, which rightly considered such work as hazardous as fighting the Germans in the air. At pilot level, opinions differed as to the merits of claiming ground kills. While most individuals agreed with the official view, almost to a man the pilots preferred to overcome the enemy in aerial combat, provided they had the choice. Ground kills were therefore treated separately and, although dozens of pilots could consider themselves 'ground aces', there were many who did not.

The Ninth Air Force was quite adamant that its fighter pilots should not seek combat with enemy aircraft unless they were fired upon first, and those same powers-that-be definitely did not allow aircraft ground kills to count towards individual scores. Consequently, far fewer pilots became aces in the Ninth than in the Eighth. Even then, pilots were often obliged to present a very good case for having deprived the Luftwaffe of several of its aircraft.

But the destruction wrought by the tactical P-38s and P-47s was very commonly reflected in lines of tiny silhouettes of trains, vehicles, boats, balloons, industrial plant and other targets stencilled on the flanks of the aircraft. Added to the scoreboard might have been brooms, indicating fighter sweeps; umbrellas, denoting top-cover sorties; and, of course, swastikas or iron crosses for aircraft destroyed in the air or on the ground. The scoreboards looked impressive and were the object of considerable pride, particularly among ground crews. It was one of the few ways that their dedication on the flight-line and the hours of 'sweating out' an aircraft's return from its missions could be recorded for all to see. Not everyone who viewed a combat scorecard on the side of a P-38 was aware that, to have accumulated such a record, individual aircraft had to have been kept technically up to the mark for dozens of sorties. Such was the pace of tactical operations in the spring of 1944 that even aircraft that had spent a relatively short time in the ETO quickly acquired a painted log of the achievements of each pilot/ground-crew team.

Kelsey led Yellow Flight of the 383rd FS on one of the D-Day patrols.

In the days after Operation *Overlord* USAAF fighters were preoccupied with beachhead support, escorting heavy and medium bombers and strafing and bombing a variety of tactical targets. Enemy aircraft were also encountered and almost routinely shot down, such sorties bringing occasional success to individual P-38 pilots. However, as all Eighth and Ninth FGs were operating over Normandy and northern France, even the 12 June claim of twenty-five enemy aircraft destroyed and ten damaged had to be shared among several units. On the debit side, the P-38 Groups lost four

Distinguishable by its deeper radiator intakes, the P-38J was a much-improved Lightning that still found operations over Europe difficult in the harsh weather conditions. This aircraft, part of the 55th FG, was used for a series of 'type recognition' photos in England. *P. Jarrett*

aircraft on that day's three separate missions, a grim statistic that never seemed to waver in its monotonous regularity. All the Lightning units continued to lose aircraft, albeit in small numbers.

Brass-eye View

As a measure of the certainty that the outline of the P-38 was unmistakable to friendly gunners below, Gens Jimmy Doolittle and Earl Partridge, respectively CG of the Eighth Air Force and his Deputy Commander, decided go up in a pair of Lightnings to see for themselves how the invasion was progressing. Finding difficulty in observing anything because of solid cloud, both officers turned back towards England to seek a break. This they found, and on return to the French coast at about 1,500ft (460m) Doolittle, who had meanwhile lost contact with Partridge, spent some 90min cruising along the Normandy beaches before returning to Bovingdon.

As the weather clamped down to hamper air operations on the days following 6 June, Allied aircraft began using a number of emergency landing strips on the French coast. These makeshift airfields removed the necessity of pilots having to nurse a crippled aircraft across the unforgiving Channel, and saved many lives. Late in June a P-38 became the first fighter to touch down on the emergency strip at St Laurence sur Mer.

The enormous air support effort over the Normandy bridgehead continued throughout the rest of June, though the P-38 units also continued to fly escort missions for their B-17 and B-24 charges. On the 18th, for example, the first strategic mission since D-Day was flown and the Eighth's P-38s flew four separate operations,

escorting all three divisions of bombers and carrying out fighter-bomber attacks in company with P-47s, primarily against rail bridges in the St Quentin area.

Success in aerial combat for the P-38 pilots still did not match those of the P-47 and P-51 units, despite a sterling effort, 180-plus Lightnings not being untypical of the numbers aloft on certain days during the post-invasion period. Then a maximum effort by Eighth Fighter Command led to there being over 1,000 fighters over France on a single day, dividing their time among escort, sweep and fighter-bomber sorties.

'No-ball' sites continued to appear in combat reports during late June, the P-38s joining the escort force to support the heavies blasting the French V1 launch sites. The occasional use of P-38 Droop Snoots continued, as on 29 June, when eight of the 364th FG's aircraft bombed shipping at Imjuiden. Less than 3 tons of bombs were released, and only half the fighter sorties were deemed effective.

In the days immediately following D-Day the presence of the Luftwaffe had been sporadic and of little real threat to the Allied juggernaut. However, there was much subsequent enemy activity as the German high command desperately shuffled units, many decimated by pre-invasion combat, to offer some resistance in Normandy. The Luftwaffe also faced the awesome responsibility of providing a degree of protection for the German ground forces, which were being decimated by streams of Allied fighter-bombers. In addition there was the USAAF strategic bomber force, which showed no sign of reducing the amount of high explosive (HE) being unleashed on the Reich's vital industries at home. The bombers still had to be intercepted by an increasingly hard-pressed Jagdwaffe because the high command

perceived this to be the greatest threat to further prosecution of the war in western Europe.

July 1944

A large-scale raid on German industrial targets on 7 July brought the Luftwaffe up in force to attack the heavies, but the strong US escort claimed seventy-five of them destroyed. All VIII Fighter Command Groups were deployed, and the P-38 pilots of the 20th FG, shepherding 2nd Bomb Division Liberators, had cause to celebrate claims for seven of the enemy downed for the loss of one P-38. Such one-sided success, though the actual total of enemy aircraft was modest, remained the exception, and some of the long-suffering personnel at King's Cliffe, Nuthampstead, Honington and Wattisham might have been forgiven for feeling that another fighter type might be more effective than the P-38. In the higher echelons of the Eighth Air Force much the same view began to prevail.

Even though the 'second-generation' Groups had come to Europe equipped with more-capable P-38Js, rather than the early models issued to the 20th and 55th FGs, the air war had changed dramatically by mid-1944. Although the deployments of the Eighth's last two P-38 Groups were separated only by a matter of months, the pace and nature of aerial combat and the number of available aircraft had increased. All Groups converted to the P-38J, but with the P-51 increasingly taking on long-range escort duty and the P-47 cutting a swathe through a lengthy list of ground targets in Europe, the plain fact was that the Eighth Air Force no longer really needed the Lightning as an escort fighter.

In July 1944 VIII Fighter Command all but removed the P-38 from its inventory when the 20th, 55th and 364th FGs began converting to the P-51. The last Lightning missions are shown in the table on page 97. That left only the latecomer 479th, the last fighter unit to join the Eighth Air Force and the last to fly missions in the Lightning in the ETO, but this, too, became a P-51 outfit in October.

Out with a Bang

Before the change-over to Mustangs, Capt Arthur E. Jeffrey of the 479th had a spectacular combat with a Messerschmitt Me 163 rocket-powered interceptor. On 29 July he was part of the escort to bombers attacking targets in the Merseberg area, and had picked up a straggling B-17 flying at 11,000ft (3,300m) over Wassermunde. One of the diminutive rocket fighters made an abortive side pass on the Fortress but stayed near, the pilot clearly intending to have a second try at shooting the bomber down. Jeffrey dived after it, caught up and opened fire. Climbing to 15,000ft (4,600m), the Me 163 circled to the left but the P-38 turned inside and cut it off. Jeffrey fired another burst, and the German pilot executed a split-S and rolled into a near-vertical dive.

Following the enemy aircraft down, Jeffrey fired more rounds and observed hits, but the Me 163 continued to pull away. Now concerned with the steep angle of his own dive, Jeffrey managed to pull the P-38 out at 1,500ft (460m) before momentarily blacking out. Recovering, he saw no sign of the Me 163 but felt that a 'destroyed' or 'probably destroyed' claim was justified.

The Victory Credits Board upheld Jeffrey's claim and he was duly credited with the only jet or rocket fighter destroyed by an Eighth Air Force P-38. Postwar analysis of Luftwaffe records confirmed, however, that the Me 163 (belonging to JG 400) had escaped destruction despite the damage Jeffrey claimed to have inflicted. Other P-38s in the area that day had seen Me 163s but had been unable to catch them.

At that point there were more than a few pilots who mourned the passing of the aircraft they had flown for many tough months of operations, having come to terms with the unreliable performance of its Allison engines above 25,000ft (7,600m). Although the move by Eighth Air Force commanders made operational sense, there were enough combat-proven P-38s with good records to make men such as Arthur Heiden, Jack Ilfrey and Robert Riemensnider (55th FS) feel a little let down.

They had all flown P-38s cared for by skilled, sympathetic ground crews, and had experienced few, if any, technical troubles while doing so. This representative trio of pilots could cite the fact that not all P-38s were prone to malfunction, while others would have pointed out that numerous fighter pilots had now gained the necessary experience to anticipate and offset engine problems, and took great pride in this. Not everyone took to the P-51 or the P-47!

The decision to remove the P-38 from the Eighth Air Force's inventory did not meet with approval everywhere. Blinded by the belief of what constituted a successful long-range escort fighter, certain USAAF chiefs with the responsibility of protecting the bomber fleets operating in Europe had continued to favour the Lightning over the magnificent Mustang; a mistake fortunately corrected before too much damage was done. Such individuals could be forgiven for views that stemmed from ingrained pre-war thinking, which had always emphasized that to fly any distance in safety an aircraft had to have at least two engines. European combat presented a great many challenges that nobody had anticipated. And for the P-38's backers the stark truth was that their dogma had to concede to circumstances which proved that what might seem obvious 'ain't necessarily so'.

What should have been much easier to grasp was the plain fact, borne out by plenty of combat statistics, that an aircraft twice the size of a Bf 109 or Fw 190 was not as manoeuvrable as either of the Luftwaffe single-seaters. That statement should be qualified and set in a time frame, for, as the quality and number of Luftwaffe pilots decreased, the P-38 had less opposition with which to contend. Moreover, away from exacting escort work it was a formidable ground-strafer favoured by many of its pilots.

The official USAAF view was unsympathetic, but the protestors complained that the P-38 was all-American, with the enormous prestige that that implied. Unfavourable comparisons were made with the P-51, which had been built to order by a foreign power and was still regarded with some reservations, amazing as this may seem in hindsight. Such individuals had difficulty in accepting the fact that this particular single-engine fighter could not only fly further than the P-38, but had a far better chance of knocking down the enemy in combat and returning safely to its base.

Few Aces

The low aerial victory tallies in the Eighth and Ninth Air Forces tended to reflect both the technical problems with the P-38 in the strategic Eighth and the tactical Ninth in the ETO, and the relatively short period of service in some units. Only eleven pilots from both air forces managed to become aces while flying from bases in England or continental Europe, and several of those boosted their scores with victories in other theatres.

In the Eighth Air Force the leading P-38 scorers were: James Morris, Lindol Graham and Jack Ilfrey of the 20th FG; Gerald A. Brown and Robert Buttke of the 55th; John H. Lowell of the 364th; and Robin Olds and Clarence O. Johnson of the 479th.

A further factor militating against high scorers on Lightnings in the ETO was the gradual re-equipment of nearly all Fighter Squadrons with other aircraft types. As a result, all four Groups had a shorter length of service in the Eighth than other fighter units.

Three of these individuals, Jack Ilfrey, Clarence Johnson and Joseph Miller, had transferred into the Eighth Air Force after achieving some of their victories while flying P-38s in the MTO.

By way of international comparison of the figures of the top-scoring pilots, the tiny Thirteenth Air Force in the Solomons ended the war with twelve P-38 aces, while the rosters of the CBI's 'independent' 449th and 459th FSs included four and seven aces respectively.

All of the Twelfth Air Force Lightnings were transferred to the Fifteenth Air Force when the second US strategic bombing organization was established in England in October 1943. Aerial victory scores became harder to achieve as the Germans gradually abandoned the southern front and Italy surrendered, splitting her air force into pro- and anti-Fascist elements. Here again the P-38s on bomber escort duty had to share a dwindling number of enemy aircraft, mainly with the Mustang Groups, but at least they all retained their Lockheed mounts until the war's end. By all accounts the men of the 1st, 14th and 82nd FGs believed this was exactly as it should have been.

CHAPTER SIX

Smile for Photo Joe

The outbreak of war in Europe saw most of the combatant nations relying on modified aircraft to perform PR sorties. Few true PR versions appeared for the first year or so of hostilities, but by 1941 the RAF had taken an early lead with adaptations of the Spitfire. Several marks had been successfully converted, and the first PR de Havilland Mosquito was coming into service.

As the British had established a small but enthusiastic PR unit at Medmenham, Buckinghamshire, before the war and expanded its activities when hostilities broke out, it was natural that the USAAF would turn to their ally for advice when establishing its own such organization. By 1942, having built up considerable expertise not only in gathering photographic evidence but in interpreting the images captured by aerial cameras, the RAF was streets ahead of all other combatants, particularly in being able to turn PR into targets for subsequent air attack. Increasingly the Axis forces were unable to do this, owing to Allied strength and flexibility. With the war rapidly broadening in scope and area, an American contribution became vital.

Lightning PR variants

With the USA's entry into the war in December 1941, the USAAC was also unable to field an aircraft type to fulfil this role, though the configuration and performance of the P-38 appeared to lend itself to the carriage of aerial cameras if its nose armament was removed to accommodate them. Lockheed personnel, and particularly the irrepressible Kelly Johnson,

worked on this version. Hearing that Col George W. Goddard of Wright Field had been trying for some time to turn the Douglas A-20 into an effective PR aircraft (and had not found the project greatly encouraging), Johnson was not slow in recognizing the P-38's potential in such a role.

Johnson and Kelsey had previously determined that the all-important need of a PR Lightning was range extension, and the next step was to produce the hardware. By adapting the existing contract for P-38E fighters (AC-15646) by means of Change Order 11, the first P-38 PR conversion was carried out on the 116th production P-38E around December 1941, with K-17 cameras replacing the fixed armament. The result was the F-4-1-LO. Johnson's team had envisaged a number of different camera installations, tailored to various aerial photography requirements, and, to an air arm lacking any other PR aircraft with a performance good enough for it to survive in hostile airspace, the F-4 was a godsend. Consequently the USAAF issued a contract for ninety-nine P-38Es to be completed without armament. Four K-17 cameras were installed in a nose modified with ports for the camera lenses, and power was provided by 1,150hp (860kW) V-1710-21 and -29 engines. Most of the resulting F-4-1-LOs were given 'restricted' status and used for pilot conversion training as RF-4-1s in the USA. Twenty F-4A-LOs initiated a series of further conversions based on the early-model Lightnings.

The F-4s were first delivered to the USAAF in March 1942, and in the main the variant was used to train pilots in the exacting art of photographic reconnaissance work in the peaceful skies over the USA, although several saw combat.

One of the F-4s loaned to No 1 PRU, RAAF, in 1942, A55-3 makes a low pass over base, probably en route for another PR sortie over New Guinea. A. Pelletier

Principal Version

The main production version of the P-38 for the PR role was the F-5, following the modification of a single P-38E airframe to produce the F-5A-2 in January 1942. It was powered by the same Allison V-1710-21 and -29 engines installed in the fighter equivalent, and was followed by 180 examples based on the P-38G, these having 1,325hp (990kW) V-1710-51 and -55 engines. Comprising twenty F-5A-1s, twenty F-5A-3s and 140 F-5A-10s, these machines had provision for five nose-mounted cameras, instead of the F-4's four. All F-5 derivatives incorporated the technical updates of the corresponding P-38 production blocks upon which they were based.

The F-5B-1 was also built by Lockheed with a camera installation similar to that of the F-5A-10, but was otherwise configured as the P-38J-5. A Sperry automatic pilot was standard on the first ninety F-5Bs and the subsequent 110 F-5B-1s that completed Lockheed's direct participation in the PR Lightning programme. All subsequent conversions were made after delivery by the Dallas Modification Center, rather than by the parent company.

cameras as standard with a tri-metrogen installation as an alternative. Five hundred F-5E-4s were built. After a single F-5F a conversion, itself based on F-5B-1 42-68220, a short run of 'F' series aircraft brought the PR Lightning conversion programme virtually to a close, first with the F-5F-3, which combined the P-38L-5 engines and airframe and the F-5F camera installation. Finally came the F-5G-6, based on the P-38L-5, with a revised, elongated nose section enabling a wider selection of cameras to be fitted.

Photographic Reconnaissance Operations

New Guinea Debut

The first PR Lightnings to become operational were in the Pacific. Three F-4-1-LOs were rushed to Australia between April and August 1942 to equip the 8th Photographic

given the temporary RAAF serial numbers A55-1 to A55-3, but two were written off in hard landings, only A55-2 surviving to be returned to the USAAF after nearly four months of sterling service.

Several other F-4s went overseas to fill a need that had become acute immediately the USAAF found itself at war. The Eighth Air Force in England took delivery of thirteen F-4As, intended to equip the 5th PRS at Podington, Bedfordshire, in September 1942. Barely two months later this unit was transferred to the Twelfth Air Force and moved base to Steeple Morden, Hertfordshire, on 2 November. The unit became part of the exodus to North Africa to support the *Torch* invasion, American PR operations only really getting started after this operation. Before Pearl Harbor there had been little activity of that nature, apart from the practice of aerial mapping. Pilots with experience of such flights found themselves in demand on tactical and strategic reconnaissance operations, and it

An uncharacteristically pristine F-4 at Hergla, Tunisia, on 13 June 1943. H. Levy

Dallas Variants

The next PR variant, the F-5C-1, was similar to the F-5B-1 but had an improved camera installation. Approximately 123 aircraft were modified, based on the P-38J airframe. The F-5E-2 was a conversion of the P-38J-15, 100 being completed at Dallas. The F-5E-2 was similar to the F-5C-1, as was the F-5E-3, 105 of which were based on the P-38J-25 airframe.

Three PR Lightning versions were based on the P-38L airframe, the F-5E-4, the F-5F-3 and the F-5G-6. The first used an L-1 airframe and had either K-17 and K-18

Reconnaissance Squadron (PRS), commanded by Maj Karl Polifka. Meeting an urgent need for aerial reconnaissance of Japanese positions in New Guinea, the unit was loaned to No 1 Photographic Reconnaissance Unit (PRU), RAAF, for several months. Polifka took over the sole available F-4 before the other two arrived in June, and flew it extensively in the intervening weeks. He photographed a large part of eastern New Guinea virtually single-handed, and was responsible for surveying sites for likely future bases on the coastal area between Oro Bay and Cape Ward Hunt. The three Lightnings were

took a special temperament to fly over hostile territory armed with only a set of cameras.

Helped immeasurably by the British, the US Navy and USAAF sent a steady stream of trainees to England to form the nucleus of an equivalent US organization dedicated to the art of photographic interpretation, or 'PI' as it was commonly known. When the USAAF began operational PR flying in North Africa, several understandable but annoying gaffes were committed owing to pilot inexperience. Operating independently from the RAF, the Americans needed much more time

A 15th PRS, 3rd PRG F-5A-10 at Ponte Olivio, Sicily, on 14 August 1943. The short bars to the national insignia with red surround complied with official changes, but there was little room on the Lightning's booms to squeeze them in without a repaint. H. Levy

Gerbini, Sicily, was the base for this F-4A, photographed on 3 September 1943, which clearly had had no changes made to its national insignia by that time. H. Levy

and help to interpret their reconnaissance photographs correctly. This led to the amalgamation of British and American units into the first Allied PR Wing, formed in February 1943.

In charge of the Wing was Col Elliott Roosevelt, the president's youngest son. A pilot with considerable mapping experience, Roosevelt was highly enthusiastic over what was still a new concept in the USAAF. He took to heart the widely-held belief that a good PR pilot needed to combine the fast reactions and tactical skills of the fighter pilot with the deliberate, methodical approach and accuracy of the bomber pilot. He also needed to take sole and complete charge of the mission without reporting to higher authority if an emergency arose.

Some American pilots did not appreciate the degree of individualism or maturity required, considering the job 'sissy'.

And not everyone thought the PR Lightning was up to the task. Although the aircraft was capable enough for low-level 'dicing', at altitude it could not always outpace enemy fighters. Pilots reported that the F-5 had a tendency to wallow about and, as they put it, become 'duck soup for the '109s'. Such a comment would have been all too familiar to men flying Lightning fighters, but the reconnaissance role had to be fulfilled and the USAAF then had little alternative to the PR Lightning.

Elliott Roosevelt was the driving force behind the steady expansion of USAAF PR in the Mediterranean, and early in 1944 the organization was able to move to Foggia, the huge complex of airfields in southern Italy. Almost the entire town of San Severo was requisitioned by the PR unit, which was by then under the command of 'Pop' Polifka. Then a lieutenant colonel, Polifka, who had many hours of

mapping flying under his belt as well as the previous command of the F-4A Lightnings operated with the Australians, was ideal for the job. Roosevelt needed a good second-in-command, as he was increasingly busy, commuting between Washington and the war theatres to broaden the USAAF's PR base. Polifka was equally active on similar business even when he was not flying missions.

Although considered a little old for operational flying at the age of 33, Polifka and Lt Col Leon Gray, another outstanding PR pilot, indulged in a form of rivalry to see who could get away with the maddest risks. This served to inspire the other pilots, who delighted in aping Pop, who thought nothing of flying so low over the Adriatic that his F-5, named *Rosebud*, created a wake, or diving into Apennine valleys to dislodge a few boulders and set them rolling.

Eighth Air Force PR

Following the F-4's brief debut in Europe, the 13th PRS at Podington took delivery of thirteen examples of the improved F-5A-3 in January 1943. These served the unit until June, when the first F-5A-10s were obtained from the 7th Photographic Reconnaissance Group (PRG) at Mount Farm. This Oxfordshire airfield became the centre for the USAAF's PR force in the European theatre, Lockheed F-5s and Spitfires dominating the scene for the remainder of the war. Many of the top US PR pilots, including Leon Gray (who eventually flew 146 sorties), Sandy Arkin, Joseph Terrett, Howard Vestal and, of course, 'Pop' Polifka, flew from Mount Farm.

Once a range of reliable cameras had been successfully adapted for aerial use, the business of gathering photographic evidence of activity in enemy territory (anywhere in the world) went into high gear. The USAAF came to rely very heavily on the Lockheed F-5 variants, and every theatre acquired a reconnaissance force centred on these aircraft. Pilots became highly skilled at finding what the enemy wished to hide, and the outstanding work of the photo interpreters on the ground remains one of the many unsung contributions to victory that can truly be classed as 'war-winning'.

In the weeks before D-Day, F-5 operations on behalf of the Eighth Air Force gradually increased in frequency, the 7th PRG despatching both Lightnings and Spitfires to reveal the damage the bombers had done and film untouched targets for future operations. It proved necessary to adapt some F-5s to take photographs of objects directly in front of the aircraft, and a suitable port was cut to take the camera lens, positioned behind a protective Perspex screen.

On 27 March twelve F-5s and a Spitfire covered a range of airfields in France, the bombers having blitzed a dozen or so Luftwaffe bases during the course of the day. Ten F-5 sorties were undertaken the following day, when the target list was broadened to take in E-boat pens at Imjuiden as well as airfields. The number of PR sorties varied for the usual primary reasons; aircraft serviceability and weather.

Good aerial photography remained dependent on clear conditions, though PR coverage was not needed on every day that VIII Bomber Command operated. Sometimes the highly-tuned Allisons in the F-5s worked almost too well, as on 12 April, when the 357th FG supplied eight P-51s to escort two PR Lightnings to the Munich area, and all but two of the Mustangs were unable to keep pace with the F-5s.

May 1944

Another May milestone for the Lightning was the first arrival of an F-5 at the Russian 'shuttle base' at Poltava on the 25th. The 7th PG's Col Paul Cullen claimed that particular record. He touched down at the Russian base in his aircraft, *Dot & Dash*, having flown via Italy.

The 7th PRG had a busy day on 30 May 1944, when no fewer than twenty-two F-5s were sent to photograph areas of France, Germany and the Low Countries. In addition there were three Spitfire sorties plus weather reconnaissance flights by Mosquitoes and B-17s. The same number of F-5s flew on the 31st, the job of the pilots being

ABOVE: **A group of F-5 pilots indulge in a game of 'horseshoes' at an unknown base in 1943; it was most probably Mount Farm.** IWM

LEFT: **An F-4A of the 5th PRS, 3rd PRG, painted in haze camouflage with white spinners, on Malta in May 1943.** IWM

Long-time companions in the PR business, the F-5 and Spitfire were complementary in European reconnaissance operations. This pair was from the 7th PRG at Mount Farm, Oxfordshire, which operated as part of the Eighth Air Force. USAF

BELOW: When pilots climbed in and out of Lightnings across the wing roots they gradually wore away the camouflage paint, but that was probably the last thing on the mind of Maj Robert Smith, CO of the 13th PRS, 7th PRG, after a long and perhaps hazardous flight. IWM

mainly photo mapping and bomb-damage assessment.

French bridges were sought by the F-5 cameras on 2 June, the Lightning pilots keeping at low altitude. Despite this precaution one aircraft was damaged. Two days later one of fifteen 7th PRG F-5s briefed for targets in France did not return to Mount Farm, putting down in Sardinia.

The 7th lost an F-5 on D-Day, and on 7 June the Photo Joes ranged out to France, Holland and Germany, eight F-5s being accompanied by five Spitfires. Eighteen F-5s were out on 8 June, two aircraft failing to return from sorties to France. Bad weather set in on 9 June, and although the 7th PRG despatched five aircraft they were all forced to return owing to poor visibility over the Continent.

The sortie total of the 7th Group's F-5 and Spitfire in Europe rose to twenty-nine on 12 June, targets in France and Germany being covered. An F-5 was lost on the 13th, but there was no bad luck on 14 June, when twenty-nine F-5 sorties were flown. The F-5 that had previously flown to Poltava returned to Mount Farm on 19 June.

For the rest of June F-5 missions remained in double figures on several days, this hectic pace being maintained at a momentous time for the Allied cause. On 22 June the PR pilots were warned to keep a look-out for V-1s actually in the air, the German flying-bomb offensive against England having begun after D-Day. Several F-5 flights were made to Italy and the Soviet Union during this intensive period of operations, the Allies having taken Rome on 5 June as well as completing the first phase of *Overlord*.

The F-5s of the 12th PRS had mapped 80 per cent of Italy before the invasion, flying 300 sorties.

Most of the PR work by Lightning pilots centred on the tactical situation in France, though strategic targets in Germany were not neglected. The daily number of F-5 sorties dropped to an average of less than ten in early July, but rose to forty-one on the 17th, when massive coverage of France and Germany was required. This reflected renewal of the VIII Bomber Command campaign against targets in the Reich, after the brief lull when the heavies were sent mainly against tactical targets during the immediate pre-invasion period. Several F-5s failed to return from these operations, though statistically the loss rate was minor, considering the number of sorties and flying hours completed.

Aborted sorties were rare, as the F-5 pilots sought to get through the weather come what may, but on 25 July ten out of forty-six

what the Germans were doing. First Lieutenant Gerald M. Adams of the 14th PRS took off from Mount Farm and pointed the nose of his F-5 towards Germany, specifically the Merseberg–Leipzig area.

The cloud persisted over the Channel and well into Germany, but it was breaking up as Adams approached the target area. He had two potential bomber targets to cover, and made an initial photographic run at 30,000ft (9,000m). As he lined up for the second an aircraft appeared, too far away to catch his F-5; or so the American thought. Having completed his second run, Adams noticed that the bandit had closed up and was now uncomfortably close. Mission completed, he firewalled his throttles and turned for home. Meanwhile

the bogey was. It was still there, and he was obliged to dive again to seek more protective cloud cover at 8,000ft (2,500m).

Loitering in cloud, Adams finally lost his adversary and turned for home. Back at Mount Farm the intelligence officer wanted full details. Adams was grounded pending tests, as it was suspected that he might be suffering from fatigue, or worse. He described the 'funny-looking 'plane' to anyone who would listen, but there was still much head-shaking. Then someone remembered similar reports by members of the 359th FG, who had witnessed German rocket or jet-powered aircraft attacking B-17s in the Merseburg–Leuna area.

Such encounters between the Eighth Air Force and the Me 163 remained few and

Unloading the cameras from an F-5 in order to process their precious film was an almost daily occurrence around the world by the middle of the war. This typical scene was photographed at Mount Farm, Oxfordshire. IWM

aircraft despatched were forced to turn back. Double-figure mission days continued into August, and thirty-four were mounted on the 5th, twenty-five on the 6th, thirty-two on the 7th and twenty-two on the 8th.

Pilots' stories about flying the F-5 are legion, but there is space here to mention only a few. One memorable mission took place on 14 August, a day when, as regards missions by the Eighth Air Force bombers, 'even the birds were walking'. Although the forecasters confirmed that the entire European Continent seemed to be covered by low cloud, headquarters ordered a reconnaissance sortie to keep abreast of

the enemy aircraft had opened fire on the F-5, and 30mm cannon shells were coming too close for comfort.

The great speed of the German interceptor was mystifying, as Adams knew that, if pushed, the F-5 could touch 400mph (640km/h), but the bogey on his tail seemed capable of at least another 200mph (320km/h).

At 12,000ft (3,600m) the F-5 pilot sought the sanctuary of cloud, but pushing down the aircraft's nose tended to fog the instrument panel and the inside of the canopy. Coming out of the cloud, Adams wiped away the condensation to see where

far between, as the tiny interceptor, though capable of phenomenal performance, had very limited endurance. It could be outmanoeuvred and outrun by Allied aircraft if it was seen early enough. The idea of a point-defence fighter *par excellence* remained another enemy threat that was 'too little, too late'.

After the war Gerald Adams met Rudolf Opitz, erstwhile commander of the only operational Me 163 unit, JG 400, based at Brandis. Although Opitz himself had been based further north in August 1944, the cause of Adams's scare must indeed have been an Me 163 from Brandis.

Saga of the 33rd

Increasing availability of the F-5 meant that the USAAF could deploy units overseas specifically to provide a photographic service for each different air force. The Ninth AAF had the 33rd PRS of the 10th PRG assigned to it in the spring of 1944. The unit was the first to fly dual day and night PR missions, though the F-5s were restricted to operating in daylight. The 33rd flew its first day sortie, a 'local', on 9 May with the squadron CO, Maj Leon H. McCurdy, leading a flight of F-5s. The

ground war, the 33rd then moved to the grass airfield at Charleroi/Gosselies in Belgium, from where it operated from 21 September. A measure of how intensively the unit's F-5s were used during this period is shown by the number of aerial negatives and prints obtained in that one month; 24,532 and 74,755 respectively.

On 16 October 1944 Maj McCurdy's fine leadership of the 33rd PRS was rewarded by his promotion to lieutenant colonel and appointment to the post of 9th Air Force Director of Reconnaissance. Captain Theodore A. Rogers took over

undertaken by Ninth Air Force PR units. The pilots were to map 1,200 miles (1,930km) of the Ruhr Valley in a co-ordinated sweep. The F-5s began taking off at 09.30hr, led by the 363rd's group commander, Lt Col James M. Smelley. To avoid German radar the Lockheeds maintained 200ft (60m) altitude en route to Y-32 Asche, which was then the temporary home of the 452nd FG. This mass-formation tactic was intended to fool the enemy into believing that the F-5s were simply another P-38 formation, and to mask that fact that they were unarmed and unescorted.

A 7th PRG F-5 at Mount Farm in 1944. via P. Jarrett

major also flew what the squadron recorded as its first combat mission on 23 May, the results being reported as excellent.

On D-Day the 33rd was out over the Channel, but the pilots found the briefed targets obscured by cloud. The unit lost its night element on 12 June, whereupon it became a regular F-5 squadron and the following day joined with the 30th PRS to become part of the 67th Tactical Reconnaissance Group (TRG).

Having put 135 missions 'on the board' between 2 and 28 June, the 33rd moved to Normandy to operate from airfield A-9 at Le Molay between 12 and 28 August. Paris was liberated before the squadron moved again, and this time it occupied Toussus-le-Noble aerodrome, 4 miles (7km) from Versailles. Following the course of the

command of the 33rd, which from 30 October had the responsibility of supplying its services to the US 9th Army as part of the 363rd TRG. This new assignment coincided with another move, on 5 November, to Y-10 Le Culot-Est, some 30 miles (48km) east of Brussels. Major Rogers had to hand his command to Capt T. A. Roberts after he and other 33rd personnel were involved in a C-47 crash.

Photo Flood

By December 1944 the 33rd had produced 239,565 photographs since D-Day. A 'maximum effort' day for the squadron was 22 February 1945, when thirteen F-5s were airborne for the largest mission ever

After overflying Asche the formation climbed to 25,000ft (7,600m), and when the Rhine came in sight each pilot nosed down to gain extra speed, took up his own flight 'lane' and turned on the cameras. In less than 15min over 1,000 square miles (2,590sq km) of Germany's notorious 'Happy Valley' had been photographed, though the usual industrial haze had obscured many of the checkpoints. Thirty Fw 190s and two Me 262s were sighted and some gave chase, but no F-5s were brought down.

The F-5 was not, of course, immune from interception, particularly by the Me 262 jet fighter, but this threat largely failed to materialize. It nevertheless caused no end of worry, because the enemy's revolutionary new aircraft could have had a very detrimental effect on Allied PR, photographic aircraft always being a natural target for fast enemy interceptors.

The total of twenty-three sorties flown by the 33rd PRS on 22 February produced 7,204 negatives and 22,177 prints, plus a Silver Star for Lt Col Smelley for his leadership.

When the 363rd TRG moved to Y-55 Venlo on 10 March it claimed to be the first USAAF unit to operate from German soil, Venlo then being a vast base that straddled the border with Holland. Although

pilot dive between them and promptly bale out. Unsure whether they had survived an attempted ramming or if the pilot had lost control, Austin and Foster each claimed half an enemy aircraft destroyed.

Then the Me 262 threat materialized. In a clear demonstration of how lethal a new generation of fighters could be, John Austin's F-5 was shot down in flames on 8 April. Two of the German jets had made the interception.

On 16 April the unit moved across the Rhine to operate from Y-99 Gutersloh/

airfields in the Middle East, Warburton visited Mount Farm and became friendly with Elliott Roosevelt. With the heady responsibility for all PR assets in Europe, the American was always on the lookout for experienced PR pilots, and they did not come much better than 'Warby'. Roosevelt was delighted to have Warburton on his team.

The British PR ace had first flown a familiarization sortie from La Marsa in a war-weary F-4 on 6 July 1943. This had resulted in a take-off crash in which Warburton was forcibly ejected from the wreckage because he had not closed the cockpit roof hatch or tightened his seat straps. His would-be rescuers found him sitting on a wingtip, smoking while the centre-section of the F-4 blazed away.

Before joining the Americans in England, Warburton had risen to command 336 PR Wing at La Marsa, but had suffered a broken pelvis in a road accident on 26 November 1943 and been hospitalized. This enforced and frustrating rest from operations resulted in Warby losing his command. He discharged himself from hospital in January 1944 and by the spring had pitched up at Mount Farm. By then he had flown some 375 operational sorties (1,300 flying hours up to 6 August 1943) and become an ace, with seven victories.

Warburton was not only made very welcome at Mount Farm but was recommended for a decoration. Citing his part in gathering photos and data for the invasion of Sicily and the reduction of Pantelleria, Roosevelt recommended him for an American DFC.

Warby needed little persuasion to return to operations, and was seconded to the USAAF from 1 April 1944. He was quickly checked out in the F-5 before flying his first mission for the Americans. His official position was Liaison Officer with the 7th PRG, but this irrepressible pilot had no intention of remaining on the ground. Elliot Roosevelt also made him Deputy CO of the 325th Reconnaissance Wing.

Having seldom flown during the first two months of 1944, it was 12 April before Wg Cdr Adrian Warburton took off in F-5B 42-68205. His mission was to obtain photographs of the German airfields at Erding, Landau-Ganacker, Regensburg-Obertraubling (where Messerschmitt had an Me 262 production line) and Schwabisch-Hall. Afterwards he was to continue south and land at Alghero in Sardinia.

One of several unusual aspects of this mission was the fact that the USAAF

To fulfil large orders for an increasing number of F-5 conversions, Lockheed put the work in the hands of the Dallas Modification Center, seen here during a busy shift.
IWM

this claim was disputed by a Ninth AAF Fighter Group, the 33rd's F-5s were up on 14 March, certainly making it the first Allied PR unit to operate from within the borders of the Reich. March's sorties brought about the 33rd's own all-time record number of prints, when 151,344 were developed from the negatives exposed by the F-5 pilots.

Whenever possible F-5 pilots tried to avoid contact with the Luftwaffe, but on 7 April a pair of 33rd PRS pilots, Capt John G. Austin and Lt James Foster, were jumped by eleven Bf 109s. Trying their best to evade enemy fire, the Americans saw one German

Marienfeld. Staying only until the 24th, the 33rd's F-5s were finally based at R-37 Brunswick, where the squadron remained until the war's end.

The RAF's Best

On the RAF side, few PR pilots equalled the outstanding exploits of Wg Cdr Adrian Warburton, whose main war service was not at the controls of an F-5 but who, ironically, lost his life while flying one on secondment to the Eighth Air Force. Having flown at least 360 sorties from Malta plus others from

ABOVE: **Another Mount Farm F-5 sortie having been completed, a Jeep waits to whisk the camera magazine away to get the film developed.** IWM

organized a flight of P-51s of the 357th FG to escort the F-5, which was also accompanied by a second F-5B, 42-67325, piloted by Capt Carl Chapman. One or two PR aircraft would have not have aroused enemy suspicions, but a fighter escort most certainly would have, to the point of attracting unwelcome attention. Nevertheless, this was laid on.

Chapman and Warburton flew together before splitting up to cover their designated targets. The American completed his photo runs and circled for a while, calling Warby on the R/T. When the other F-5 did not appear, Chapman proceeded to Sardinia. He returned to Mount Farm later that day, photographing a number of French airfields en route. Warburton, meanwhile, had not arrived at his intended destination.

Speculation as to Warburton's fate continued for some time. Unfamiliarity with the F-5 was believed to have been a factor in

ABOVE: **Lockheed F-5B-1 42-67331 of the 27th PRS, 7th PRG, in the summer of 1944. This aircraft was lost on 24 September 1944, its pilot, Lt McDonald, being posted as MIA.** J.V. Crow

RIGHT: **An F-5 in anonymous overall blue camouflage and with white or yellow spinners was almost certainly a 7th PRG aircraft.** R.L. Ward

ABOVE: With more space in the nose, the F-5G could also shoot film from head-on, overcoming a drawback of preceding versions. P. Jarrett

OPPOSITE PAGE:
TOP LEFT: Royal Air Force PR ace Wg Cdr Adrian Warburton (centre) with American pilots in an F-5 revetment made out of stacked petrol cans, Malta, 2 April 1943. IWM

TOP RIGHT: Warburton is shown the controls of an F-5 by Lt Sculpone on 2 April 1943, during his secondment to the USAAF in Malta. A brilliant pilot with over 350 sorties to his credit, Warby was lost in a PR Lightning the following year. IWM

BOTTOM: The final wartime version of the PR Lightning was the F-5G, a conversion of the P-38L-5. Here, the first of the breed overflies the camera during a test flight. Lockheed

his loss, and figured in many theories of how and why he disappeared. The Americans were criticized for allowing the flight at all, though they were hardly to blame. They were understandably in awe of Warby's abilities and his outstanding record as a PR pilot.

Such had been Warburton's unconventional approach to Service life outside of operational flying that he was not posted as missing in action until 1 May, seventeen days after he was presumably lost. This was because the USAAF and RAF authorities fervently hoped that he would turn up somewhere, having gone off on one of his jaunts not fully covered by a detailed flight plan. But nothing more was heard of Warburton before the war ended and for decades afterwards.

Then, on 19 August 2002, a German aviation archaeologist began excavating an aircraft crash site in the Landsberg district of southern Germany. The field in question lay south-east of Egling on the

River Paar, and it was on record that an Allied aircraft had come down at about 11.45hr local time on 12 April 1944. At that time several boys reported seeing an aircraft flying low from the direction of the airfield at Lechfeld. It was trailing smoke, and flak bursts were seen. The aircraft flipped, inverted and dived into soft earth, creating a shallow crater. Parts strewn about the field were pushed into the crater by the Wehrmacht troops who found it.

Some larger sections of the aircraft were cleared during land consolidation work in 1951–52. Later investigation of what then remained confirmed that it was indeed an F-5B, and that some human remains were that of Warburton, who was finally laid to rest at a military funeral on 28 February 2003.

French Lightnings

Apart from the French officials who visited Burbank during the early stages of YP-38

production in 1939, the next Frenchmen to have close contact with the Lockheed Lightning were pilots based in North Africa. Stationed in Tunis when the *Torch* landings took place, GR II/33 was something of an élite unit, and with the backing of Elliott Roosevelt its *1st Escadrille* received PR Lightnings, in the form of six F-4s, in April 1943. These were used for familiarization training at Laghouat in Algeria, several pilots having previously had some tuition on the F-4 with the USAAF at Oujda, Morocco.

Equipped with the F-5A when it was pronounced operational, the French unit moved to Marsa to share the base with the US 3rd PR and Mapping Group. Moving forward to cover targets in Sicily, Italy and Sardina, the *1st Esc* was based at Foggia by 8 December 1943 and Naples (Pomigliano d'Arco) on 13 February 1944. Missions to photograph German installations and troop movements in southern and central France usually entailed flights of four to six

Among the thousands of 'out-to-grass' Lightnings in the USA at the end of the war were F-5Es, some of which were bought by survey companies. This helped extend the post-war life of the type into the present era. WTL via R.L. Ward

BELOW: When the Eighth Air Force wanted improved coverage of German targets, both bombers and fighters were adapted. Lockheed P-38J-15 44-23139 was given an extended nose to house H2X and an operator. *Aeroplane*

Although the dozen P-38 Pathfinders were shipped to Europe, they were found less effective than bombers because their radar was unable to scan the full 360 degrees. Lockheed

BELOW: Lockheed F-4As were used by the French unit GR I/33 to fly numerous missions in support of ground forces during the last stages of the war in Europe. ECPA

hours, but flying times were reduced by the use of forward airfields. It was official policy to send French pilots to locations in their homeland, and the number of sorties over Italy remained modest. By 31 July about eighty F-5 sorties had been flown for the loss of two pilots, the second of whom was the noted poet and author Antoine de Saint-Exupéry, lost on 31 July.

When the south of France was invaded, on 15 August 1944, GR II/33's main task was to support the First French Army and US forces in attacks on German positions, PR sorties to that end having begun on 1 August. With Allied forces pushing swiftly north, *1st Esc* was able to operate from le Luc, 20 miles (32km) inside France, two

weeks after the landings. Moving to Valence and then Dijon, the unit soon began to fly over the Rhine and Danube valleys, becoming part of 'XII TAC French Section' on 1 September 1944.

When the USAAF formed the 1st Tactical Air Force (TAF) to support the campaigns of the Sixth Army Group, GR II/33 became an integral part of the component 1st French Air Corps, under the command of Brig Gen Paul Gerardot. He in turn planned tactical reconnaissance sorties with 1st TAF CO Maj Gen Robert M. Webster.

Undergoing various changes of title, all of which were ignored by its pilots, GR II/33 supported operations into the Mulhouse, Colmar and Strasbourg regions before

becoming *Groupe de Reconnaissance I/33 Belmont* on 1 January 1945. From then until the war's end the French Lightnings sought out German activity up to the Swiss border. Hard flying did nothing for the inventory, and by 16 April only one Lightning remained operational. By VE Day the unit's sortie total reached 431 for the loss of five pilots, one of whom was a prisoner of war.

The French received an unknown number of F-5s under Lend-Lease arrangements and eventually flew the A, B, F and G variants.

When Saint-Exupéry failed to return from an F-5B mission to the burning town of Arras (scheduled to be his last with the unit), there were fears that his poor physical condition had been a contributory factor in his disappearance. He was really too tall to fit comfortably into an F-5 cockpit, and numerous injuries he had suffered in past combat flying still plagued him, but the circumstances of his loss remained a mystery for decades.

In October 1998 the remains of what was believed to be an F-5 were found by a Marseilles fishing boat between Bandol and Marseilles. Speculation that the aircraft parts pulled up by the nets were from Saint-Exupéry's machine was reinforced by a bracelet with his name engraved upon it, together with the name of his US publisher in New York. What, if anything, a further search for the wreckage revealed is unknown.

Antoine de Saint-Exupéry taxies out in his F-5, which is marked with tiny GR I/33 unit badges to record sorties. 'St-Ex' went missing on an F-5 PR sortie in 1944.
ECPA via A. Pelletier

US Navy Use

One of the more obscure programmes concerning the PR Lightning centred on the FO-1 for the US Navy. Having looked askance at Lockheed's proposal to adapt the P-38 for a role as a carrier-borne fighter, on the grounds that it was far too large and was not powered by the air-cooled engines almost universally favoured by that Service, the navy did acquire four F-5Bs from the USAAF in North Africa. These, allocated BuAer Nos 01209, 01210, 01211 and 01212, were theatre transfers assumedly used for normal photographic duties, which paved the way for the specialized postwar variants of first-line naval aircraft.

World-wide Coverage

Various versions of the Lockheed F-4 and F-5 were operated by USAAF units around the world. In terms of numbers of operational squadrons the distribution was biased towards the European theatres, mainly owing to the number and diversity of the potential targets that needed to be covered. Another factor was the inherent risk of using lower-performance types against the formidable German defences. While not being the fastest type in the

Allied inventory, the F-5 was usually able to evade Luftwaffe interceptors.

Europe and the Mediterranean were well served by USAAF PR Lightnings, and their pilots obtained some of the most vital (and dramatic) photographs of the war. Sufficient full sets of pre-D-Day prints were obtained by low-flying ('dicing') F-5 sorties to issue to all ground commands before the assault. Particularly useful were the close-up shots of the numerous anti-personnel obstacles or 'hedgehogs' strewn about the French beaches by the Germans. Rigged with explosives, these obstacles had a secondary anti-tank use.

Both the Eighth and Ninth Air Forces built full photographic reconnaissance forces around the F-5, these Lightnings eventually becoming the catalyst for all USAAF PR flying around the world. 'Focus cat' Lightnings were supported by such stalwarts as American-manned Spitfires and the Douglas F-3 Havoc, which undertook a variety of special day and night duties in the ETO. In turn, the USAAF PR force co-operated with the RAF's Spitfires and Mosquitoes and other types. Every aircraft used on PR duties tended to concentrate on a specific role, invariably tailored to its range, performance and altitude capabilities, though there was some back-up in the event of unserviceability and so forth.

Bomber Support

Much of the USAAF's PR effort in Europe was in support of the strategic bomber offensive, and while the other aircraft types brought back data on weather conditions and the extent of passive opposition in the form of electronic countermeasures, enemy radar activity and so on, the 'Photo Joes' at the controls of unarmed Lightnings concentrated almost entirely on taking pictures. For certain targets the resulting prints were used to form overlapping mosaics and panoramas showing entire factory complexes, airfields, harbours and marshalling yards, plus hundreds of miles of coastline and other geographical features.

Photographic reconnaissance was laced with operational hazards, these tending to increase in proportion to the ever-widening need for new target coverage. The USAAF's long-term answer was to provide the F-5s with (usually) a P-51 fighter escort, but a means of 'self protection' was also investigated. After a number of F-5s were lost on operations, several aircraft at Mount Farm were fitted with gun pods under the outer wing panels. Containing two 0.50in machine-guns, these pods added unwelcome weight and drag and were not generally adopted for service.

When a fighter escort was deemed necessary, PR pilots would hardly complain, though 'going it alone' had become second nature to them. There was also the undeniable risk that several aircraft would be more likely to be detected on enemy radar. The lone aircraft minimized the risk of being recognized for what it was and therefore put in greater danger. It became something of a deadly sport practised by both the Allies and the Axis to try to bring down the other side's PR aircraft, either by airborne patrol or a 'scramble' and high-speed climb by specially lightened and polished interceptors. Potentially, the Luftwaffe's jet interceptors made that particular job that much easier.

Post-Strike Bomb-Damage Assessment

When bombing missions had been completed the F-5s went out and obtained post-strike evidence of how accurately the target had been hit. There were occasions when the PR aircraft brought back positive proof that further attacks were necessary, though estimating the degree of damage,

TOP: **An F-4A of GR I/33 undergoes servicing at a forward airbase.** ECPA

ABOVE: **An F-5's camera magazine is unloaded at a base in the Vosges foothills of eastern France during the winter of 1944–45. At that time GR I/33 was part of the 1st French Air Corps and assigned to the US 1st Tactical Air Force, formed on 6 November 1944.** IWM

particularly inside apparently 'gutted' factories, was later shown in some cases to have been quite optimistic. Cameras could not always record in detail the degree of damage to vital machine tools, for example, and it was only by completely wrecking those that a factory line would be forced to shut down. Postwar analysis proved how notoriously difficult it had been to assess such damage, however low the PR aircraft had passed over the target.

On the southern front F-5s were very active before, during and after the assault on Monte Cassino and the Gothic Line, the Twelfth Air Force's photographic Lightnings coming home with a fine visual record of the fighting and its aftermath.

To the French and Walloon people of Holland, who saw many P-38s/F-5s over their shattered countries during the war, the aircraft was 'Le double queue' (the twin-tailed one), an unmistakable symbol of Allied victory.

China-Burma-India

The CBI Theater placed considerable demands on PR, its vast area of operations involving shuttle sorties over 'the Hump' as units carried out temporary duty with the Tenth and Fourteenth Air Forces. Each air force was assigned its own PR squadron, these being the 8th and 21st respectively.

F-5s Join the Fifth

In the Pacific most aircraft, including heavy bombers and especially medium bombers, were fitted with cameras to enable comprehensive dossiers of target assessment photos to be built up. A vast number of prints recorded ground attacks on airfields, gun emplacements, bridges, buildings and so forth, often capturing amazing detail for minute intelligence interpretation. A broader canvas of prints was required as the Allies advanced deeper into regions that had hardly ever been covered by the camera lens, and certainly not in the detail required. Several USAAF PR squadrons flying the F-5 were sent out as soon as

A late-war (or possibly post-war) line-up of F-5Fs and Gs of GR I/33. Both versions used P-38L-1 and L-5 airframes, making them among the most capable of the PR Lightnings. A. Pelletier

trained crews and aircraft became available. The first such units in the Pacific arrived on 5 Dec 1942, and from these early beginnings the Lightning was deployed anywhere that US forces required its particular specialized service. There were few other aircraft with the necessary range and, particularly, performance to evade enemy fighters, and the adapted Lightning, usually in single squadron strength, became an integral part of the planning of air operations from the South West Pacific to the Sahara.

Among the Fifth Air Force's PR Lightning units the 8th PRS, the famed 'Eightballers', built an enviable reputation as a 'can do' outfit when it came to providing the combat groups with visual evidence of Japanese activity in some of the most difficult terrain in the world.

Obtaining pictures of small potential targets surrounded by dense jungle involved a high standard of flying skill and an intimate knowledge of areas that seemed completely featureless to the untrained eye.

In the Solomons the only new Lightning Group to join the Thirteenth Air Force early in 1943 was the 17th PRS, with F-5s. Operating from the strip known as Fighter Two from January, the PR pilots soon found their new area of operations to be quite a challenge. One member of the squadron, Capt Eugene R. Brown, was flying one of the

early missions to obtain pictures of enemy activity at Kahili. Taking advantage of an overcast that he thought would have hidden him from any enemy aircraft flying above the cloud, Brown was suddenly jumped by two A6M 'Zekes'. The Japanese pilots had him squarely in their sights, and their fire shot out the F-5's port engine and a 20mm shell nicked the aircraft's starboard propeller, throwing it out of balance.

Fortunately the enemy pilots either abandoned the chase or lost sight of Brown when he dived to 300ft (90m) over the ocean, at which point he regained some control of his dangerously vibrating F-5. He was then about 400 miles (640km) from home, with only one good engine, but he managed to nurse the crippled aircraft home, later being presented with a well-earned DFC.

Invasion Intelligence

Among the air units working towards building a comprehensive mass of data for the invasion of Iwo Jima in February 1945 was the 28th PRS, which, like the combat groups, moved forward to remain within range of targets. The 28th mapped the entire island, using five F-5s working in relays to take 1,720 photographs. The PR aircraft were escorted by twelve P-38s and four Boeing B-29s.

During the assault on Okinawa F-5E 44-23280 of the 28th PRS was escorted by US Marine Corps F4U Corsairs to reconnoitre dug-in Japanese positions. Marine 1st Lt David D. Duncan squeezed himself into one of the F-5's drop tanks to secure visual and photographic confirmation from as low as 100ft (30m).

Drop-tanks had originally been modified with clear nosecones to carry urgent medical cases to rear areas for treatment. They were rarely used for that purpose, but had secondary uses, as the intrepid Duncan demonstrated.

Photographic Lightnings also made a modest contribution to the final defeat of Japan by collecting evidence that the atomic bomb had indeed done its deadly work at Hiroshima on 6 August. The exact nature of the 'super bomb' was not widely publicized, however, and several pilots who were airborne that day had little idea of what they were witnessing. These included Charles Lerable, a member of the 25th PRS, who was on his way back to base after taking shots of the home islands. His sortie was part of the intelligence-gathering exercise to prepare for an invasion of Japan scheduled for 1 November. Noticing a strange, mushroom-shaped 'thunderstorm', Lerable started his cameras and the F-5 returned with some unusual prints of the Hiroshima explosion.

CHAPTER SEVEN

Zero Feet

As the P-38 was in greater demand in other war theatres, particularly the Pacific, it made sense to change the emphasis in Europe. From late 1943 pilots destined to serve in the ETO trained for operational duties that were fundamentally different to the role of escort/interceptor fighter. This was particularly true of P-38 units, which, though they did not entirely abandon the escort role, generally provided support to medium bombers rather than the heavies.

The tactical force in Europe now concentrated on the ground-support role, the bombing and strafing by fighters of a variety of ground targets, particularly Luftwaffe aircraft and airfields.

In pursuance of the official policy of hunting the German air force to extinction in the air and on the ground as a prerequisite to a successful invasion of the European continent, the P-38 proved ideal. If carried out with careful planning and intelligent execution, continual ground strafing of aerodromes could wreck the best part of Luftwaffe strength in the west. Once *Overlord* had been deemed a success and German counterattacks had failed to dislodge the Allied armies, the tactical air forces could offer a support service that would prove unstoppable.

As the only fighter in the USAAF inventory fitted with a 20mm cannon, the P-38 made an excellent strafer. In addition, the latest P-38J, which equipped the Ninth Air Force Groups, was capable of carrying up to 3,000lb (1,360kg) of bombs.

Other Weapons

Several types of ordnance had been combat tested on the P-38, including the triple-cluster M-10 rocket launcher. This weapon had enjoyed some success in Burma, but overall results were not significantly better than those obtained with a range of free-fall bombs. Moreover, the P-38's configuration somewhat limited the available carrying points for external loads. If the inboard wing racks were fitted with drop tanks, the

only free area was the fuselage pod. Field engineers had consequently bolted an M-10 launcher on to each side of the lower fuselage, but, although this was practical,

it did little for the aircraft's aerodynamics, though the tubes were designed to be jettisoned *in extremis*. Officially, it seems that the reluctance of ETO commanders to

First Lieutenant James Morris of the 77th FS, 20th FG, confers with his crew chief, Staff Sgt Joe McCarland, in front of *Black Barney*, Morris's personal P-38, coded **LC-B.** IWM

clear this weapon on P-47s because of its inaccuracy in the close confines of rural France extended to the P-38. Had an aircraft so configured come up against high-performance enemy fighters it could have been dangerously disadvantaged, and no such rocket-tube fittings were cleared for use on the P-38 in Europe.

Nevertheless, as ground attacks by fighters developed, ordnance was increasingly used to good effect. In all theatres the 4.75in HVAR was regarded as a useful weapon for fighters and attack aircraft, and Lockheed returned to the drawing board to establish whether the outer wing panels of the P-38J could take a conventional battery of rockets on 'zero-length' launchers. As detailed elsewhere in this volume, such installations were tested, but with unsatisfactory results.

The preferred alternative was to group rocket rounds on the multiple-tiered 'tree' installation. This arrangement was approved for later-model P-38Js and Ls

shortly before the war's end, after most of the campaigns in the west had been completed. Consequently no operational use of rocket projectiles by P-38s is known to have occurred in the ETO.

Combat operations in all theatres in 1944–45 therefore saw the P-38 units, in common with those in Europe, relying almost exclusively on guns, with bombs as their 'heavy' offensive load. Napalm appeared on the scene in mid-1944, the tanks of jellied petrol being similar in configuration and weight to drop-tanks. In addition there were several 'combination' weapons, whereby armourers would rig fragmentation bombs to drop with external tanks to create an anti-personnel weapon.

Napalm was first used by P-38s in the ETO in July, when the mission planners thought that fire from the skies would create a useful conflagration on the ground. Oil-filled drop tanks were used occasionally for a similar purpose.

Two-Man Lightnings

The advent of the more versatile and technically improved P-38J enabled a revision of tactical deployment in Europe, to encompass fighter-bombers attacking selected targets *en masse* independent of the bomber escort mission. And if fighters could be navigated to their targets by a 'pathfinder' aircraft matching their performance, rather than a vulnerable heavy bomber, then the installation of a Norden bomb sight in a P-38 made sound tactical and economic sense. Thus was the 'Droop Snoot' conceived, a precedent having already been set with the hybrid conversion of an F-5A-10 (42-12975), which became the sole XF-5D-LO experimental two-seat armed reconnaissance model. The second crew member was seated in a glazed nose compartment to act as camera operator and, if necessary, a gunner, using the two 0.50in machine-guns provided. Three K-17 cameras were carried,

'The Rebel Kids' may refer both to the pilot (Lt Marvin Glasgow) and ground crew of this 55th FG P-38J, which bears the widely adopted nose markings to make it resemble a Droop Snoot bombing leadship. USAF

A P-38J of the 343rd FS, 55th FG, flown by Lt William H. Allen.
J.V. Crow

one mounted to take pictures below the nose and one in each tail boom.

This particular configuration was not adopted for production, but the XF-5D, minus the armament, formed the basis for the Droop Snoot P-38 bombing leader conversions.

In January 1944 the Eighth Air Force's ever resourceful Operational Engineering department at Bovingdon took up the idea of providing an unarmed pathfinder leader for deployment by the Eighth Air Force P-38 Groups.

A wooden mock-up was built to specifications drawn up by Cass Hough and armament and ordnance specialist Col Don Ostrander. Hough flew to Langford Lodge to discuss the idea with Lockheed Overseas Corporation (LOC) engineering personnel. James E. Boyce was then manager of LOC, with J. D. 'Jack' Hawkins as chief engineer. George McCutcheon carried out the necessary design work, and the mock-up was completed to confirm the basic layout of the interior. The next stage was to modify an aircraft, and P-38H-5 42-67086 was fitted with a dummy nose conforming to the design contours.

With the aerodynamics of the new nose section approved, a prototype (42-68184) was fitted out, using an example of what would be the initial 'production' aircraft, the P-38J-10. After being tested at Bovingdon, the aircraft, which was originally camouflaged, was stripped of paint and used for bombing trials at Bradwell Range, flown by Cass Hough and with Col Ostrander manning the Norden sight.

Two standard P-38Js accompanied the lead ship, and to make the test realistic the Droop Snoot was furnished with a formation-bombing system. This triggered a light in the cockpits of the following P-38J fighter-bombers, the pilots releasing their bombs when the lights flashed. A later system developed by the Eighth's Technical Operations Unit used radio signals to trigger all the bomb toggles, permitting the lead ship to fly within a formation for extra protection, rather than being stuck out in front and exposed to flak, if not to fighter attack. At least twenty Droop Snoot conversions were undertaken for the Eighth Air Force fighter Groups, and the number may have extended to a further five, though no exact records of the programme appear to have been kept.

The result of the Droop Snoot programme was a neatly reconfigured P-38 lacking any fixed armament but retaining standard bombing capability. From his seat in the nose a navigator/bombing leader would lead a formation of standard fighter-bombers, pinpoint their target and, using the Norden bomb sight, release his ordnance first.

By overseeing the entire operation from an airborne perspective, selecting the primary and secondary target(s) and acting as lead bombardier, the Droop Snoot crewman enabled greater bombing accuracy than fighter pilots might have achieved individually. On the way home the main formation of aircraft could undertake strafing runs. A degree of surprise was also anticipated, as the enemy would be hard put to detect that the Droop Snoot was not a standard Lightning until the bombs began to fall. Much was made of the fact that a P-38 could carry a similar bomb load to a B-17 on ultra-short-range missions, with eight fewer men in the crew; or so went the theory.

To sustain the element of surprise, P-38 fighters were given a white nose ring and a highly polished nose tip to make them resemble Droop Snoot aircraft. From a distance, sunlight reflecting from polished metal noses and Perspex was similar, and the ETO Lightning force was commonly given the shiny-nose treatment.

Six more conversions were made at Langford Lodge before both the 20th and 55th FGs carried out the first Droop Snoot combat missions in the ETO on the same day, 10 April 1944. The target for the former unit was Florennes/Juzaine aerodrome, but the Lightning pilots found it obscured by cloud and returned home, dropping their bombs in the Channel en route. The 55th had better luck at Coulommiers aerodrome, sixteen aircraft releasing 17 tons of bombs. This was the secondary target, the primary at St Dizier being cloud covered. The 20th also claimed one enemy aircraft destroyed, but the 55th lost two P-38s in its attack.

The Eighth Air Force continued to send the P-38 groups on irregular Droop Snoot missions, but on 25 July one led the Thunderbolt-equipped 56th FG. It was flown by none other than 'Hub' Zemke, who was to sight for twelve P-47s carrying oil-filled belly tank 'bombs' destined for the aerodrome at Montdidier, but German flak all

dive bombing normally used by Thunderbolts and was apparently not repeated.

Otherwise, the P-38 Groups interspersed escort sorties with ground attacks as the days leading up to D-Day passed. On 31 May a strong fighter attack on German airfields included the Droop Snoot-led 20th FG, which dropped 19 tons of HE on Rheine-Hopsten and strafed to claim five enemy aircraft destroyed on the ground without loss to its own numbers.

controlled heavy bombers as giant flying bombs.

A crew of the 36th Bomb Squadron, 25th BG, took off in a Droop Snoot on 13 August, the day after the disastrous loss of Lt Joseph Kennedy, the future US president's brother. They were seeking clues as to what had caused the explosive-packed PB4Y-1 Liberator in which Kennedy was flying to explode in mid-air without warning, before any of the crew had a chance to

Bellied-in P-38J-5 42-67232 of the 384th FS, 364th FG. All too often missions ended like this for individual Lightnings in the Eighth Air Force Groups.

An oil-streaked wheel indicates that this P-38J of the 385th FS, 364th FG, had a recent rough mission and only just made it home.

but wrecked the mission. Zemke's Lightning was hit on the approach to the target, and the starboard propeller blown off. Regaining control, he headed home, but on touching down at Boxted the Droop Snoot's brakes failed and it ploughed into a field. The attack was carried out at the relatively high altitude of 12,000ft (3,600m), which differed from the shallow

All four Eighth Air Force P-38 Groups received Droop Snoot Lightning 'lead ships', but their success in combat was mixed. The upshot of the Droop Snoot experiment was that the Eighth ultimately relinquished all but three of its converted aircraft, the latter including P-38J-15 43-28490, used in connection with the Aphrodite project, which utilized radio-

bale out. Using their monitoring equipment, the Droop Snoot specialists aimed to detect any radio signal that might have been strong enough to trigger the electronic detonators in Kennedy's aircraft by accident. They found some evidence to suggest that navigational-beacon transmissions could have been the cause, but there was no definite proof.

Operational Engineering retained a second P-38J-15, 42-104075, for its own use, while the third (serial number unknown) was reserved for the Dilly project.

Four Droop Snoot conversions were loaned to 100 (Bomber Support) Group, RAF, for electronic intelligence (ELINT) operations, primarily to monitor German radar defences. Originally assigned to the 7th PRG, they retained USAAF markings and were flown by American pilots on secondment. The aircraft comprised two P-38J-15s (43-28479 and 44-23156) and two P-38J-20s (44-23501 and 44-23515). The second J-20 was posted missing in action at an unknown date.

One of two P-38s to fly operationally with the RAF, J-20 44-23517, was the

Down in a field on return from a mission, a 343rd FS, 55th FG, P-38J seems to have its starboard engine feathered, a sure sign of trouble in the cold skies over Europe. Author

BELOW: Despite losses, the USAAF could usually maintain its P-38 inventory, and depots such as that at Langford Lodge in Northern Ireland did their bit to keep the combat units supplied with new or refurbished aircraft, such as this P-38J-10. via R.L. Ward

Known USAAF ETO Squadron Use of Droop Snoot Conversions

P-38J-15	42-104075/Q3-B *Droop Snoot*	8th AF Tech Ops
P-38J-10	42-67450/LC-E *Eze Does it*	77th FS, 20th FG
P-38J-15	44-23156/R4-X	36th BS, 25th BG
P-38J-10	42-67704/CL-K	338th FS, 55th FG
P-38J-20	44-23507/4N-Z(bar) *Trail Blazer*	394th FS, 367th FG
P-38J-15	43-28483/J2-?	435th FS, 479th FG

New P-38Js and F-5s poured into England in 1944 to maintain the units of the Eighth and Ninth Air Forces. This view shows a busy depot, probably Bovingdon in Hertfordshire. IWM

A longer view of the same base reveals a small Lightning jam on the taxiway as an F-5 confronts a P-38J, while ground crew prepare fighters for final assembly. IWM

personal mount of Air Cdre Sharp when he commanded No. 54 Base. This, formed on 1 January 1944, controlled the bomber bases at Coningsby, Metheringham and Woodhall Spa in 5 Group, which had its own target-marking force more or less independent of the regular Pathfinders. Sharp, previously a liaison officer with Eighth Air Force headquarters, accepted the P-38J upon taking up his new appointment, the aircraft being delivered in the summer, when No. 54 Base Lancasters were engaged on tactical support for the armies in Normandy. Air Cdre Sharp's Lightning was flown on several of these raids during the first week of August by Sqn Ldr Owen.

On 6 August a second P-38, L-1 44-24360, arrived at Coningsby for trials. Recorded as a 'PB-38' this aircraft had Droop Snoot configuration and retained US markings. Owen flew it on several unspecified trials and on 15 August Wg Cdr Guy Gibson, VC accompanied ninety-four bombers to raid Deelen and other Luftwaffe night-fighter bases. Gibson was then No. 54 Base Air Staff Officer.

The 'PB-38' was returned to the USAAF at the end of August but it had impressed the staff at Coningsby who sent 'their' P-38J to Langford Lodge for Droop Snoot modification. When it returned to Coningsby the aircraft had Loran and Gee as well as twin VHF radios and was given an overall coat of PRU Blue paint and RAF markings. It then began target-marking work, Owen flying it on 23/24 September on a 5 Group raid on Munster/Handorf airfield. The aircraft flew regularly, assumedly in the target-marking and bomber controller roles and was well liked by its crews.

When Air Cdre Sharp moved to Northolt, his Droop Snoot Lightning went with him; after the war '517 was flown to 51MU at Lichfield for disposal, then in natural metal finish but retaining RAF markings. It was apparently returned to US control having meanwhile acquired the as yet unexplained code letters 'DPA'.

On operations, a formation of P-38s led by a Droop Snoot aircraft (known locally as a 'B-38' for a time) was felt to be less effective than medium bombers in terms of the weight of explosives they could deliver. Targets such as airfields were notoriously difficult to render completely untenable in a single strike, as the pilots of both fighter-bombers and medium bombers found. It was true that after bombing the Lightnings could use their heavy armament to strafe with marginally less risk than larger aircraft, but, even so, attack bombers such as the A-20 Havoc carried respectable batteries of forward-firing machine-guns if 'down on the deck' strafing runs were necessary. The USAAF believed implicitly in this duality, and perpetuated it in the Douglas A-26 Invader, the 'second-generation' attack bomber.

In summary, the Droop Snoot mission offered little or no real tactical advantage in an arena rapidly filling up with combat aircraft able to meet all foreseeable sortie requirements. Not that the two-seat Lightnings became extinct; a number of combat groups, not all of them P-38 units *per se*, acquired examples, and these continued to be used in several 'home front' roles, including flying members of the top brass to forward airfields for conferences in the minimum time.

ETO Swansong

On 11 August 1944 Robin Olds started a run of aerial victories that were to make him the last P-38 ace in the Eighth Air Force. During a freelance sweep over France he became separated from the rest of his flight, and from that none-too-envious position he surprised two Fw 190s. Opening fire on the rearmost aircraft, Olds kept the trigger down for five to eight seconds and observed strikes on its port wing. Shifting his aim, he then poured lead into the German fighter's fuselage. Large pieces of airframe broke away and black smoke poured from his quarry, which executed a wild half roll and dropped off to Olds's right-hand side from an altitude of no more than 100ft (30m).

As this attack developed, the pilot of the second Focke-Wulf attempted to evade, executing a violent right-hand skid, which Olds followed. As the first Fw 190 fell away below Olds's starboard wing, he opened fire on the second from 350yd (320m). Firing as he closed to 200yd (180m), Olds observed strikes. The enemy pilot made a 360-degree turn and flew off straight and level, with the P-38 in hot pursuit. Both aircraft were still at low altitude as Olds fired a 5sec burst from dead astern. This brought a familiar shower of debris from the German fighter, which then zoom climbed with the Lightning following. As the Fw 190 reached the top of its climb the pilot baled out. His parachute opened almost at

Pre-D-Day operations gave individual P-38s impressive mission totals in a short time. This 20th FG aircraft, the personal mount of Maj Delynn E. Anderson, bears umbrella, broom and bomb symbols to denote different sorties. USAF

once and Olds had to 'cock up a wing' to avoid him, but he saw this second aircraft hit the ground and explode.

Skies of Fire

A red-letter day for the P-38 in the ETO was 25 August, when the 367th and 474th FGs ran into a mass of Bf 109s and Fw 190s during a low-level sweep over central France. One squadron of the 367th was set upon by aircraft of JG 6, the pilots of which obviously knew their business. The 393rd FS answered the call for help and waded into the dogfight.

One man who had a field day was the 393rd's CO, Capt Lawrence 'Scrapiron' Blumer, so nicknamed not only because he often returned from missions with his P-38 damaged, but also because he had the name painted on the nose of all the Lightnings

he flew. He was credited with five Fw 190s and became an 'ace in a day'.

This combat was all the more remarkable because it was said to have taken place within the confines of Bourges airfield and none of the participating aircraft ever got higher than 3,000ft (900m).

Other pilots of the 367th FG, which was awarded a Presidential Unit Citation for the action, claimed another fifteen enemy fighters. That these victories did not come cheaply is shown by the loss of eight P-38s. The 474th FG claimed twenty-one victories for the loss of eleven P-38s on this hectic and memorable day of incredible action, the heaviest since the invasion.

Over Rostock that same day, Robin Olds became an ace when he downed two Bf 109s. The second victory could have ended in disaster, as the canopy of Olds's P-38 ripped itself away while he was diving to rescue a P-51 that was being attacked by the Messerschmitts. One latched on to his tail, but Olds out-turned the German and shot him down to become the first ace in the 479th.

The final aerial victories for an Eighth Air Force P-38 unit came on 26 September 1944, when the 479th ran into a bunch of enemy fighters south-west of Munster. Only the 434th and 436th were flying Lightnings, the 435th having changed to Mustangs. The 479th was temporarily based at Wattisham, sharing the airfield with the 370th FG's Lightnings, and the sweep was flown in support of the airborne assault on Arnhem. Ranging over Holland, the pilots found little action, but war with the Eighth Air Force was all but over.

When the 479th entirely re-equipped with Mustangs in October, the three Ninth Air Force Groups were left to carry the torch for the P-38 in Europe, apart from a handful of 'special duty' aircraft.

Chances for the tactical force to shoot down enemy aircraft continued to be relatively rare, and in any event there was always the watchful eye of authority to discourage the practice. That did not prevent 'Scrapiron' Blumer seeking the Luftwaffe on 19 November, when the 367th FG clashed with several Fw 190s that were about to attack a group of US light and medium not until early 1945 that the change-over to other fighter types began, when the 367th received P-47s in February. After the 370th, alias the 'Dynamite Gang', converted to Mustangs in March, only the 474th remained flying the P-38 as a front-line fighter in Europe, a distinction most of the Group's pilots relished.

Switching to a totally different type of fighter could be a challenge, and the change did not sit well with many pilots, though there was general approval when the capabilities of the P-47 and P-51 became apparent. Given the choice, however, pilots with lengthy experience of the Lockheed twin would undoubtedly have stayed with it.

The wartime caption to this photo states that it was the first P-38 to land in France post-invasion, having been flown over the Channel by Maj Gen 'Pete' Queseda, boss of IX Fighter Command. It belonged to the Ibsley-based 367th FG, which moved into Beuzeville on 22 July 1944. USAF

over Germany the force bounced two gaggles of enemy fighters and a swirling dogfight developed. The result was a claim for twenty-seven enemy fighters for the loss of a single P-38, seventeen falling to the 434th FS. The Group received its third Distinguished Unit Citation for this operation, which was almost the last with the P-38. Although the 479th did not fly its first all-Mustang mission until 5 October, and there was a late September 'damaged' claim by 2nd Lt Eugene Wendt, the P-38's bombers. In the vicinity of the German town of Merzig the P-38s chased down the enemy, the US pilots claiming six downed. Blumer nailed one of the Focke-Wulfs for his sixth and final victory of the war. No bombers were lost, the Lightnings successfully breaking up the enemy fighter attack.

Thereafter the number of P-38s in the ETO began to decline as the Ninth Air Force also chose to phase out the Lightning in favour of the P-47 and P-51. This process was delayed in the TAF, however, and it was In their view, by early 1945 the P-38J had reached the peak of its capability, and an experienced pilot knew how to get the best out of it.

Lightnings remained familiar enough in the theatre, but many operations up to the end of the war were undertaken for reconnaissance purposes, a role for which the USAAF had no replacement for the capable F-5. That left a few Droop Snoot two-seaters that were used for second-line duties or ferried away to other theatres.

Combat Period, ETO P-38 Groups

Assignment	First and last P-38 mission (replaced by)
Eighth Air Force	
20th Fighter Group	28 Dec 43–21 July 44 (P-51)
55th FS	20 July 44
77th FS	20 July 44
79th FS	21 July 44
55th Fighter Group	15 Oct 43–15 July 44 (P-51)
38th FS	15 July 44
338th FS	15 July 44
343rd FS	15 July 44
364th Fighter Group	3 March 44–27 July 44 (P-51)
383rd FS	27 July 44
384th FS	27 July 44
385th FS	27 July 44
479th Fighter Group	26 May 44–3 Oct 44 (P-51)
434th FS	28 Sept 44
435th FS	21 Sept 44
436th FS	3 Oct 44
Ninth Air Force	
367th Fighter Group	9 May 44–23 Feb 45 (P-47)
392nd FS	11 Feb 45
393rd FS	23 Feb 45
394th FS	16 Feb 45
370th Fighter Group	1 May 44–25 March 45 (P-51)
401st FS	24 March 45
402nd FS	24 March 45
485th FS	25 March 45
474th Fighter Group	25 April 44–8 May 45
428th FS	8 May 45
429th FS	8 May 45
430th FS	8 May 45

NB Dates for some squadrons differ due to aircraft changeover being phased over several days/weeks.

Lockheed P-38J-10 42-68017, flown by Capt George Cueleers of the 383rd FS, 364th FG. He eventually achieved 10½ victories, but only one and a half were achieved on the P-38. USAF

Statistically, each Group's final figures showed the enormous effort that had been put in over a relatively short period. The 474th is a good example, as it enjoyed the continuity of flying the P-38 as its singular aircraft type throughout its entire combat period. In addition, it had only three commanding officers during that time. Colonel Wasem, who had taken over on 1 August 1943, handed over to Lt Col Earl C. Hedlund on 17 February 1945. Hedlund's tenure lasted until 18 April, when Lt Col David L. Lewis became the 474th's last wartime leader through the German surrender and up to 3 November 1945.

The Group produced three aces, each with five victories: Lenon F. Kirkland, Joseph E. Miller and Robert C. Milliken. Kirkland and Milliken scored all their victories while serving with the 474th, while Miller got one, the other four being credited while he was with the 14th FG. This trio of pilots made the 474th top in terms of the number of Group aces in the Ninth Air Force, and joint first with the 20th FG, Eighth Air Force, which also produced three.

From March 1944 until May 1945 the 474th flew 12,954 sorties in 822 missions, dropped 3,920 tons of bombs and expended 241,897 rounds of 0.50in ammunition and 36,656 rounds of 20mm cannon shells. The Group was credited with the destruction of 113 enemy aircraft in the air plus 90 on the ground; 4,643 pieces of equipment including tanks, armoured fighting vehicles and other military vehicles, locomotives, rail cars and gun emplacements were denied to the enemy, and damage was done to another 5,681 pieces. These figures and similar ones for other units showed that a P-38 Group unleashed under favourable conditions could cause an awful lot of damage to most tactical targets.

continued overleaf

Combat Period, ETO P-38 Groups *continued*

Top cover, sweeps, escort missions, a couple of busted locos and a single aerial victory are marked up on P-38J-10 *One Man Posse*, flown by Lt Robert E. Miles of the 55th FS, 20th FG. USAF

Lieutenant John Armstrong flew this P-38J-15 as part of the 79th FS, 20th FG, in 1944, aided and abetted by his ground crew, T/Sgt L. Kergewski, Sgts C. Wilder and C. Lawler, and Cpl Cresniali. USAF

RIGHT: Completing every sortie without once having to turn back through mechanical failure, Art Heiden of the 79th FS, 20th FG, had a dedicated ground crew and a superb example of the P-38J. Here Heiden congratulates M/Sgt Max Piles for his help in completing sixty-five missions.
Heiden

BELOW: The ingenious Droop Snoot broadened the scope of the P-38, with a second seat and a bomb sight to enable it to lead standard Lightnings to tactical targets. This was the first conversion carried out in England.
Lockheed

Combat Period, ETO P-38 Groups *continued*

TOP: A P-38J-20 (44-23517) Droop Snoot believed unique in acquiring RAF markings, seen at 51MU at Lichfield, Staffordshire, after the war. IWM

ABOVE: An uncamouflaged P-38J shows what the Droop Snoot looked like from head-on. USAF

LEFT: Although they were used successfully on several occasions, Droop Snoot-led P-38 formations could rarely deliver the same amount of bombs as a small force of medium bombers, and the idea waned. USAF

CHAPTER EIGHT

Southern Front Finale

By the spring of 1944 fifteen Groups of B-24s and six equipped with B-17s constituted the main wartime bomber strength of the Fifteenth Air Force in Italy. In addition to a special bomber squadron, there were seven Groups of fighters, including the trio of original Twelfth Air Force units flying the P-38. The 5th PRG, flying F-5s, joined them in September, and a second special unit with B-24s appeared the following January. Last but not least was the 154th Weather Reconnaissance Squadron, which was equipped with Lightnings throughout much of the year and operated both F-4s and standard P-38 fighters.

ground forces on the ropes. Progress into northern Italy had previously been slow as the weather changed for the worse and slowed everything down, but the troops who had made such great sacrifices were now strong enough to withstand local counterattacks. They could hold on and await support, and if the air forces could offer less of it for several days, even weeks, because of bad weather, then so be it. Time was on the Allies' side.

By September 1944 the P-38 pilots of the Fifteenth Air Force had for weeks been filing encounter reports of combat with Fw 190s, even though this particular German

As for the Fw 190, although this excellent fighter was the subject of a limited Luftwaffe deployment in the area, it was unable to affect the Axis reversals. What Allied pilots frequently encountered at this late stage was the radial-engined Rumanian IAR 80, the subject of numerous mistaken sightings. This cannon-armed interceptor and its similar IAR 81 derivative flew combat missions as part of the Axis until the country changed sides in late 1944, and it was obvious that the finer points of aircraft recognition, including markings and national insignia, were being overlooked by American flyers in the heat of battle.

Black Day

During 1944 it fell to the P-38 groups based in the MTO to undertake one of the war's few all-fighter air strikes on a strategic target. This was none other than the notorious oil-producing complex at Ploesti, Rumania. The bane of the Fifteenth Air Forces' heavy bombers, the refineries had been heavily damaged by the time of the Lightning raid on 10 June. It was an ambitious operation for fighters to undertake, and it proved to be a black day for the participating Groups.

Marshalling forty-six bomb-laden P-38Js at Foggia 11/Vincenzo airfield, the 82nd FG took off shortly after dawn to rendezvous with the 1st FG's Lightnings, forty-eight of which were to escort them. The 82nd FG aircraft, led by Lt Col William Litton, CO of the 96th FS, were drawn from all squadrons. Each aircraft carried a single 1,000lb bomb on one wing rack, balanced by a drop-tank on the other side.

Although he did not normally fly missions, the group commander, Lt Col Ben A. Mason, Jr, also went along on what promised to be a memorable operation. Specifically, the P-38 strike was to be directed against the cracking and distillation plants and the boiler house of the Romano-Americano refinery, which was located well

Still bearing the US national flag on the fin, obscuring the serial number, this is a P-38F of the 71st FS, 1st FG. Applied for the *Torch* landings to show that the USA was not at war with Vichy France, the markings did not prevent brief combat taking place.
P. Jarrett

By 1944 the P-38 escort Groups in the Fifteenth Air Force were flying a proportion of ground-attack sorties. It was not that the Axis no longer appeared in the air, but the bulk of the German units were pulling out of Italy to defend the Reich. Many Allied pilots based in the region were destroying more enemy aircraft on the ground than in the air, and by the autumn the Allies also had the German

fighter was all but extinct on the southern front. In fact the Luftwaffe in general was a shadow of its former self in Italy, but the USAAF fighter pilots continued to report German aircraft. This was correct, but the pilots flying the Bf 109s that opposed US bomber formations were predominantly Italian, with Bulgarian, Hungarian and Rumanian units bolstering the Axis order of battle in northern Italy and the Balkans.

Lockheed P-38F-1 41-7555 of the 27th FS, 1st FG, in Algeria shortly after the *Torch* landings in November 1942. P. Jarrett

away from the rest of the complex and had so far escaped serious damage. There had been previous attempts to knock out this same target, but from 25,000ft (7,600m) the B-24s and B-17s had not had much success. Someone thought that a 'precision' dive-bombing attack at low level by smaller aircraft would do the trick. The main problem was that each refinery was well spaced from its neighbour and difficult to knock out from high altitude. A high degree of precision was required to destroy specific buildings and plant, and this often proved impossible to achieve with heavy bombers,

which had to run the gauntlet of very heavy defences. The latter would be present in great number, but it was estimated that the swiftness of the Lightning attack would catch many of the gunners off guard and create an element of surprise. Whatever the hazards, neither Ben Mason or deputy group CO William Litton intended to miss this particular mission.

As briefed, both Lightning Groups were to meet up over the Adriatic, fly across Yugoslavia, traverse the Transylvanian Alps and finally drop down low for the target approach across the flat plains of the

Rumanian border region. Owing to range considerations, the route from Foggia to Ploesti was straight, with no diversions to confuse the enemy as to the 82nd's target. This represented a 1,300-mile (2,090km) round trip.

Ever since the *Tidal Wave* B-24 strike of 1 August 1943 the Rumanians had ensured that a strong aerial defence force was maintained for Ploesti. Nearly ten months after that epic Liberator attack that responsibility was in the hands of the pilots of Grupul 6 of the Rumanian Air Force, equipped with about seventy IAR 80/81s. Also available was Grupul 1, with thirty Bf 109s, but only on an 'as required' basis. The two units therefore mustered about 100 fighters. In addition to the interceptors there were numerous flak positions, plus smoke generators to hide the refineries from aerial attackers.

The German early-warning system in Yugoslavia was still intact, and this detected the Lightning force even before it entered Rumanian airspace, despite the American pilots maintaining an ultra-low target-run-in altitude of 50–100ft (15–30m). The loss of the element of surprise was a setback, compounded by the fact that the two elements of Lightnings had become separated.

Dropping tanks, the P-38s spread out to make their approach as the Rumanians scrambled their fighters. As they had not at that point positively identified the Lightnings' target, the German radar controllers believed that a Jabo attack against their airfields was imminent. Aircraft from airfields likely to be hit were therefore scrambled, and the 82nd's pilots saw a procession of fighters, bombers and transports coming right at them. Despite orders to the contrary, the temptation to engage with them proved irresistible to some, and several pilots attacked. Subsequently, claims including a Henschel Hs 126, a Messerschmitt Me 210 (almost certainly an Me 410), a Heinkel He 111 and a Bf 109 were filed by the participating pilots.

An earlier incident north-west of Nis had caused Lt Walter Leslie to break formation, pull up and bale out before his P-38 fell away and exploded as it hit the ground. This action may well have 'painted' the Lightning force on the Axis radar screens.

The Rumanian pilots of Grupul 6 were led off from Popesti-Leordeni airfield by Capitan Aviator Dan Vizante, who then had fifteen kills to his credit. In the emergency the Bf 109Gs of Grupul 7 were recalled from the Russian Front, while two

Buzzing was a favourite way of letting off steam for a USAAF pilot, as one of the 97th FS's aircraft appears to be demonstrating by this low pass across Hergla, Tunisia, on 17 June 1943. Levy

Lutfwaffe Gruppen, I./JG 53 and III./JG 77, were scrambled from Pipera airfield near Bucharest. Leading the JG 53 element was Gruppenkommandeur Maj Jurgen Harder, then with sixty-four victories to his credit.

Within minutes of taking off, Vizante spotted the P-38s and positioned to attack. As the 1st FG passed over Popesti, six Dornier Do 217s were observed going into land, and three flights of Lt John Shepard's 71st FS broke away for some easy victories. All six Dorniers were downed just before the IARs of Grupul 6 fell upon the P-38s. Four 1st FG machines were shot down in that first pass, and the others dropped their long-range tanks, the better to manoeuvre with the IAR 80s. The dogfights spiralled

for the whole mission. On the other hand, 2nd Lt Herbert 'Stub' Hatch, Jr, element leader for Craigmore Green Flight of the 71st FS, claimed five IAR 80s. Hatch shot down all the IARs the Rumanians lost that day, and was the only pilot to return home to Salsola. (Inevitably the IARs were identified in combat reports as 'Fw 190s'.) The Rumanian fighters almost wiped out the 71st FS, Vizante claiming two P-38s to become the Rumanian Air Force's top ace. This engagement also marked the high point in that air arm's lengthy battle with the Fifteenth Air Force.

The interception wrecked the 1st FG's planned escort mission (only the 71st's Blue Flight and the 27th FS remained with the

Of the original forty-eight Lightnings despatched on the Ploesti mission, only twenty-four were able to bomb the refinery. Nine were lost to a combination of flak and fighters, and another ten were badly damaged. One Bf 109 was claimed shot down.

Despite these diversions, the 82nd pressed home its attack and dropped thirty-six bombs, hitting the cracking plant and a storage building and damaging three refinery buildings. Considering the reduced size of the force, the bombing was well executed.

Excessively risky though this operation might appear to have been (it certainly seemed so to the pilots at the time), with hindsight there were many variables, and it might have been more successful had

Another Hergla resident, on 1 August 1943, was this P-38G-15, probably belonging to the 37th FS, 14th FG.
Levy

upwards from 100 to 300ft (30 to 90m), the opposing aircraft being drawn into a narrow valley, which at one point contained an estimated forty P-38s and IARs. Attacking while trying to avoid collisions made combat that much harder, and two P-38s crashed when their wingtips scraped the ground. Two of the Rumanian machines were lost through colliding and several were hit by their own ground fire. But the USAAF formation was being hit hard.

When the four-minute battle was over the 71st FS had lost nine of its sixteen Lightnings, the highest unit casualties of the day, the 1st FG losing a total of fourteen

82nd FG force), and surviving pilots had no choice but to limp back to Italy, some nursing damaged aircraft.

Unaware that their escort had been depleted, the pilots of the 82nd ploughed on, starting their climb to altitude before dive-bombing the target. The approach took the P-38s over Pipera airfield, which looked quiet as the American fighters swept past. This was because the forty Bf 109Gs of Grupul 7 and the two Luftwaffe units had taken off and were waiting above. When Ploesti's Rumanian flak batteries joined in the fray, the 82nd's pilots 'felt as though the roof had fallen on us', as one of them put it.

surprise been achieved and the enemy fighters evaded. As it was, the 82nd's reduced level of bombing through battle attrition was as good as could have been expected in the circumstances. But 10 June 1944 was remembered as the worst loss of US fighters in a single day for the entire war. No more Ploesti-type precision attacks by fighters were planned.

The pace of operations was such that the groups on the Ploesti mission were particularly hard-put to marshal the basic sixteen squadron aircraft for the following period of escort missions. The 71st FS suffered futher losses before June was out.

On 14 June the 14th FG escorted aircraft of the 55th Bomb Wing to the Petfurdo oil refinery in Hungary and had a memorable day, particularly those in the 49th FS.

As smoke billowed up from the target, rising to 20,000ft (6,000m), the 14th split up, the 37th and 48th FSs flying east of the target and the 49th heading west – and the fifteen P-38s ran headlong into forty or fifty Bf 109s. Don Luttrell was one of the pilots, with Lt Louis Benne leading. He became separated in the Germans' first pass as Lt Clyde Jones called for a break right and brought the Lightnings round to form a Lufbery circle. As the Flights formed up and dropped their tanks Benne was embroiled in a dogfight. He shot down two

Messerschmitts, but a third was on his tail. Fire knocked out his P-38's starboard engine, the instrument panel was shattered and Benne took shrapnel in the left shoulder. To cap it all, his port engine was on fire. Spinning out of the melee, Benne dived, recovered at 14,000ft (4,250m) and throttled back. His aircraft was clearly doomed, so he crawled out of the cockpit, over the wing, and dived through the tail booms before opening his parachute. Benne was captured almost as he hit the ground, his predicament not being improved by being buzzed by the Bf 109 that had shot him down.

Meanwhile, Jones had troubles of his own. The swirling mass of aircraft seemed

to contain more Bf 109s than P-38s. One of them fired at Jones and set off the incendiary device that was only supposed to burn the aircraft after it had been shot down. That fire set off a chain of events that demonstrated the difficulties a pilot might face in baling out of a crippled P-38. With much of his instrument panel also shot away, Jones headed straight for the deck, trying his best to bale out. Finally popping the canopy and being sucked out by the slipstream, Jones fell back across the canopy, the seat belt holding him in – or rather outside – the Lightning. He managed to undo the belt, but the force of the slipstream smashed his feet against the control wheel and broke both of his legs.

LEFT: The barely discernible boom code 'HV' marks this P-38G as an aircraft of the 27th FS, one of thirty Lightnings putting down at Gerbini, Sicily, on 6 September 1943 to refuel after a sweep. Levy

BELOW: There was always interest when an unfamiliar aircraft diverted to another airfield for whatever reason. This seems to have been the case when Lt Martin Collis of the 97th FS, 82nd FG, landed his P-38, *Mickey*, at an airfield seemingly manned by RAF personnel. IWM

Being thrown over the canopy also broke Jones's back, and then his head smashed against the elevator mass-balance, rendering him unconscious.

Plunging downwards, Jones came to and lost fingernails clawing at the D-ring of his parachute before he gathered his wits and pulled the ring, whereupon the 'chute opened. Although he descended safely, Jones was discovered by irate civilians and handled roughly before the Germans rescued him and sent him to hospital in Budapest. After that, Clyde Jones became a guest of Stalag Luft III.

Back at altitude the pilots continued the gruelling turning match in two circles, one right-hand and one left-hand, formed at 18,000ft (5,500m). American pilots later reported seeing Bf 109s at every quarter, and all swore they fired at at least eight of them. When one of the Lufbery circles dropped to 14,000ft (4,250m), Lt Thomas Purdy called for the P-38s to climb back. It went on for 25min, an eternity of combat that exhausted everybody. When they finally turned for home the pilots of the 14th saw that the Germans did not follow. The 49th FS claimed thirteen destroyed for the loss of five P-38s. None of the bombers was lost.

Road Strafing

Strafing raids had been going on for some weeks, and on the 15th the 1st FG sent all its squadrons into France to hit Plan de Dieu aerodrome. Again the attack was carried out at low level, the 71st maintaining high cover while the 27th and 94th dropped down to shoot-up the target. An Fw 190 shadowing the strafing Lightnings was shot down by Lt Robert Spitler, but two P-38s were hit by flak and went down over the aerodrome. Seven enemy aircraft were claimed on the ground, and the Group afterwards sought targets of opportunity and found some rail traffic to shoot up.

On 16 June the 1st was back on escort, shepherding the bombers to the Labau oil-blending plant near Vienna. Some thirty enemy aircraft challenged the mission, and the 94th FS, which had the high-cover slot, became embroiled in a 20min running battle in which three P-38s were lost for three Bf 109s destroyed and several damaged. Pilots reported their first sightings of the Me 262 and marvelled at the speed and altitude of Germany's first operational jet fighter, though none of them attacked the Americans.

Shuttle to Russia

The 82nd FG drew an unusual mission on 4 August, namely the Fifteenth Air Force's one fighter shuttle run to Russia. For Operation *Frantic IV* the Lightnings, plus P-51s of the 52nd FG, were to strafe two enemy airfields at Focsani in Rumania. Lying about 70 miles (110km) north-east of Ploesti, the airfields were beyond the range of fighters based in Italy unless bases further east, such as those in the Ukraine, could be used.

Shortly after 08.00hr that morning the 96th FS led the Group off from Foggia 11 to rendezvous with the Mustangs, which it did without delay. Their escort did not last,

as the aircraft of the 52nd disappeared, not to be seen again.

The 82nd had two aircraft abort with mechanical problems en route, and experienced ground fire when passing north of Ploesti. Flak bursts split the formation, and the pilots went down to strafe their secondary target, the trains plying the many tracks in that area. After five locomotives had been destroyed the Group came upon Focsani and attacked in line-abreast formation. Heavy flak greeted the P-38s and several aircraft were hit, but four enemy aircraft were claimed destroyed and four were damaged. Installations were also damaged as heavy-machine-gun and cannon fire

There was a narrow escape for Lt Thomas W. Smith of the 37th FS when a Bf 109 collided with his P-38 during an escort mission to Klagenfurt on 16 January 1944. With his Lightning hanging together, Smith reached an Italian wheatfield before the shattered airframe finally gave in. IWM

raked the airfield. Lieutenant Larry Noel of the 96th FS, destined to become the 82nd's leading loco-buster, claimed three destroyed on this mission.

Colonel William P. Litton, who was on his fiftieth mission, had an amazing escape after his aircraft was hit in the port engine, which burst into flames. When the starboard Allison followed suit, there was nowhere to go but down. Litton put the Lightning on the ground, but its 200mph (320km/hr) momentum took it straight into the side of a hangar. The impact sheared off the wings but the fuselage careered on, skidding to a halt on the far side of the hangar with Litton still in the seat. None of the pilots who witnessed the crash gave much for the colonel's chances,

Willsie was still being shot at from the ground, and he concentrated on making as good a landing as possible under the circumstances. Despite cracking his nose on the supposedly cushioned gunsight and spilling much blood, he retained the presence of mind to discharge a tiny phosphorous bomb, a canister carried in the cockpit and activated by a ring-pull for the purpose of destroying the aircraft in just such a situation. The bomb exploded near a wing fuel tank, and Willsie watched as Andrews landed. His rescuer had seen Willsie cross the field's ploughed furrows, and elected to land along them to minimize the risk of the P-38 nosing over.

Andrews realized the danger in which he had put himself, as the Rumanians and

flaps down, he gained enough lift to enable his P-38 to clear the trees bordering the field. Having joined other 82nd aircraft, Andrews was notified that his undercarriage was still down. Once its wheels were retracted, the two-man Lightning headed for the Ukraine. Crossing both the German and Russian lines, and getting shot at from both, the P-38 flew on for 2½hr before touching down at Poltava.

Frantic IV was not considered a great success for the 82nd, which lost five P-38s and four pilots, including the group CO. Several other aircraft were damaged, and repairs to these kept key personnel in Russia for some days. But on 6 August the Group was again airborne from Foggia 11, flying a thirty-ship sweep to the Ploesti region.

MTO Droop Snoots

With enemy air activity lessening but ground fire seemingly becoming more deadly, especially on low-level strafing missions, the 82nd carried out the Fifteenth Air Force's first Droop Snoot mission in the MTO on 29 August. It was believed that attacking targets from a higher altitude should reduce losses, so a single modified P-38 was flown out from England and the Group eventually acquired two more two-seaters, one for each squadron. The target for the initial 'bomb on leader' mission was a railway bridge. The 96th FS dropped from 15,000ft (4,500m), its Lightnings adopting three-ship sections flying in 'V' formation. This first mission was disappointing, as all the bombs missed the bridge, but the 82nd was encouraged by the Droop Snoot concept and the Group became much more adept with practice. There was already a good deal of experience among the Droop Snoot crews. All of the bombardiers, who were generally preferred to be of small stature, as there was little room to spare in the P-38's nose, had previously flown in heavy bombers. There were also enough pilots in the squadron who had flown B-17s or B-24s to pass on their invaluable knowledge. The 82nd's roster aimed to have two pilots and two bombardiers assigned to the Droop Snoot ships.

The 96th FS flew its second Droop Snoot mission on 30 August, a more successful attack on another railway bridge, at Kraljevo, Yugoslavia. The structure received several direct hits.

Further Droop Snoot missions were flown by the Fifteenth, the official view of this type

A P-38H named *Marion III*, of the 94th FS, 1st FG, dispersed on a typically barren Tunisian airfield early in 1943. R.L. Ward

but he survived to end up in a Rumanian hospital. Told he would have to have his right arm amputated, Litton threatened the doctors that, if he lost it, he would have them executed when Rumania capitulated in a few weeks' time. He kept his arm.

Lieutenant Tommy Vaughan of the 97th also bellied-in beyond the airfield to become a PoW, a fate shared by his squadron mate, Lt Alfred Ellison.

Better fortune attended Lt Dick Willsie, who also lost an engine to the intense ground fire at Focsani. With his second engine streaming coolant he called in his intention to crash-land. Back over the radio came Fg Off Dick Andrews: 'Pick a good field and I will come in after you'.

Germans were shooting at him and six Bf 109s were prowling, waiting for a chance to strafe his aircraft. One dived, only to be shot down by a Lightning of the 95th FS. Lieutenant Jim Hardin of the same squadron died when his Lightning was hit by flak and exploded in mid-air.

While the rest of the Lightnings strafed the soldiers now heading for Andrews' aircraft, Willsie was hauling himself aboard. Amid a tangle of arms and legs Willsie somehow managed to reach the controls and ease the throttles forward. Power had to be applied carefully to avoid the wheels digging into the soft earth. Full nose-up trim kept the nosewheel out of the mud. Hauling right back on the stick, with combat

of P-38 operation being more positive than in the Eighth Air Force. The southern-front commanders were particularly pleased with the modified Lightning's dual ability to provide weather information. There was, however, agreement in principle with one of the Eighth's strong recommendations, that a Droop Snoot formation be provided with a top-cover escort. The problem was that, in the event of the force coming under attack by enemy fighters, the necessary close bombing formation could easily be broken if the P-38 fighters were forced to defend themselves. In that event, re-forming a tight formation for a good bomb pattern might prove difficult.

As it transpired, few enemy fighter attacks were made on Fifteenth Air Force Droop Snoot-led P-38 formations, and although there were casualties these were slight. Of the twenty-one Droop Snoot missions flown between 1 August 1944 and 21 January 1945, eighteen were undertaken by the 82nd FG and three by the 14th. Double missions, sometimes to the same target, were flown on four days during the above period.

'Are We on the Same Side?'

As the north-western and southern European war fronts came together before merging into a more-or-less single theatre centred on Germany and Austria in the spring of 1945, so the Red Army's westward advance brought Allied pilots into contact with their eastern counterparts. When Stalin's tanks crossed into Europe the old Eastern Front ceased to exist, and Soviet attack aircraft and fighters increasingly began to appear over Berlin and other German cities. Russian fighter regiments could now reach their patrol areas within minutes after take-off. Such sorties over potential targets in built-up areas were novel for the Russian fighter pilots, who had traditionally been deployed as a battlefield support element for their assigned army groups. As the powerful Red Army penetrated into Germany the fighters found more flexibility as the Luftwaffe's appearance in the air became scarcer.

On occasion the Russian pilots met aircraft of their western Allies flying, so to speak, from the opposite direction. These were not always the friendly, passive encounters of allies they should have been. Neither side was very well informed about the other, and recognition of the respective aircraft types was not all it could have been. To the Americans, the Russians were largely an unknown factor.

The P-38 pilots of the 82nd FG found this out the hard way on 7 November 1944, when the two sides exchanged fire. There was a degree of irony in that the mission flown that day had been at the request of the Russians, who had previously been impressed by the firepower of the P-38. Complying with the request for air support, the 82nd embarked on a 4hr mission to attack German columns and rail movements between Sejenica, Novipasar, Baska and Nitrouica in Yugoslavia. The 82nd

Escort and ground-attack occupied the three P-38 Groups of the Fifteenth Air Force from 1943 to 1945. This aircraft of the 96th FS, 82nd FG, shown on the point of bomb release, was flown by a pilot claiming five victories. E.A. Munday

was led that day by Col Clarence T. Edwinson, who had some 4,000hr flying time and twenty-seven combat missions to his credit.

When they arrived at the assigned area, about 60 miles (95km) southwest of Sejenica, the Lightnings split up and hit the deck to strafe. Edwinson, flying over Novipasar, found heavily-congested roads and began strafing targets at Krusevac, continuing through to Cicevan and finally Nis. As the squadron pulled off target it was attacked by Soviet Air Force (Voenno-Vozdushnye Sily (VVS); Military Air Forces) Yakovlev Yak 1s scrambled from the nearby airfield at Nis to protect their convoy.

One P-38 was shot down in the initial firing pass by the Yaks, but instantaneous reaction by the Americans brought down three Yaks. Edwinson quickly recognized the 'enemy' aircraft for what they were, but was powerless to stop the dogfights developing once the two sides had engaged. When things quietened down, however, the leader of the Yak unit pulled up alongside Edwinson's aircraft and waggled his wings. Both pilots realized the mistake and the firing ceased before the situation deteriorated further.

Subsequent investigation showed that the 82nd had attacked the wrong target and shot up Russian, rather than German, troop columns. A British map had been used to brief the pilots, most of whom believed that their co-ordinates had been right. Only later, when gun-camera film had been developed, was the error there for all to see, though the terrain in the 'right' and 'wrong' areas was remarkably similar. It was determined that the incident was primarily the result of a navigational error compounded by non-existent intelligence on the exact position of the rapidly moving Red Army spearheads. By 7 November these forces were some 60 miles (100km) further forward than they were expected to be.

Investigation of the P-38-versus-Yak combat determined that the Russian formation had been from the 866th IAP (Fighter Air Regiment) attached to 17 VA (Air

Army), then led by ace Capt Alexandra Koldunov and based at Nis.

The US pilots lost that day were Lts Gene Coulson and Phil Brewer, both of whom were killed. Lieutenant Ken Latschke of the 97th shot down the Yak that had accounted for Brewer's Lightning, and Lt John Blumer cleared a Yak from the tail of Lt Tom Urton's aircraft, the little Russian fighter falling away in flames. Urton fired at another two Yaks, one of which was probably destroyed. Lieutenant Bill Blurock broke into the Yaks that had fired on Col Edwinson's Flight and observed one pouring smoke with its wheels half-down. It looked to Blurock like another probable.

The fact that the Fifteenth Air Force's record against the Germans in Yugoslavia and Hungary had been good made the occasional 'friendly fire' incident all the more regrettable. Between 18 August and 11 November the fighters flew thirty-seven bombing/strafing missions near Soviet lines, claimed the destruction of 621 enemy aircraft and damage to 306, and laid waste much railway rolling stock and a great many vehicles of increasing importance to the retreating Germans.

After a strong Russian protest the incident resulted in the departure of Col Edwinson on 22 November. Following standard procedure, he was recalled to the USA to explain the circumstances surrounding the 7 November mission, though his fellow pilots felt he had no choice but to react the way that he did, given the speed of air combat, which allowed no time for hesitation.

New Year 1945

As 1945 began, so escort duty intensified for the Fifteenth Air Force fighters, the performance of the heavy bombers improving in line with better weather. On the last day of January, the Fifteenth was launched against the Moosbierbaum oil refinery, the bomber force dropping 1,398 tons in the heaviest single attack on one target by the US component of the Mediterranean Allied Strategic Air Forces (MASAF).

In February the Fifteenth was able to carry out an almost unprecedented thirteen days of continuous operations, a total of 8,850 B-24s and B-17s dropping 14,681 tons of bombs on a variety of targets during the month.

As many of the targets for the Italian-based heavies lay on the other side of the Alps, the reassurance of having two engines

in their escorting fighters was not lost on bomber crews; or indeed on the fighter pilots. There were several occasions when P-38s with combat damage tucked in close to a bomber formation to share the protection of their formidable batteries of heavy machine-guns. The trio of P-38 Groups continued to draw escort duty, though the four Groups of P-51s in the theatre meant that the squadrons of the 1st, 14th and 82nd FGs could regularly be released for ground-attack missions. As a consequence the quantity of locomotives and rolling stock on Italy's rail system laid waste by Lightnings began to spiral alarmingly from the German viewpoint. An intricate network of railways with sidings, marshalling yards, tunnels, bridges and depots served the Axis armies between Austria and Italy via the Brenner Pass, feeding the battlefield troops with virtually all of their supplies. Much of this network wound its way through mountain passes, making accurate bombing difficult, but it was systematically interdicted by the Allied air forces to the point where the enemy could move only with the utmost difficulty.

On 24 March the Fifteenth's heavies headed for the German capital, which lay over 700 miles (1,125km) from the main Foggia complex of bomber airfields. With strong support from Fifteenth Fighter Command, this was the longest escorted mission ever flown in the Mediterranean theatre of war.

Records continued to be set by the MASAF, and on 15 April a massive support operation to assist Allied troops in both Italy and southern Germany recorded sorties by 1,848 bombers and fighters. Despite this being the highest single daily total for the Fifteenth Air Force, the bombers were briefed for tactical targets and they consequently dropped a modest total of 2,369 tons, while the fighters were active on ground attacks.

As well as improved weather for visual bombing (disregarding the fact that the Fifteenth Air Force now led the Eighth in terms of accuracy in blind bombing by radar), the heavies enjoyed far less interference from Axis fighters. Reflecting this aerial supremacy, the four-month (January to April 1945) figures for Allied fighter sorties showed that escort missions occupied 80 per cent of the total effort in January but gradually dropped to 57 per cent by April. Losses of fighters per 100 sorties also fell, from 1.11 per cent in January to 0.64 per cent in April, an average of 0.83 for the four-month period. Actual losses of P-38s

and P-51s while flying 77,309 sorties in the same period totalled 232 aircraft.

Germany Kaput

By April 1945 there was little to distinguish between the former ETO and MTO war fronts, as fighters from both former theatres were operating from German airfields. There was further contact between US and VVS fighters above the remnants of the Third Reich, but probably as a result of earlier, tragic incidents, these were usually warily friendly.

On 17 April the *Stars & Stripes* reported on what was described as the first meeting between Russian aircraft and the Ninth Air Force, in the shape of four P-38s of the 474th FG, led by Lt Robert L. Freeman. The Lightnings were returning from a mission to the Riesa area when they encountered ten Lavochkin LaGG-3s over Oppelhaun, the geographical boundary of what soon became the US and Soviet zones of occupation. Initially doubtful as to the identity of the small fighters, Freeman watched them form a Lufbery circle, with scissors and figure-of-eight manoeuvres thrown in for good measure. He was impressed, as none of the LaGG pilots climbed above 1,000ft (300m). The formation would have been hard to crack had the P-38s been obliged to attack, but the Russian pilots waggled their wings enough to show off their red star national insignia. Satisfied, the Americans returned to base to check the identity of their allies' aircraft in their recognition manuals.

P-38 Statistics, ETO

Operations by P-38s in the European theatre totalled 129,849 sorties, during which 20,193 tons of bombs were dropped. On such operations 1,758 Lightnings were lost, against 1,771 aerial victories and 749 enemy aircraft destroyed on the ground. The aerial loss and claims were extremely close, and in percentage terms of loss rate per sortie it meant that, for virtually every enemy aircraft destroyed, a P-38 went down. This produced a figure of 1.4 per cent, worse than comparable figures for all other US fighters in the ETO. This virtual 'one-for-one' balance might have reflected the difficulties the P-38 experienced in Europe, many weather-related, but the figure is believed to have included losses to all causes, including accidents, rather than air combat *per se*.

CHAPTER NINE

Kenney's Kids

Lightnings in the Islands

The US Seventh Air Force was charged with the defence of Hawaii for the early part of the war, the attack on Pearl Harbor naturally creating a perceived need for fighter defences able to ward off another Japanese attack. When the possibility of such an event faded, the Seventh's Fighter Groups sent their component squadrons into forward areas to gain combat experience. The first major deployment of a full Seventh Group occurred in June 1944, when the P-47D-equipped 318th FG shipped out to become the front-line USAAF element in the invasion of the Marianas. The P-38 was not part of the organization until the war literally moved out of range of the Thunderbolt, and the 318th FG temporarily equipped with J models that November. With Lightnings the Group's squadrons, the 19th, 73rd and 333rd FSs, were better able to escort B-24s flying from the Marianas to targets on Iwo

Jima. These particular Lightnings were loaned by the 21st FG on Ohau, and thirty-six aircraft, twelve to each squadron, flew their first mission on or about 22 November. This was a seven and a half hour bomber escort mission to the Japanese naval anchorage at Truk, during which the P-38 pilots claimed four A6M 'Zekes' shot down.

Realizing that the USAAF's main intention of using Saipan as a B-29 base put the home islands in great danger, the enemy retaliated. The P-38s helped ward off several air raids in the period up to February 1945, and claimed a small number of victories before the enemy raids more or less petered out. For the 318th the main job in hand was to neutralize Japanese resistance to the forthcoming US amphibious assault on Iwo Jima, and to this end the group's Lightnings flew 253 sorties, each one entailing a round trip of 1,600 to 1,700 miles (2,575 to 2,740km). Half of the sorties included strafing attacks on the island's defensive positions, particularly 20mm and

40mm gun emplacements. The group shot down thirteen enemy aircraft for the loss of four P-38s during this short campaign. The best day in terms of aerial combat was 11 February, when the 318th intercepted an escorted Japanese strike force heading for Saipan and shot down four bombers and three fighters, breaking up the attack before it had even begun.

Thereafter the P-38 bowed out of the Seventh Air Force, the 318th FG converting to the P-47N in April. Back in Hawaii, although the 21st FG was equipped with P-38s it did not take them into action, but awaited the arrival of P-51s before joining the war in late 1944.

The China-Burma-India Theater

Denied adequate resources until the Allied situation had stabilized elsewhere, especially in the Mediterranean, the CBI received

Flying P-38s over Burma as part of the Tenth Air Force before other units did so, the 459th FS entitled itself the 'Twin Dragons'. Here, one of the unit's P-38Js is prepared for a ground-attack sortie. IWM

its first P-38s in the summer of 1943. General Claire Chennault, of 'Flying Tiger' fame, had lobbied Washington long and hard to send him more aircraft and personnel, and felt that the arrival of Lightnings was long overdue. One of the few people with influence to get things done, Chennault faced complacency and a mountain of red tape, despite the fact that China remained the one area where the Japanese Army could pursue offensive operations with a real capacity to threaten Allied endeavours.

Superior US airpower was the key to preventing such a disaster, but various parties decreed that until the war in North Africa was won, thus releasing American units for combat elsewhere, China had to more-or-less fend for herself. At best, the supply of war materiel remained at a trickle.

August 1943

By 14 August news reports mentioned that a 'Squadron X', equipped with Lightnings, had been organized at Lingling. This was the 449th FS, which had been in China since 25 July, when the first aircraft had arrived.

As usual the P-38's reputation had preceded it, but Chennault, not a man to accept anything at face value, decided to arrange a fly-off between a P-38 and a P-40. This had unfortunate connotations, as wily ground crews had stripped a Warhawk of all surplus equipment and put a very able pilot at the controls. The mock combat demonstration saw the P-38 easily outclassed, which apparently coloured Chennault's view of it for the duration of the war. This is curious, because the Fourteenth Air Force had been obliged to accept the P-47, which was not overly favoured owing to its high fuel consumption. Every gallon of petrol consumed by the USAAF in China had to be hauled over 'the Hump', as the Himalayan mountains were universally known, and, given the Thunderbolt's thirst, the P-38 would surely have seemed a better prospect. Of course, Chennault might have wanted to be certain that he would continue to receive improved P-40s if the supply of P-38s faltered, and this view has some credence. Indeed, he might have been told that Lightnings were still in short supply and that he would be unlikely to see too many of them in China.

This almost seemed to be the case, as deployment of the Lightning in the CBI remained modest in terms of both aircraft numbers and units. Nevertheless the P-38Gs of the 449th FS, part of the 51st FG, had by then seen combat, and in August came the first confirmed victory. Led by Maj Edmund Goss, ex-CO of the 75th FS with six kills to his credit, the theatre rookies claimed three 'Zeros' (almost certainly Ki-43 'Oscars') in return for one P-38 shot down while taking off. Goss himself attacked a 'Zero' over Hengyang while flying a P-38G on 21 August and was awarded a 'probable'. He was one of a number of pilots in this and other Far Eastern areas who was awarded claims for Japanese fighters listed as 'Army Zero' in official records. This suggests that either intelligence data was being ignored by individuals at unit level who were convinced that pilots had indeed encountered the Imperial Navy's A6M, or that deeper checks were not made into claims at the time. There was no such animal as an Army 'Zero'.

September 1943

Co-operation between the P-38s and the P-40s of the 23rd FG, the premier fighter unit in China, paid off against several

Under-cover servicing was something of a luxury for the USAAF in Burma, but this crew have stripped the panels from one of the Allisons of a 459th FS P-38J in comparative comfort. IWM

important targets. On 5 September 1943 another demonstration of getting 'the mostest out of the leastest' (which could have been the Fourteenth Air Force's motto) saw Col Bruce K. Holloway's 23rd FG carry out a guerrilla strike on the Shihhweiyao dock and iron works on the Yangtze River. To be successful, the attack required that the Japanese flak surrounding the target somehow be distracted from the aircraft carrying the bombs. In addition to the fixed defensive guns the enemy had moved a destroyer and two gunboats down the river and positioned them right opposite the dock, ready to pick off any US aircraft that put in an appearance. The problem was solved by the six Warhawks that broke formation over the target at about 5,000ft (1,500m).

Diving individually on the iron works, the P-40 pilots opened fire and created enough racket with their racing Allison engines at maximum 3,000rpm boost to gain the gunners' full attention and create confusion. While they did so, four Lightnings sneaked in at angles of 45 to 60 degrees to the works and released their eight 500lb bombs right on the nail. The P-40 circus continued as the P-38s made good their escape, their approach having been specially chosen to avoid exploding debris. The attack was typical of the small-scale but effective tactical war the Fourteenth fought. On this occasion no USAAF aircraft were lost.

On 9 September the 449th dive-bombed the docks at Canton, the 500lb bombs falling accurately while the Japanese harried the Lightnings to little effect. There were several claims against enemy aircraft in the ensuing dogfights, and a Japanese transport fell to the guns of Lt Billy Beardsley. This aircraft had Gen Takuma Shimoyama as a passenger, and his death robbed the 3rd Air Division of its commanding officer. Although this was not known by the Allies at the time, it had an adverse effect on future Japanese air plans.

The following day P-38s again raided Canton docks, and Lt Lee O. Gregg found that he had a fight on his hands. Up against an estimated sixteen enemy fighters, he managed to shoot one down after a hard fight with Japanese pilots who seemed to be skilled combat veterans. One got on the tail of Gregg's wingman but was shot down by his would-be victim, who had to crash-land his badly-damaged P-38G at Kunming.

October 1943

The 449th FS carried out another dive-bombing mission on 30 October, the target being Kiukiang. Eight P-38s were jumped by a mixed formation of Ki-43s and Ki-44s, and four of the USAAF fighters were shot down. However, three of the remaining pilots exacted revenge to the tune of four 'Tojos' and two 'Oscars'. Lt Tom Harmon claimed two 'Oscars' before being forced to bale out. He returned to Lingling after a 32-day trek through the jungle.

Hanging beneath his parachute, Harmon feigned death while Japanese fighters circled ominously; stories of Allied airmen being shot in their 'chutes were legion, and he was taking no chances. On his way to earth Harmon witnessed victories over two 'Tojos' by Bob Schultz.

In October 1944 the 449th FS was officially transferred from the umbrella of the 23rd FG to the 51st FG, which otherwise flew P-40s. The 51st maintained only two squadrons of Lightnings when the others re-equipped with Mustangs. In total, only four units flew Lightnings in the CBI for any length of time, the 51st FG's 26th FS also re-equipping in late 1943.

November 1943

On 24 November an F-5 returned with evidence that the Japanese had about 200 aircraft at Shinchiku, on Formosa, and the following day the USAAF despatched fourteen B-25s, eight P-38s and eight P-51As to deal with some of them. It was the Fourteenth Air Force's first attack on Formosa, the island having been made into a substantial base by the Japanese, with several good airfields. Flying low over the straits between Suichuan and Shinchiku to avoid detection, the Americans came upon a Japanese transport going into land at Shinchiku. Bob Schulz was detached to shoot it down, which he did, then rejoining his flight.

Schulz witnessed the hapless enemy aircraft lined up in front of the Americans' guns as another airborne victim, a Kawasaki Ki-32 'Mary' single-engine light bomber/trainer, floated into his sights. This was also shot down in short order.

As top cover to the Mitchell bombers the P-38s swept the airfield first. The attack took the enemy completely by surprise and all of the US force returned home safely. The pilots claimed ten more airborne

Not all of the 459th's P-38Js got the elaborate green dragon decoration that stretched the length of both booms, as it was time-consuming to apply. This aircraft had been 'dragonized' when it was photographed in May 1944. IWM

victims before strafing the airfield as the bombers released their loads.

On 4 March 1944 Lee Gregg became the 449th's first ace, when he shot down an 'Oscar' during an engagement over Shihhweiyao. Minutes later the squadron had its second ace when Bob Schulz destroyed another Ki-43, his fifth victory.

Dragons over China

Unlike almost all other USAAF fighter squadrons, the second P-38 unit to serve in the CBI was activated in-theatre, on 1 September 1943. This was the 459th FS, which

Tenth Air Force in Burma and the Fourteenth in China. The 459th was later attached to the 33rd FG when the latter was transferred in its entirety from North Africa.

The P-38Hs with which the 459th FS was first equipped carried little in the way of distinctive markings, but early in 1944 the green dragon insignia appeared on the cowlings and tail booms. Becoming operational in November on new aircraft shipped from Kurmitola in India, the 459th was attached to the 80th FG. It was as part of that unit that three P-38s flew the squadron's debut mission, led by Lt Hampton Boggs, who had previously flown P-40s. Familiarity with the Curtiss fighter was a

more would follow to place him as the theatre's second-ranking ace.

Despite losing several P-38s in accidents, the 459th's morale was high and good reports from RAF instructors at the gunnery school at Armada Road served only to boost confidence in the pilots' skills and the squadron's adopted tactics. It was with the RAF's 224 Group that the Twin Dragons saw their next bout of air action, from 1 March 1944. The Lightnings' role was the destruction of enemy aircraft on and over their bases in Burma, He Ho and Meiktila aerodromes proving to be particularly good hunting grounds. Based at Chittagong, the squadron was led from 11 March by a new

Well-posed P-38J-15 *Melba Lou* of the 449th FS, 51st FG, at Comilla in India on 14 August 1944. H. Levy

was also unusual in being deactivated within days of VJ Day and therefore never serving time in the USA. Nicknamed the 'Twin Dragons', the 459th drew its pilot cadre from the 311th Fighter-Bomber Group and the parent 80th Group and added a few freshly trained men who had come in directly from the USA. Because of its virtually unique origins the 459th tended to operate as though it was an independent organization, which was in the nature of the CBI, with regular unit rotations between the

Tenth Air Force stock-in-trade, few individuals, either pilots or ground crew, being familiar with the somewhat more complex Lockheed twin.

December 1944

On 1 December Boggs scored his squadron's first victory when he destroyed a Mitsubishi A6M3 'Hamp' ('Zeke 32') fighter over Rangoon. This was his own first victory; eight

CO, Lt Col Verl Luehring. Numerous fighter sweeps and airfield attacks kept the squadron busy over the next few months.

These missions were not always challenged, because the JAAF's fighter assets in Burma were gradually withdrawn as the situation on the ground brought the Imperial Army little progress against increasingly stiff Allied resistance. Despite this, Japanese units such as the crack 64th Sentai were based in Burma at various times. The Japanese pilots flew their Ki-43s with great skill, giving no quarter and never shying away from a fight. Nor were the Japanese averse to setting traps to bloody the noses of Allied fighters that became a wearisome source of annoyance. Such a trap was sprung on 6 June 1944, a momentous day on the other side of the world, but something of a disaster for the Twin Dragons over Burma.

During a mission to Meiktila by some twenty P-38s, a superior force of 'Oscars' ambushed the Americans and proceeded to shoot down Capt Walter Duke, the squadrons's ranking ace. Also missing after the raid was ace Burdette Goodrich, who was subsequently to die at the hands of his captors.

Duke had managed to extricate himself from the initial enemy attack, but two P-38s had reportedly gone down. 'Wally' Duke set out to locate them, and while engaged in this task he was jumped by several flights of 'Oscars', which overwhelmed him. The death of high-scoring pilots was a blow to both sides, and the JAAF did not emerge unscathed in this respect, for Goichi Sumino, a twenty-five-victory ace, was one of the Japanese casualties.

The Twin Dragons recovered from such setbacks and went on to carve a high reputation in combat. It was one of the few squadrons of P-38s to operate over the vast

Expert tuition. Pilots eagerly gather round the cockpit to hear Capt George W. Prentice's views on the P-38's controls soon after Lightnings arrived in Australia to equip the 475th FG. IWM

Major Lynn Witt at about the time he took command of the 35th FS after it had converted to the P-38 in mid-1944. He was an ace with six victories, two of which were scored on the P-38. J. Stanaway

This P-38H taking off from Tezgoan, India, on 25 April 1944 hails from the 459th FS, which introduced an aircraft tail numbering system that spring. H. Levy

Tommy Lynch was an outstanding exponent of the P-38 with the 39th FS, 35th FG, flying G, H and J models in combat and scoring twenty victories before his death on 8 March 1944. IWM

CBI area, and its pilots felt they had a reputation to uphold.

While much bitter ground fighting lay ahead to secure all of Burma, by early 1944 the Allied armies had contained the Japanese and prevented any repeat of the defeats of 1941–42. In the air the enemy could do little to prevent constant interdiction of his supply lines, dumps and troop concentrations. Imperial Army troops became increasingly isolated on the remote jungle battlefields, lacking the kind of air support and supply that rapidly became a cornerstone of Allied success.

With a vast front line to patrol, the RAF was the predominant air force, using all types of aircraft to blockade and beat back the enemy. In its supporting role the USAAF, having to divide its assets between Burma and China, mainly deployed squadrons of P-40s and P-47s in the theatre.

As for the Lightning, the 459th soldiered on with its P-38Hs into 1944, until it was able to re-equip with the J model. The squadron continued to operate more or less independently in the theatre until it formed a fourth unit of the 33rd FG in 1945.

The 33rd FG's 58th, 59th and 60th FSs arrived at Nagaghuli in Assam, India, in November 1944 after months of the 'switchback' war typical of the CBI, and the group was informed that it would relinquish all its P-47s for Lightnings by early the following year. As was often the case, the change-over was phased over a period of months, the 58th FS receiving the first allocated Lightnings in November. It was February before the 59th and 60th FSs had completed their spells of transition training, and most of the flyers were glad to be getting back into the war.

The 33rd had recently had a thin time, with little enemy air activity over its designated part of China, but Burma represented a much 'hotter' combat theatre. The 60th was the first to move to a forward base, at Nansin, where the ground crews found that the P-38 required considerably more 'tender loving care' than either the P-40 or P-47. Missions included patrols and fighter sweeps, with selected targets being bombed and strafed. Air combat was a comparative rarity, but there were banner days in this respect. One was 15 January 1945, when Lt Daniel K. Pence and Maj Clarence T. Baker of the 58th FS ran across three Ki-43s while on patrol southwest of Meiktila. All three enemy aircraft were shot down, two by Pence and one by Baker. This was the only reported air

Six-victory ace Capt Charles S. Gallup in front of his P-38F-5, 42-12627 *Loi*, aircraft No 11 in the 39th FS, 35th FG. IWM

BELOW: Kenneth Sparks of the 39th FS, 35th FG, flew P-38Fs and Gs throughout his combat career and scored eleven victories, only to be killed while flying a P-38J as an instructor at Muroc, California, on 5 September 1944. IWM

engagement involving the USAAF over the entire Burma front that day.

March 1945

Having completed conversion to the P-38, the 33rd FG was officially proclaimed a twin-engine fighter Group by USAAF headquarters on 1 March. Thereafter there was little for the unit to do as the war in Burma wound down towards the final surrender of Japan.

Before that much-anticipated event the USAAF brought a new weapon into use in Burma, the Azon bomb. This was a relatively simple weapon designed to increase the accuracy of the traditional free-falling 1,000lb HE bomb by installing electronic guidance and a flare in the tail section. The Azon, so called because it could be controlled in azimuth (Az-) only (-on), was used to good effect by B-24 Liberators, mainly against linear targets such as bridges. The availability of Droop Snoot conversion kits for the P-38 prompted Lockheed to despatch Technical Representative Wayne Snedden, who had worked with the 459th FS in Burma, to India in January 1945. It was suggested that the Droop Snoot might

LEFT: Lightning aces of the 8th FS, 49th FG, included Capts Robert Aschenbrener (*left*), with ten victories, and William C. Drier, credited with six. The caption to this photograph, issued on 22 December 1944, noted that both pilots became aces on the same day, 24 November. IWM

BELOW LEFT: Lieutenant Colonel Gerald R. Johnson was one of the top aces flying P-38s in the 9th FS, 49th FG, in the south-west Pacific. He was credited with twenty-two victories, and, in common with some of his contemporaries, was killed shortly after the war. Author's collection

make a useful 'small-scale' Azon bomber, and Snedden consequently directed the conversion of ten P-38Js and Ls at the Southern India Air Depot at Bangladore, which had absorbed the Hindustan Aircraft factory.

Apart from the necessary nasal surgery and the fitting of the bombardier's seat and A-9 Norden sight, each P-38 needed Azon bomb directional control and automatic radio-bomb-release equipment, which required three rod aerials to be located on the underside of the port boom. All ten aircraft (one of which is known to have been P-38J-15 42-104154) were completed over a period of fifty-one days, bombardiers being trained in the meantime. It was proposed that the 459th FS would operate the Azon Droop Snoots, and to that end ten bombardiers arrived in the squadron area on 18 June 1945.

Several training sorties were undertaken with the modified P-38s, though the war in Burma was by then virtually over, both officers and enlisted men rotating home. The Droop Snoot detachment of the 459th, by then part of the 33rd FG, continued its training programme, crews dropping practice bombs into the Bay of Bengal. On 25 June heavy rainfall forced three crews to divert to three different locations until the storm had passed. Amid rumours of the unit's impending move to China and Japan's imminent surrender, the Burma air front remained quiet and, in the event, no combat use was made of the Azon Droop Snoots.

One of the Azon-modified aircraft may well have been that used by Gen George Stratemeyer, who had P-38L-5 44-25605 fitted out as his personal transport, complete with a two-star-general rank badge on the nose. For its VIP 'customer' this Droop Snoot had a special 'front seat', a leather-trimmed interior and a built-in Thermos flask.

CHAPTER TEN

Pacific Supremo

In February 1944 the US invaded Kwajelein in the Marshall Islands, the first of a series of headline-grabbing strides across the South-West and Central Pacific, the 'road back' to Japan.

Meanwhile, the Fifth Air Force reached out to secure more airfields in New Guinea, and the Thirteenth moved in the Solomons and New Britain to consolidate the Allied hold on vital coastal airfields on tiny areas of each enormous group of islands, larger areas of which remained under Japanese occupation. Operation *Cartwheel* saw Allied

admirably made up the numbers, despite their high fuel consumption and some manoeuvrability limitations. Lightnings remained in short supply.

That the 9th FS was not alone in temporarily having to fly the P-47 rather than the Lightning was shown in March 1944, when the 'Flying Fiends', alias the 36th FS of the 8th FG, was obliged to do likewise. When these decisions were taken, the degree of pilot protest (there was reportedly little in the 36th) depended on what they had been flying before. The 36th had

and unyielding. Allied ships and aircraft were the key to supplying the troops and ultimately securing New Guinea. The ground fighting for the country's most important bases raged for most of 1943 and into the first half of 1944, Australian and US troops having to wrest nearly every yard of territory from staunch Japanese defenders. But they prevailed. In the air, the pace slackened noticeably as the summer came round. The Japanese, exhausted by the previous campaigns and appalling losses, had no choice but to curtail operations and await the next disaster, when and where it was chosen to befall them, courtesy of the Allies.

During 1944 Kenney finally saw his fighter Groups generally equipped with P-38s and P-47s, the long-serving but obsolescent P-39s and P-40s gradually being phased out. Both the Airacobra and Warhawk had served the Fifth Air Force well when nothing else was available. Kenney, though grateful, wished to persuade Washington that the sooner he got ample numbers of modern fighters, the sooner he could outflank and outfight the Japanese to the point where they could be annihilated, which seemed the chosen fate of most of the jungle troops.

The technical advances that had given the USAAF improved models of the P-51, P-47 and J- and L-model Lightnings were offset to some extent by the difficulties of getting them to the combat units. A particular challenge was scarcity of good deep-water port facilities and skilled dock labour in New Guinea, and a general lack of shipping. Most supplies had to come by sea, including replacement aircraft, and though aircraft could be assembled and test-flown in relatively safe rear areas, the enormous back-up required to keep a single Fighter Group operational was sorely stretched at times. At squadron level morale was high, despite the problems, and officers and enlisted men alike appeared almost to thrive on deprivation. Few aircraft stayed on the ground as long as there was fuel for their tanks and ammunition for their guns.

Lockheed P-38L-1 44-27121, named *Charlcie Jean*, was flown by James 'Duckbutt' Watkins, twelve-victory ace of the 9th FS, 49th FG. R.L. Ward

air, land and sea forces completing the encirclement and isolation of the main Japanese bastion of Rabaul by March 1944.

An influx of newer fighters such as the P-47 to replace the valiant 'old guard' of P-39s and P-40s that had held the line since early 1942 made all the difference. George Kenney always had reservations about also operating Thunderbolts, but these were necessary to give squadrons an aircraft more capable than the P-40. Thunderbolts

flown Lightnings, but these were so worn out that any new fighter would have been welcome.

On the ground, Allied forces made good progress up the northern coast of New Guinea, airfields at Hollandia, Wadke, Biak and Nadzab being secured and occupied by P-38s and other aircraft that pounded enemy targets until the isolated and deprived forces could only mount rearguard actions. These, however, were vicious

March 1944 – the Old One-Two

The Fifth Air Force's commanding general always had qualms about losing his best fighter pilots in combat, and by March he had had both Dick Bong and Tommy Lynch assigned directly to V Fighter Command headquarters. This did not prevent the two aces flying several freelance sorties together, acting alternately as leader and wingman. The JAAF fell foul of this combination of talent on 3 March 1944 over Tadji airstrip, New Guinea. Encountering two Mitsubishi Ki-21 'Sally' heavy bombers over the strip, Lynch gave one several bursts and pulled up. Bong, flying 300yd (275m) behind, finished it off. Post-combat reports and gun-camera footage appear to have shown that Lynch's strikes were fatal to the bomber, and he took credit for the kill.

Bong became element leader as the two P-38s rejoined at 6,000ft (1,800m). While they were climbing, four 'Oscars' and a 'Tony' came on the scene. Turning into the Americans, the four 'Oscar' pilots seemed to have an advantage, but nothing is certain in air combat. Noting that only the 'Oscar' pilots had reacted to the Lightnings, while the 'Tony' continued on a straight-and-level course, Bong took his chance and gave it a deflection shot. This appears to have done little damage, as no credit was awarded to him. Bong dived away to regain speed as Lynch caught up with the 'Tony' in a right turn, closed and fired. He was officially credited with destroying it.

An 'Oscar' then latched on to Lynch's tail, but Bong reacted quickly and let him have it. The 'Tony', meanwhile, went down to crash as Lynch, now leader again, fired on another 'Sally', for which he later received a 'damaged' credit.

Tommy Lynch emerged from the afternoon combat with two fighters to add to his score, the 'Tony' and a second fighter recorded as 'unidentified', plus two 'Sallys' damaged.

This brief resume of a single combat serves to illustrate how good teamwork paid off, but it was only part of the day's tally, for Bong's record was also boosted by two 'Sallys'; his 23rd and 24th victories.

Tommy Lynch's tally had then risen to eighteen, including the two fighters. Cruelly, fate decreed that the ace would lose his life five days after the 3 March combat, and in roughly the same place. He was shot down by flak over Tadji on the 8th, with his final score at twenty confirmed, one probable and six damaged. Dick Bong was devastated at the confirmation of Lynch's demise. He had been on the mission and seen one of the propellers separate from Lynch's P-38 seconds before it exploded. He searched the area where his friend had gone in, but with little hope that Lynch could have survived.

Such blows were part of the grim side of war, and could have an adverse effect on morale, but there was a remedy. When Bong equalled Eddie Rickenbacker's First World War total of twenty-six kills, Kenney ordered the ace home to Washington forthwith. En route, Bong stopped off to offer his condolences to Tom Lynch's widow, Rosemary.

Kenney was like a mother hen to his fighter pilot chicks. He followed their progress with great interest and was never short of praise for outstanding acts of courage and flying skill. Many Fifth Air Force P-38 fighter pilots had the latter quality in abundance, as their steadily rising air-combat scores proved.

Kenney was also an astute judge of character, a trait he demonstrated on several

Robert DeHaven's P-38J was No 13 in the 7th (Screamin' Demons) FS, 49th FG. DeHaven had a total of fourteen victories. R.L. Ward

Lieutenant C. Robert Anderson's *Virginia Marie/Margaret*, alias P-38J-15 of the 433rd FS, 475th FG, on Boroka airstrip, Biak, in October 1944. R.L. Ward

occasions when he realized that the top-scoring pilots needed a rest. And if they did not leave the theatre voluntarily he would order them out for their own safety.

In marked contrast to the Americans, the Japanese aircrews found home leave an increasingly rare luxury as their fortunes waned. Although both the JAAF and JNAF aircraft remained technically excellent and were gradually modernized to increase crew survivability, the outstanding pre-war-trained fighter pilots were steadily whittled away, never to be replaced by men of equal calibre.

In August 1944 the spectacular American invasion of the Marianas brought the prize of new B-29 bases to expand the long-range bombing campaign intended to knock Japan out of the war. Saipan, Tinian and Guam lay that much nearer to Japan than either India or China, the nations that had made bases available for initial Superfortress operations.

May 1944

In May the Fifth Air Force continued to pound Hollandia, working towards the acquisition of more New Guinea airfields. A massive attack on the 3rd almost broke the back of the enemy's air power in the region, this being the culmination of several missions that netted the Americans the incredible total of 340 enemy aircraft destroyed on the ground and an estimated sixty in the air. So desperate had the enemy's position become that even half

the number of losses on the ground would have been disastrous. The continuing success of the P-38 was beyond dispute, Perry Dahl and Warren Lewis of the 475th becoming aces on the memorable 3rd.

The relentless decimation of Japanese bases and supplies by heavy and medium bombers, plus large-scale fighter activity, produced further P-38 aces by mid-April. Inclement weather over inhospitable terrain contrived to bring about a greater number of USAAF aircraft losses than the enemy, but on the 21st the US Navy began an uncontested pre-invasion bombardment of the Hollandia area. The first US aircraft landed the following day, and by the 23rd the uncompleted Tadji West airstrip was in American hands. With sterling work by RAAF and US engineers, airstrips at Hollandia and Alexishafen, among others, were made ready for Allied occupation.

By May 1944 the 8th FG had finally become an all-Lightning outfit, the 80th FS flying P-38Hs and Js and the 9th FS having also been able to trade in its P-47s. This gave the Fifth Air Force seven P-38 squadrons, all of which turned increasingly to ground-attack sorties as the strength of the enemy air forces lessened in parallel with the loss of their bases. The Japanese were not in any way out of the picture in New Guinea, but they did have to operate from increasingly remote airfields in the face of the Allied advance.

Grim nicknames laced with black humour had long given impetus to USAAF fighter squadron *esprit de corps*, and the 'Headhunters' of the 80th FS lived up to

this tradition in terms of aerial victories. Eventually the 80th boasted eighteen aces who had wholly or partly flown with the unit to accumulate their scores. Having fought its way up from Port Moresby to Dobodura the previous December, the squadron had moved its P-38s across to Cape Gloucester in February 1944. By June it was then based at Nadzab and Owi in the Schouten Islands off New Guinea.

The 39th had similarly bidden farewell to Moresby before moving to Nadzab and Gusap in January. In common with the fashion for racy names and appropriate designs for approved or unofficial unit badges, the 39th became the 'Flying Cobras'.

June 1944

With its excellent range the P-38 could undertake sorties lasting several hours. The fact that only the Lightning could handle such missions strengthened its position as the premier USAAF fighter in the Pacific. That said, aircraft and pilots were still being lost through technical difficulties that were curable without any modification to the P-38. One of the key areas where things could be improved was fuel management, and there was an individual who could command the respect of eager young fighter pilots labouring under a mistaken doctrine as to how a P-38 should be flown in terms of engine power settings. Such men had not always received the best of training before being posted to a demanding theatre of war.

Jay Robbins's 8th FG P-38J
Jandina IV. **Robbins scored
a total of eighteen victories.**
R.L. Ward

Few USAAF fighter pilots had not heard of Charles Lindbergh, the man who had made the first solo crossing of the Atlantic. Even sceptics who doubted Lindbergh's political views, patriotism and motivation (he had resigned his Army commission in April 1941 and become a reservist) had to agree that he was an outstanding pilot. In particular Lindbergh must have been pretty good at managing his fuel on his epic flight, so 'Lindy' (or 'Slim') was sent to the Pacific to demonstrate how it was done. Having already been despatched to the Pacific to solve some problems with the Vought F4U Corsair for the Marines, Lindbergh flew to Nadzab on 15 June 1944 and eventually arrived in the 8th FG's area.

When he set out to take up a P-38J for the first time, on 16 June, Lindbergh was rolling out when one of the wheels locked and blew its tyre. He took off, but had to put the Lightning down immediately 20ft (6m) off the strip so as not to block the runway. Undaunted, he grabbed another aircraft and accompanied the Group's 35th FS, which was using Nadzab's No 4 strip at that time. The mission lasted some 80min.

Lindbergh used Nadzab No 3 on 26 June and flew out to Hollandia to make contact with 'Satan's Angels', where he was welcomed aboard by Col Charles MacDonald. Lindbergh was in impressive company. MacDonald then had eleven victories to his credit, and was subsequently credited with twenty-seven, becoming the third-ranking ace in the Pacific. 'Satan's Angels' was a crack unit, one of the leading Groups in the theatre, but Mac understood the importance of fuel conservation on long overwater missions, and soon made Lindy feel an important part of the Group.

Flying a mission on 28 June, Lindy accompanied Maj Meryl M. Smith, then Group Deputy CO, with Maj Thomas McGuire, on whose wing he flew. The mission was a coastal sweep to seek out and strafe enemy shipping, barges and Fox Tare Charlie-size vessels (this last was a coding system to identify various sizes of enemy vessel). The flight lasted 6hr 24min, and Lindbergh waded in, shooting the small vessels up like a veteran. The famous aviator flew several more missions with the 475th as part of the team, recording bombing, strafing and escort duties in his journal, to familiarize him with this aspect of the Lightning's war.

Good detail is revealed in this view of a 67th FS, 347th FG, P-38J taken in January 1945. Note the hinged-down formation light panel below the fuselage. A. Pelletier

Fuel economy was second nature to Lindy, and he was soon offering his expertise to the 475th's pilots. In his book *The Wartime Journals of Charles A. Lindbergh*, the Atlantic pioneer records one occasion when he arrived back at Nadzab with 275 US gal (1,040ltr) in his P-38's tanks, and still found pilots a little edgy at having 'only' 175 US gal (660ltr) remaining. Even after a 7hr mission Lindbergh landed with about 210 US gal (795ltr) to spare, but he knew that the P-38Js the Group was then flying could yield better consumption figures than that. That went for every aircraft – and, more importantly, every pilot – in the Group.

Lindbergh lectured the pilots and demonstrated that, overall, V Fighter Command could extend the range of its P-38s by as much as 30 per cent. Basically the method was to cruise at 1,600rpm in auto-lean mixture at 185mph (300km/h) indicated airspeed. If that speed was maintained at high manifold pressures, the fuel consumption of the J model fell to 70 US gal (265ltr) per hour.

July 1944

Before Lindbergh bade the 475th farewell, the 433rd FS escorted B-24s attacking Jefman on the western end of New Guinea, and not one of the Lightnings returned with less than 160 US gal (600ltr) of fuel. Having to leave the Group for several days, Lindbergh returned and flew from Mokmer airstrip on Biak with the 433rd FS on 24 July. Another mission followed on 27 July, when the squadron flew out to Halmahera in the Molucca Islands as part of the escort to about forty B-25 Mitchells. No enemy fighters rose to challenge the strike.

For his memorable 'victory mission' on 28 July, Lindbergh accompanied Col Mac-Donald, leading Blue Flight of the 433rd with the call sign 'Possum 1'. Ceram, also in the Moluccas, was the target, and enemy fighters were expected to put in an appearance over the Elpaputih Bay area. Radio calls confirmed that the Japanese had indeed materialized, on a day when the 'Headhunters' were ironically hampered by a shortage of ammunition. In the ensuing

dogfight some of the pilots complained about their lack of ammunition, but Lindbergh's guns were loaded when his adversary seemed to appear out of nowhere and head directly towards his P-38. Lindbergh fired a burst and the shells appeared to hit home, but the enemy aircraft, presumably a Mitsubishi Ki-51 'Sonia', the type at which Charlie MacDonald had fired seconds earlier, zoomed, missing his Lightning by mere feet. It arched over Lindbergh and Lt Miller, his wingman that day, and both American pilots watched it splash down in the bay. It was a certain kill, but one that could hardly be recorded in the 433rd FS's records.

Charles Lindbergh thus became one of the few civilians to score an aerial victory with the USAAF. There was no publicity for the feat, as the brass did not look too kindly on civilians occupying the cockpits of military aircraft, but the kill was the best possible way for Lindbergh to appreciate the combat conditions the P-38 pilots were experiencing almost daily. Their respect for him went up accordingly.

A formal gathering of the 67th FS in January 1945 reflects on past glories, including aerial victories. The Fighting Cock badge was first carried into combat on P-39s. A. Pelletier

More P-38 missions for the Atlantic solo flyer followed, but George Kenney decided that it was too great a risk to have Lindbergh flying operationally in the forthcoming invasion of the Philippines, and ordered him home on 16 August 1944.

August 1944

Throughout August the relentless Fifth Air Force rolled on, temporarily held up by a spell of bad weather over New Guinea early in the month. The bomber offensive against Japanese bases, many of them bypassed as far as ground or amphibious assault was concerned, continued apace, the fighters escorting numerous missions to keep any resurgence of enemy activity firmly contained. Other locations needed to be seized to bring more Allied air bases into the picture, and on 17 August air support was provided for US landings at Wardo on the island of Biak. By the end of the month, with Noemfoor Island being declared secure, the US command could announce that the arduous New Guinea campaign was at an end.

September 1944

With many of the Japanese bases in the SWPA captured or neutralized, the Allies began to dominate. In the air, on the ground and at sea the Japanese units remaining in the vast Pacific Ocean Area faced an uncertain future, their supplies and reinforcements dwindling under the onslaught of three US air forces and RAAF and Royal New Zealand Air Force squadrons. Wherever they faced western might, the oriental enemy took heavy and unsustainable casualties.

On the 30 September Lt Col Robert Westbrook, leading ace of Thirteenth Fighter Command, shot down his seventeenth enemy aircraft over Kendari airfield in the southern Celebes. Westbrook was over the islands after leading seven P-38Js of the 67th FS on a 1,500-mile (2,400km) bomber

escort. The 'Oscar' was downed over Ambesia, and after destroying three more Ki-43s in October Westbrook emerged as the top ace of the Thirteenth.

October 1944

In October 1944 the US forces embarked on a massive amphibious assault on the Philippines, where the bloody, protracted fighting for this huge group of islands was to bring

Dick Bong shakes hands with Gen Douglas MacArthur on the occasion of the presentation of the Medal of Honor to America's 'Aces of Aces' on Leyte on 12 December 1944. IWM

the Fifth Air Force's P-38 groups considerable action and a great deal of success.

Much of the central Pacific lay beyond the reach of the Fifth's fighters until they could be transported by sea. Carrier Air Groups proved more than adept at gaining air superiority before, during and after islands had been subjected to amphibious assault. Having secured the primary

objective, the seaborne forces moved on, whereupon the USAAF took over garrison duty and mounted its own operations to prevent any Japanese attempt to regain the initiative.

Counterattacks invariably continued to be costly disasters for the Japanese, but that did not mean that they stopped. As a result the P-38 squadrons flew a spiralling total of ground-attack sorties to destroy enemy aircraft on the ground, while escort missions continued in support of USAAF heavy bomber operations, mainly by Seventh and Thirteenth Air Force B-24 Liberators. There was also a standing requirement to provide fighter support for the Fifth's own tactical bomber/attack force of B-25s and A-20s, and though both of these types were usually more than capable of looking after themselves, the Lightnings' presence was always appreciated, just in case the Japanese proved to be particularly aggressive. Moreover, any crippled bombers in danger of attracting enemy fighters required an escort. Medium bombers suffered not only from the attention of Japanese interceptors; flying at the low altitudes they routinely adopted on missions, ground fire could be murderous.

The Lockheed fighters were also required to escort numerous sorties by their unarmed F-5 brethren, the pilots of which provided a steady stream of vital visual intelligence to the campaign planners. As it did elsewhere, the F-5 itself took on the mantle of PR supremo in the Pacific, several squadrons maintaining reconnaissance cover of Japanese targets wherever they were located.

Irrespective of the nature of operations, the fighter pilots of the Fifth Air Force continued to achieve success in aerial combat. Dozens of individuals became aces, many of them wholly or partly while flying the P-38. A great many who had cut their teeth on the P-39 and P-40 were able to take advantage of an improved edge over the enemy when P-38s arrived as replacements, a situation that was also found to be the case when a unit switched from the P-47. In time a cadre of pilots, numbered among the best in the USAAF, were all flying Lightnings, to the obvious delight of George Kenney.

Tortuous Tacloban

Having been assigned to the 85th Fighter Wing for the defence of Leyte, the 49th FG took thirty-four P-38s into Tacloban on 27 October. One aircraft crashed on landing, but the remainder refuelled and took off without delay. Running into Japanese aircraft, the P-38 pilots of the 49th FS accounted for four of the six Aichi D3As and Ki-43s claimed by the Group and V Fighter Command during the day.

Tacloban had been prepared in a hurry by the 305th Airdrome Squadron, one of the army of unsung but vital engineering

bloodbath were the escort carriers of Admiral Sprague's Task Force III. Having made several courageous strafing runs on ships as large as the battleship *Yamato*, the naval aircraft could contribute little more. They could not land back aboard if their ships were about to be sunk; all they could do was to seek land as fast as possible, and Tacloban was the only place to go.

On 28 October the Lightnings of the 49th were briefed to attack ground targets in the Ormoc area. A spectacular result of one twelve-aircraft mission was massive explosions resulting from an attack on an enemy ammunition dump.

Despite overwhelming US air strength, the struggle for the Philippines was far from a walk-over for US forces. In a touch of irony the 49th FG claimed its 500th victory over Tacloban on the 29th, but a day later

November 1944

In a successful day's hunting on the first day of November, the 8th FG sent forty-two P-38s off from Morotai to strafe airfields on Leyte. The pilots destroyed seven enemy aircraft in the air, as well as claiming about seventy-five destroyed or damaged on the ground. Numerous enemy aircraft were later found to be unflyable, as they lacked vital spare parts. At some bases, however, the enemy had been astute enough to drain off fuel to prevent aircraft burning. This only brought down more fire from the Americans, who were of course unaware of the exact status of grounded aircraft.

Over in the central area of the Philippines both of the Thirteenth Air Force's P-38 Groups were active, the pilots additionally ranging out to hit Cebu in the Celebes

John Loisel's P-38J with plane-in-squadron number 140 denoting the 432nd FS, 475th FG. Loisel scored eleven victories. R.H. Strauss

units that built and operated such forward airstrips for US Army and Navy aircraft. Manning control towers and generally directing operations, maintaining and refuelling aircraft and providing an ordnance and armament provision service, these units were worth their weight in gold to the operational squadrons.

Coming into its own as a diversionary airfield while the three-day Battle of Leyte Gulf raged, Tacloban was short on luxuries but provided a haven for US Navy fighters displaced from their escort carriers when the Japanese fleet attacked. Under the Imperial Japanese Navy's *Sho* plan, designed to wreck the American landings, all that stood between the enemy battleships and a

the unit could muster only twenty P-38s, having suffered losses in numerous strafing attacks by Japanese aircraft. Accidents, too, had resulted in a growing number of Lightnings being grounded for maintenance or relegated to the boneyard to be cannibalized to keep others flying.

Fifth Air Force P-38s were active elsewhere at this time. The 8th FG, based on Morotai, sent its 36th FS to strafe Sandakan aerodrome on the north-western tip of Borneo. The Lightnings also swept a nearby harbour and claimed one ship sunk to add to a mounting tally of destruction of Japanese seaborne traffic, ranging from small coastal cutters to barges, luggers and freighters.

and shooting down several Japanese aircraft in the process.

Air combat over the Philippines intensified on 2 November as the Japanese realized the great danger that a successful US invasion of the islands represented. The 49th FG saw much action during the day, its pilots claiming the destruction of twenty-six Japanese aircraft.

The hot pace continued on 12 November, when the P-38 again demonstrated its ascendancy over the best fighters the JAAF and JNAF were able to put up. While Fifth Air Force bombers pounded various Philippine aerodromes, pilots of the 475th downed a Ki-48 'Sally' and two Ki-43s near Dulag, Leyte, at 08.15hr. A 347th Lightning

OPPOSITE PAGE:
TOP: More restrained unit markings were used by the 67th FS, 347th FG, as P-38J '163', nearest the camera, shows. A. Pelletier

BOTTOM: Having lost both engines on a 1944 combat mission, Lt James A. Posten had no choice but to ditch his P-38J-15, fortunately in shallow water. IWM

shot down an A6M over Negros/Alicante aerodrome at 12.40hr, and another three 'Zekes' fell over Tacloban between 13.30 and 13.45hr when the 475th and 18th FGs teamed up. 'Satan's Angels' had by no means finished the day's work, as four Mitsubishi J2Ms, an A6M and a Ki-43 were destroyed in an afternoon combat over northern Cebu between 17.10 and 17.40hr. A 475th FG pilot downed an A6M over Dulag at 18.20hr and, finally, Capt Frederic F. Champlin of the 431st FS became an ace when he added a Ki-43 and a Ki-48 for his fifth and sixth kills near Dulag at 18.15hr. That made sixteen.

On 14 November the 475th FG completed a five-day move to bring the 431st and 433rd FSs forward to Leyte, a situation that everyone appreciated, as the Group was now together again and at full strength. What the pilots and ground crews definitely did not appreciate was the all-invasive mud of Tacloban's ill-equipped and over-used airstrip. And the enemy was hardly passive, offering combat on most occasions that the Lightnings flew.

Calls to get steel Marston matting laid on the runway at Dulag aerodrome to relieve the ever-more-crowded conditions at Tacloban bore fruit on 21 November, when the engineers completed their work. The Lightning pilots could now operate with much less apprehension that their heavily-laden fighters would mire down in the glutinous mud.

By 31 November the 475th was able to claim seventy enemy aircraft destroyed for the month, and the figure rose to ninety during December; quite phenomenal figures for a single Group in so short a period.

December 1944

The landing at Ormoc Bay on 7 December was a daring move by MacArthur, for Japanese naval units were close enough to bombard the unloading transports, but with air supremacy the US commanders considered

---

Richard Ira Bong

With Dick Bong's tally having reached thirty-eight, V Fighter Command felt that he had more than earned the Medal of Honor, and with due ceremony MacArthur arrived at Tacloban to present him with America's highest award for bravery on 12 December 1944. In his address the general described Maj Bong as one 'who has ruled the air from New Guinea to the Philippines'. The citation to the award officially highlighted the period from 10 October to 15 November 1944, during which Bong had destroyed eight enemy aircraft.

Bong continued to fly combat missions, and in the next two weeks or so two more enemy aircraft fell to his guns, bringing his score to a record forty, more than any other US fighter pilot in any theatre. He was then posted home for the last time.

Purportedly, the Fifth Air Force commanding general had an early inkling of Dick Bong's potential as a fighter pilot, an intuitive feeling that he would go far. Bong shot down his first enemy aircraft on 27 December 1942, after which his personal score began to climb steadily. At the controls of a P-38F-5 until January 1943, the young native of Poplar, Wisconsin, flew with the 9th FS

and thoroughly learned his trade. Although he considered himself the 'lousiest shot in the Army Air Forces', his tactics and reflexes were usually sound enough to outfox and outfight the enemy. But such was his own critical view of his poor gunnery that Bong went so far as to sign himself up for a gunnery course on a Stateside leave, hoping first and foremost to improve his deflection-shooting skills. He completed the course at Foster Field in Texas between 7 July and 6 August 1944, and apparently did well enough, but his instructors might have been quite surprised to have such a student. Giving tuition to a 'trainee' pilot with an impressive string of kills to his name was hardly an everyday occurrence.

Bong remained with the 9th FS and flew the P-38G and H until November 1943, when he was transferred to V Fighter Command headquarters, under which the remainder of his victories were officially achieved. For these his mounts were the P-38J-15 and L-1. Bong was flying an L-1 when he destroyed his last victim, an 'Oscar' that fell near San Jose on Mindoro on 17 December 1944.

---

the risk minimal. Close air support was critical, and in this respect the P-38s of the 49th and 475th FGs responded magnificently. Air combat for the duration of the amphibious landings saw the Lightnings net fifty-three enemy aircraft out of an estimated seventy-five that threatened the landing beaches.

Moving On

A week or so after the invasion of Mindanao the 8th FG moved into the island's Hill and Elmore aerodromes. There were supplies to be moved in by the ubiquitous C-47s, and the 8th's P-38s provided an escort, the 36th FS positioning above the Skytrains to act as the high cover.

By the 30th the 80th FS was heading for its last aerial victories in the Pacific. These came on the penultimate day of the month, when Capt Louis Schriber, Jr, shot down an A6M to become an ace.

A census taken the following day stated that Far East Air Force (FEAF) had 470 P-38s on hand, including those in transit from the USA. Just in case this was not quite enough, the Seventh Air Force released forty-seven late-model P-38Js and Ls to the FEAF, these coming from the 18th and 318th FGs.

Combat flying in the Pacific was a fatiguing business, made worse by hazardous weather that brought poor visibility,

torrential rainfall and unbelievably high humidity levels. In addition, a range of debilitating tropical diseases drained men both physically and mentally. Operating continually from primitive airstrips was always demanding, requiring a high degree of flying skill. Then there were the Japanese, an enemy not renowned for the care of men unfortunate enough to fall into their hands. For some, such risks preyed on their minds. Others could put such things out of their minds and concentrate on the job in hand.

Despite all the drawbacks of the theatre, the top P-38 pilots indulged in keen competition to score the highest number of aerial victories. Good for headlines and *esprit de corps* though it was, the 'ace race' had its downside when individuals were tempted to take that small step beyond basic self-preservation to prove something. George Kenney was well aware that men could and did push themselves too hard to achieve victories. He came to recognize that this danger could become more acute the higher an individual's score rose. He saw that the race between Dick Bong and Tommy McGuire for the position of top ace could get out of hand, especially if the man in second place took that extra risk to equal or overtake his rival.

When Dick Bong returned to the USA to undertake a War Bond tour, McGuire's personal score stood at thirty-eight. Circumstances claimed the lives of both men within a short time, McGuire in combat and

Bong in the crash of a Lockheed F-80 on 6 August, sharing the date of his demise with that of thousands of citizens of Hiroshima.

January 1945

Like Bong, McGuire was the subject of a restraining order, but in early January 1945 he was 'just visiting' the 431st FS area on Negros Island to talk to his friend, Maj Jack B. Rittmayer. Captain R. F. 'Pappy' Cline had taken over as CO of the 431st the previous December, replacing McGuire, who was no longer officially on the squadron rolls.

Fifth Air Force headquarters did not condone operational flights intended merely to run-up personal scores, but if there was

breeze'. Douglas Thropp, Jr, Capt Edwin Weaver, Rittmayer and McGuire were among those present. Inevitably the shop talk turned to the ace race, and gradually the idea of one more P-38 flight led by Mac to lure Japanese fighters into action took form. If McGuire could destroy three enemy aircraft he would have forty-one to clinch the title, beat Bong and pass the torch to the 475th. At one point McGuire turned to Thropp and said: 'Do you want to go?'

'Hell, yes' was the prompt reply.

'OK then,' answered McGuire, 'you be tail-end Charlie, on Rittmayer's wing.'

McGuire himself organized the sweep, which was to patrol the Japanese fleet anchorage at Mindoro in the Philippines. It was reasoned that Japanese fighters would

that the aircraft might have over-extended his luck (McGuire had not scored a victory for some months) and even reversed it. Instead he took P-38L-1 44-24845/112.

Even though the flight was not authorized by the Fifth Air Force, the high-ranking ace still had the 'pull' to lay-on such a mission. That said, Pappy Cline was not apparently at Negros at the time, and it remains something of a mystery as to who actually condoned the mission. Ground crews would have been alerted to fuel and arm the Lightnings, and wake-up calls for the four pilots would have been arranged, all in the knowledge that 'Mac' was about to fly while on restricted flight status. Ace Fred Champlin was Operations Officer, and he might have had a hand in it, as it

Lingayen was a busy airfield in January 1945 as the fight for the Philippines continued to rage. Among the residents were the Lightnings of the 431st FS, some of which carried the full 'Satan's Angels' markings. The nearest P-38L was possibly that of Chris Herman, with Bob Werner's '139' behind it. A. Pelletier

the slightest chance that McGuire could knock down more of the enemy and beat Bong into first place, then officialdom had little cause to complain. The chance of becoming America's 'Ace of Aces' was a powerful incentive, and McGuire intended to take every opportunity to gain the title. The scene was set on the night of 6/7 January, when a get-together of 431st FS pilots led to some drinking and 'shooting the

be sent up to protect the ships as soon as US aircraft appeared. Each of the 431st's P-38Ls would carry two 150 US gal (570ltr) drop-tanks to extend their patrol time over the enemy fleet. Had the flight been merely a sweep across Negros, extra tanks would not have been needed.

McGuire elected not to fly his personal P-38L-1, 44-24155/131 *Pudgy* (V), on the mission, as he had earlier voiced the opinion

was his P-38L that McGuire flew on the mission. In any event, it would have been difficult to deny Mac his request, as he had been a highly respected member and CO of the squadron. As he was due to rotate home in February, it was common knowledge that he would have few more chances to increase his score.

'Daddy' Flight took off at dawn on 7 January. All of the P-38 pilots were experienced and, in addition to Mac's thirty-eight kills, Doug Thropp had two, Jack Rittmayer three and Ed Weaver two, a combined total of forty-five victories.

The flight levelled off at 10,000ft (3,000m) over Negros, which lay beneath high cloud cover. McGuire ordered them down through gaps in the cloud, and in the dive the flight became separated. Thropp, flying on Rittmayer's wing, stated that his element was more than a mile (1.6km) away from Mac and his wingman. Rittmayer throttled back, cautious about flying through cloud. As McGuire pulled ahead he called: 'Close it up'.

Rittmayer then said he had trouble with one of his engines. McGuire told Thropp to move in to element lead as number three in the flight. Thropp was able to close the gap, and the flight's intergrity was all but restored.

Some 500ft (150m) below the manoeuvring Lightnings was a Ki-43 'Oscar' flown by Akira Sugimoto of the 54th Sentai, who had been ordered to search for an American convoy apparently en route to Mindoro or Lingayen. Having discovered nothing, he was heading home to Fabrica aerodrome.

While he was closing up to McGuire and Weaver, Thropp spotted the Japanese fighter, which closed fast and flashed under McGuire's element. Neither Thropp or Rittmayer had time to react, unlike Sugimoto. The Japanese pilot went after McGuire and Weaver, who formed a left-hand Lufbery.

The book said that if you split the elements when under attack, and if the attacking enemy aircraft turned in front of either Lightning, the other can shoot it off his wingman's tail.

Seeing the beginnings of such a move, the Japanese pilot pulled away and opted to attack the second element. Thropp's aircraft was struck by a burst of fire that damaged one of his P-38's turbochargers. Sensing a sure kill, Sugimoto closed in. Thropp later reported thinking: 'He's so close I could hit him with a rock'.

Thropp was about to toggle his drop-tanks to improve his manoeuvrability when McGuire called over the radio: 'Daddy Flight; save your tanks'. This surprising order only emphasizes McGuire's intention of gaining several victories that day. Dropping tanks would have restricted range and lost the chance to clash with enemy aircraft over the Mindoro convoy. Thropp reluctantly complied, but at low

level the P-38 was heavy and sluggish. He saw McGuire and Weaver still circling and wondered why, as Rittmayer fired at the 'Oscar', which then broke off its attack on Thropp.

Sugimoto now dived on the circling element and got on Weaver's tail. Reacting, Weaver (who reported the enemy aircraft as a 'Zeke') turned and went into a shallow dive. Seeing the danger to his wingman, McGuire reacted by throwing his Lightning into a steep banking turn, hoping to cut off the enemy aircraft and persuade it to attack him. The ruse failed. With its wings near-vertical the Lightning stalled, flipped over and nosed down. Without height, McGuire had no chance to recover. Weaver noticed a flash of flame as his leader hit the trees. Thropp also saw the crash, but at the time did not know who had gone in. Only later did they piece together the details of McGuire's last flight, and the fact that there were two Japanese fighters involved, rather than one.

So perished the USAAF's second-highest-scoring ace, seemingly without a shot being fired at his aircraft, though there was a report of some ground fire that might have contributed to his disastrous stall; or may have been mentioned merely to make the loss of so skilled a pilot more plausible. The fact that McGuire elected not to drop his external tanks, as was normal practice with the P-38 when combat was imminent, was assumed to be a major factor in his demise.

Although McGuire himself had often stressed this rule on the grounds that a pair of large and heavy tanks understandably limited the P-38's manoeuvrability, the compliant pilot could face the grim prospect of a landing far short of base if fuel ran out. This was probably uppermost in McGuire's mind as he manoeuvred the heavy Lightning, bent as he was on getting those few final victories to put him ahead of Bong. To do that he had planned for a longer flight. The ultimate irony was that the Japanese had obliged, but had appeared unexpectedly early in the mission.

McGuire's 'victor' had scant little time to savour his victory, as he was obliged to clear the area and make an emergency landing. Unfortunately his aircraft was seen by Filipino guerrillas, who promptly exacted revenge on one more hated Japanese by putting six bullets into Sugimoto's chest.

McGuire's wingman had come up against a Nakajima Ki-84 'Frank' flown by Sgt Mizunori Fukuda of the 71st Sentai. The

heavily-laden P-38 was out-manoeuvred and shot down by one of the enemy's best fighters, though Fukuda himself was forced to crash-land at Manapla, his aircraft having been damaged by fire from Ed Weaver's guns.

Unassailable Score

George Kenney and the USA at large was stunned at the news of Tommy McGuire's death. His loss left Dick Bong as the virtually unassailable USAAF 'ace of aces', it being unlikely that his score of forty would be surpassed by any other US Army, Navy or Marine fighter pilot before the war ended. As the pilot who had come nearest to Bong's score, McGuire was recommended for the Medal of Honor.

At the time of McGuire's death there were several up-and-coming P-38 aces with scores in double figures. They included the 475th's CO, Charles MacDonald (final score twenty-seven), Francis J. Lent (eleven) and John S. Loisel and Elliot Summer, with ten each. Behind Dick Bong in the 49th FG were Gerry Johnson (twenty-two), Robert M. DeHaven (fourteen) and James A. 'Duckbutt' Watkins (twelve).

MacDonald, who scored all his kills flying P-38s despite earlier combat service on the P-36 and P-47, succinctly summed up the qualities of the Lightning by setting down his chosen tactics in a Fifth Fighter Command study entitled *Twelve to One*. This manual, which took its title from the enormous kill ratio USAAF pilots achieved over the JAAF and JNAF, was not published until 1 August 1945, and thus was a near-final report on what 'Kenney's Kids' had achieved during the last year or so of the war. In part, MacDonald said: 'The main reason we beat the enemy is because we work as a team, using the good qualities of our airplanes and keeping him from using the good qualities of his own. I think if the Japanese had P-38s and we had Zeros we could still beat them because the average American pilot is a good team worker and is always aggressive.'

Some of the most skilled P-38 pilots committed to paper their definite views about their aircraft, American pilots and the Japanese. Urged to 'tell it like it was', these men pulled few punches.

Throughout the war the two top qualities of the P-38 were speed and firepower. Almost every pilot agreed that wading into even a large formation of Japanese aircraft usually succeeded in breaking them up. In that case, scattered enemy aircraft had no time to re-form for mutual protection, allowing the P-38s to select their targets. Then the attackers often had things all in their favour, provided a few golden rules were followed. In combat, speed and aggressiveness were paramount, but the astute pilot also knew the limitations of his own aircraft and the most dangerous points of the enemy fighters he encountered. The lesson every USAAF fighter pilot had drummed into him upon arrival in the Pacific was that anyone flying P-39s or P-40s should 'never dogfight with a Zero'. This timely warning saved many lives, but it could largely be set aside by 1944–45. When pitted against the superb late-model P-38J and L, the P-51D and P-47N, the one Japanese fighter that had been the scourge of the Pacific in 1941–42 met its match. It was not that the dogfighting abilities of the IJN's A6M and the JAAF's Ki-43, Ki-44, Ki-61, Ki-84 and so forth were denied by Fifth Air Force fighter pilots, it was simply that all the American types were superior on most counts, as were the tactics, not to mention the superiority in numbers. And the rank-and-file Japanese pilots of 1943–44 were no longer the élite corps they had been some two years earlier.

That said, things did not always go according to plan for the US fighter pilots, even one as good as Dick Bong. On one occasion Bong, who then had twenty-one victories, was escorting Allied shipping in Oro Bay, New Guinea, when enemy fighters were intercepted some 20 miles (30km) out to sea. In the ensuing melée Bong found he had an 'Oscar' instead of a wingman behind him. He pulled ahead of the Japanese fighter at 15,000ft (4,500m) altitude. Unable to shake it off, he dropped down low over the ocean. When he was about half a mile (0.8km) from his pursuer Bong executed a very tight 180-degree turn, in effect heading off the enemy fighter to come around and bring his guns to bear.

As the turn was completed the enemy pilot himself attempted to cut off Bong, who suddenly found the situation changed. Coming down on his P-38 were nine Japanese fighters. Bong had no choice but to abandon his original prey and fire at the leader of the diving pack. His fire was accurate, and the enemy aircraft went down. Continuing head-on into the formation, Bong fired, fatally hitting a second and damaging a third. Fire was coming the other way and finding its mark, but, hav-

ing made the best of a potentially disastrous situation, Bong evaded the rest of his attackers. Back at base he reflected on the folly of becoming target-fixated and failing to scan the sky adequately for other dangers. Bong's ground crew replenished the coolant lost from the P-38's port engine and patched up the holes, but it was a lesson the American ace did not forget.

The enormous effort by the Stateside training schools to provide enough fighter pilots for the war zones is illustrated by the fact that, since the summer of 1944, 265 new P-38 combat pilots were posted to FEAF units. This rate was exceeded in the next half-year period (to June 1945), when another 498 Lightning pilots arrived in the theatre.

In the 8th FG, accumulated P-38 kills had brought Jay T. Robbins twenty-one victories, George Welch sixteen, Ed 'Porky' Cragg and Cyril Filcher Homer fifteen apiece, and Richard L. West fourteen. These scores were the tip of the iceberg for the leading Pacific-based Lightning Groups, all of which had a galaxy of aces and scores running to several hundred kills.

The P-38's poor ratio of enemy aircraft kills to losses in Europe was completely reversed in the Pacific, where the 49th FG accounted for 678 Japanese aircraft, mostly but not entirely while flying Lightnings, while the 475th was credited with 545.

Capping-Off the Enemy

One element in the process of clearing out remaining Japanese garrisons in the Pacific (or, at least, those that could potentially threaten Allied air operations) was extensive aerial reconnaissance of areas hitherto attacked only infrequently. One of these was Singapore, on the tip of Malaya. Eternally infamous for being surrendered to Japan in 1942, in Britain's most humiliating wartime defeat, this important naval base had been largely left alone ever since, particularly by tactical air forces. This was primarily because of the remoteness of Singapore from any Allied fighter bases for much of the war. But in the summer of 1945 the Thirteenth Air Force decided to find out what enemy activity remained there. Accordingly, an F-5 reconnaissance sortie was undertaken in July, but the aircraft failed to return. A follow-up mission by an F-5 on or about 1 August ran into trouble, the damaged aircraft crash-landing on Palawan Island, but the film taken by its

pilot revealed that there were 125 enemy fighters on four concrete runways at Singapore, the base having been one of the finest in the Far East before the war.

Although P-38s of the 347th FG, based on Palawan, had been attacking such enemy shipping as still plied the ocean within an 850- to 900-mile (1,360- to 1,450-km) radius from Puerto Princesa aerodrome, they could never get much further afield without ideally staging through Borneo.

That territory was in Japanese hands until an Australian invasion in June 1945. Having repaired the runway at Labuan aerodrome, the Australians were happy for the USAAF to use it when an order from Thirteenth Fighter Command on 12 August 1945 called for a strike on Singapore.

Such missions had begun for the 'Sun Busters' earlier that month, the Group's 67th FS having sent eight P-38s on a fighter sweep to Singapore on the 4th. On that occasion the fighters staged through Brunei Bay.

Six days after the atomic-bombing of Hiroshima, rumours of Japanese surrender were strong, but no definite move had been made and the war continued. Responsibility for undertaking the Singapore strike fell on the 68th ('Lightning Lancers') FS, equipped with P-38Ls.

The briefing for the mission revealed that two IJN cruisers and several other ships were in place off Singapore, and these, along with the 125 fighters and the port's formidable AA defences, made the operation no milk run. Moreover, the squadron was sending only eight P-38s, which the participants felt was far too few. Even though the 68th was to rendezvous with sixteen RAAF Mosquitoes, sceptics still rated the P-38s' chances as slim. They reckoned that seven Lightnings could be shot down if the enemy intercepted.

Unusually, Operations Officer Richard F. Brown, who was to lead the mission, called for volunteers. He had no cause to fear that a full complement of pilots would not 'sign up', and he soon had his full team. Another epic long-range P-38 mission was in the making.

On 13 August the pilots were driven out in Jeeps to revetments containing three P-38Ls each. The primary target was the shipping in Singapore Harbour, and the small force of Lightnings took off in the dark from Puerto Princesa's muddy runway, covered mostly by pierced steel planking which fortunately negated the effects of the frequent rainfall. By daybreak the P-38s were in sight of Labuan and lining up to land, noting the airfield pock-marked with craters made by American bombs. Some aircraft stuck in the mud but were extricated after some effort, and all eight were refuelled. As Scamper Red Leader, Richard Brown now had the Australian Mosquitoes, which would fly as four flights to follow the Lightnings, making twenty-four aircraft to fly the mission. Start engines was at 06.25hr, and take-off at 06.30hr. Singapore was 850 miles (1,360km) away. On a mission such as this, Charles Lindbergh's advice came into its own. Brown reminded the P-38 pilots to follow cruise-control procedures after climbing and throttling back to 1,900rpm and 32in of manifold pressure. For long-range cruise the power would go down to 1,600rpm/30in. Radio silence was to be observed.

On take-off Brown and the other pilots quickly reached the magic 125mph (200km/h), the speed at which the P-38 could still be flown if one engine cut. At that speed there was enough rudder control to manoeuvre. Up at 10,000ft (3,000m) the light rain turned heavy. There had been a 'no weather' note at briefing because such data was not available. Then it grew worse, the poor visibility forcing the RAAF Mosquitoes to turn back. The Lightnings ploughed on, their tight formation helping the pilots to see each other and stay together.

Some 25 miles (40km) from Singapore the aircraft dropped to 100ft (30m) above the sea, and the pilots saw a ship dead ahead. By then they were fast burning fuel from both their drop-tanks; Brown dropped his, still containing about 15 US gal (57ltr), on the deck of the ship. The Lightning flight strafed the vessel and set it on fire. They descended to 50ft (15m) as the target came racing into sight.

Pilots spotted two ships being loaded with 50-US gal (180ltr) drums of petrol from a dozen barges. The renowned quietness of the P-38's approach was an advantage, as the Japanese workers seemed unaware of the impending danger. Opening up their formation and increasing speed, the P-38 pilots selected their target ships. Brown and his No 2, 'Steve' Stevenson, attacked the largest freighter, of some 10,000 tons displacement. A second vessel of about half the size was moored close by, but sufficiently distant for Brown to fly between the two after strafing. Stevenson was hit as the ships opened up with everything they had. Despite calls from his

wingman and a seemingly well P-38, he had been hit. Brown watched helplessly as the Lightning dropped away, exploding as it hit the water.

Pilots were strafing the barges and stoking up fires on the larger vessels. All the freighters had been loaded with fuel, and this had been set ablaze in the holds of both ships. Eleven of the barges were also burning. They had done enough. Brown called a join-up and five other P-38s appeared, throttles set for long-range climb. At 10,000ft (3,000m) heavy clouds were present to threaten the ten-minute fuel reserve the pilots had. But the weather improved, with no strong headwinds to ruin the precise planning necessary for an operation such as this. Soon the force was approaching Borneo. There was clear weather at Labuan, and seven P-38s landed safely.

Fuel trucks appeared and topped-up the tanks ready for the 68th to return home the following morning. When they landed at Palawan on the 14th the pilots learned that the Singapore strike had been the Thirteenth Air Force's last mission of the war. In 11hr 35min the Lightnings had flown 2,300 miles (3,700km).

Philippines Finale

Spearheaded by the P-38 groups, Fifth Fighter Command had moved up to support the lengthy operation to secure all of the Philippines. The 49th FG had reached Linguyan on Luzon, a base large enough to accommodate all of the three squadrons' aircraft and located near enough to the remaining targets. Having enjoyed a break in casualties for several weeks, the 49th almost inevitably suffered more losses of pilots and aircraft. Now, though, the Philippines witnessed the appearance of a strange flying machine that could quickly assist downed pilots by taking off vertically and, upon reaching the scene of a crash, actually hover over it. This freakish contraption was a Sikorsky R-4 helicopter, the first of its kind to undertake operational trials in the Pacific during the war.

Fields of Fire

Some of the late Philippines fighter missions were spectacular and lethal to the Japanese, who stubbornly held out in fortified areas and caves, with little hope of

being relieved. Their plan was to take as many Allied soldiers and Filipino civilians with them as they fought to the last man. But the US wanted to avoid playing that deadly game whenever possible, and if the enemy wished to die rather than surrender, so be it. In the last week of April the 49th was called upon literally to scorch the enemy out of a fortified camp at Ipo Dam. This earthen structure at the confluence of the Ipo and Angat Rivers was held by 4,700 fanatical troops. The reservoir supplied much of Manila's fresh water, and there were fears that the Japanese might poison it, so capturing the dam became imperative.

To persuade the enemy that further resistance was useless, the Fifth planned a massive fire-bombing of the area, a deluge of napalm and HE against which there could be no practical defence. The 49th's P-38s took off on 3 May to become part of a force of 270 fighters for the first of the saturation strikes. The result created awesome fields of fire running south-west from Ipo village through the surrounding foothills for 45 miles (70km), out to the village of Santa Maria. For four days the fires raged as the fighters bombed and strafed anything that moved.

As the early May fire raids had been a success they were repeated on the 16th. Again the 49th's P-38s swept in, and forty-eight pilots watched their bombs stoking the conflagration, caused this time by a total of 680 fighters. From their lofty vantage point the pilots saw a vision of hell unfolding as a 5-mile (8km) square of jungle disappeared under a shimmering heat haze. Each attacking Lightning was buffeted by the rising thermals as the big silver tanks of jellied petrol tumbled away from fighters flying straight and level.

Several more carpets of fire were laid before the enemy in the highlands near Santa Maria succumbed to Allied troops, who suffered only light casualties, and the Ipo Dam was taken virtually unopposed. Nearly half the defenders had been incinerated.

Strafing several ground targets in succeeding weeks was something of an anti-climax for the 49th, although a big operation lay ahead. In June, after a bitter fight, the US finally secured the island of Okinawa.

Last Damned Island

Although virtually no airmen involved in the capture of Okinawa were aware of the fact, Ryuku Island, which formed part of greater Japan, would be the last island invasion of the war. Beginning on 1 April 1945 the assault troops rapidly captured Kadena and Yontan airfields in the face of suspiciously light resistance. This materialized into a series of bitter, no-quarter battles as the troops drove south, and Okinawa was not finally secured until the end of June, after terrible loss of life on both sides. The air forces meanwhile used 'Okie's' captured airfields and turned the tiny off-shore island of Ie Shima into a veritable floating air base.

The Fifth Air Force acted mainly in an important diversionary role during the Okinawa operation, sending numerous strikes to Formosa to paralyse Japanese air power and devastate enemy seaborne traffic. It was 3 July before the Fifth was able to put Lightnings over Japan, when the 35th FG flew a sweep to Kyushu. By moving about 60 per cent of his entire force to Okinawa and Ie Shima, George Kenney was positioning his squadrons for the forthcoming invasion of the home islands, planned for 1 November. In the meantime the Lightnings mopped up pockets of Japanese resistance in the Philippines, where the Luzon fighting did not finally end until 11 July.

Preoccupied as they were with helping to secure Luzon, the Fifth's P-38 Groups tended to remain based in the Philippines until the last minute, rather than moving up to the Ryukus. Ie Shima became terribly crowded with the Seventh Air Force's Fighter Groups, and Okinawa was crammed with US Marine fighter squadrons, USAAF nightfighters and US Navy patrol bombers. The Mindoro/Luzon-based P-38s had the range to reach Japan if they were needed, and there seemed little point in adding to the overcrowding. But the top brass had its roster of groups for the invasion order of battle, and the 475th duly shipped out for Ie Shima in July, where Group personnel found that there was indeed little room for anything but aircraft. The 8th FG's late August move to Ie Shima coincided with the end of hostilities and the arrival of a Japanese surrender delegation, which left only the 49th to see out the end at Linguyan, although everyone knew (or thought they knew) that the Group would move into a new combat area sooner or later.

There was considerable frustration as the P-38 Groups awaited the call to move into what was anticipated to be the last and bloodiest battle of the war. Group intelligence in the 49th forecast a spree of aerial victories that would top 1,000 when the invasion, Operation *Olympic*, finally got under way. Events on Tinian in the Marianas in the first week of August ensured that fighter pilots, be they eager or apprehensive, would not have to risk their necks in any such contest.

After the atomic bomb strikes against Hiroshima on 6 August and Nagasaki on the 9th, the Second World War had but days to run. The 'super bombs' all but wiped out the two Japanese cities, and the end was almost a foregone conclusion. But the fighting continued while the Japanese deliberated on what concessions they could wrest from the victorious Allies amid the ashes of their country.

On 14 August five P-38s of the 35th FS, 8th FG, were escorting two rescue aircraft off the coast of Japan when six enemy fighters were spotted. The Lightnings' attack at 12.15hr resulted in four Ki-84s being shot down; the last air-combat victories for USAAF fighters during the war. The Japanese surrendered in the early hours of the following morning.

On 25 August personnel at the Japanese airfield of Nittagahara on central Kyushu observed the unmistakable sight of two P-38s preparing to land. Lieutenant Colonel Clay Tice, Jr, and his wingman, Fg Off Douglas C. Hall, of the 49th FG put down after reporting they were low on fuel. Both pilots had been out on a sweep of southern Japan, with orders not to shoot unless they were fired on first. Tice had only 240 US gal (910ltr) remaining, and Hall was soon down to 120 US gal (455ltr). As their base on Okinawa was 550 miles (880km) away, they would not make it without fuel. Tice radioed a rescue B-17 crew and asked them to fly to Ie Shima for fuel and bring it to Nittagahara, where the P-38 landed around noon.

Curious locals might have wondered at the huge red name *Gloria* painted on Tice's Lightning, but the erstwhile enemy aircraft were attended to by now-friendly and smiling Japanese, who helped to refuel the two aircraft. Although 'C' rations and candy were exchanged and everyone chattered, neither side could understand a word spoken by the other.

At the time it was reported that Douglas MacArthur was furious when he heard about the emergency incident, believing that it somehow stole the thunder of his triumphant entry into Tokyo as Supreme Commander of the Allied Powers. Few people believed the P-38 pilots' story, preferring to accept that the real reason for the unauthorized landing was that Clay and Hall had wanted to be flying the first USAAF aircraft to touch down in a defeated country. They were.

Occupation Duty

The end of the war did not mean instant rotation home for all the combat groups. Some were required for occupation duty in Japan, a chore that first befell the 49th, which went to Atsugi, Honshu, on 8 September. At that time FEAF had 808 P-38s on strength, but this number gradually dwindled as the aircrafts' support, both human and technical, melted away. As the men who had sustained the Lightning Groups through months of combat gradually rotated home, the nature of the units inevitably changed. Rules and regulations that had gone by the board in wartime suddenly appeared to irk everyone.

Then the 475th received orders to ship out to Korea, where an unexpected hazard awaited. With a degree of irony the Group's remaining P-38Ls were suddenly (and for the first time) obliged to fly in bitterly cold, damp conditions, and they did not take to them. In a repetition of the experiences of the pioneering Lightning units in England in 1943–44, the 475th's P-38Ls began to suffer engine malfunctions, with problems of congealing oil that would have been all too familiar to crew chiefs who had served in the ETO. This time, however, it hardly mattered. The Lightning had finished its war and was being replaced by the Mustang, and although North Korea would soon invade the south to launch another conflict, 'Satan's Angels' and its all-conquering Lightnings would be but a memory when hostilities broke out in 1950.

When the war ended, the Fifth Air Force P-38 Fighter Groups turned in the following total scores for enemy aircraft destroyed in aerial combat: 475th FG, over 500; 49th FG, 678, and 8th FG, 443. The latter two had, of course, achieved their totals on aircraft other than the P-38, which gave 'Satan's Angels' an unassailable lead despite the overall total being less – but denying the enemy over 1,500 aircraft was an impressive achievement.

CHAPTER ELEVEN

Special Duties

Lightnings at Night

Following the combat debut of the makeshift P-70 nightfighter in the hands of two nightfighter units over New Guinea early in 1943, the Fifth Air Force cast about for something more able to intercept nocturnal Japanese raiders. The converted Havocs equipping both of the 6th Night Fighter Squadron's (NFS) detachments proved to be much too slow for the work, taking nearly 45min to climb to 20,000 ft (6,000m). One detachment operating from Guadalcanal in February managed to obtain several war-weary P-38Gs, and decided to adapt them for a night role. It seemed logical to operate the Lightnings at high altitude and the P-70s lower down. Operationally the P-38s were deployed on orders from a local filter centre, which alerted the 6th that the Japanese were on their way. A Lightning took off and orbited a given point, the pilot endeavouring to pinpoint the target by means of his eyesight and the island's searchlight batteries. It was primitive stuff, harking back to pre-radar days, but there was really no alternative. What was supposed to happen when the incoming raiders were detected by the ground filter centre was than an outer ring of searchlights would attempt to illuminate the enemy aircraft and preferably to 'cone' it with three lights, whereupon AA fire would try to bring it down. If the guns were unsuccessful they would cease fire and 'hand over' to the circling P-38. In practice the gun crews continued to blaze away, forcing the hapless fighter pilot to fly through their bursts.

A similar frustration arose among the members of the other 6th NFS detachment in New Guinea, but its personnel decided to make the interception more scientific. They took the SCR-540 AI radar from a P-70 and installed it in the belly tanks usually carried by the Lightning. This makeshift arrangement appeared to work well enough, but both detachments were disbanded before it could be proved in combat.

Meanwhile, a USAAF nightfighter training programme had been started in

Orlando, Florida, in anticipation of the P-61 being available by the time the bulk of the students graduated. Delays with the Black Widow meant that the P-38/P-70 combination had to be called upon again.

Two new nightfighter squadrons, the 418th and 419th, were sent to the Pacific at the end of 1943, to New Guinea and Guadalcanal respectively. New P-70As proved hardly less capable than the original 'secondhand' aircraft used by the 6th NFS, and again the P-38 was called upon. Several G and J models were pressed into service, but by 1944 Japanese activity over the Solomons was definitely on the decline, and the first two units plus the 421st NFS marked time, awaiting the arrival of the P-61. All the crews put in what amounted to extra training in the exacting art of night interception in a war zone, and they were no worse off for that.

It was almost the end of 1944 before the first night kill was obtained by a P-38. This distinction went to the 547th NFS, which was posted to New Guinea via Townsville, Australia, in September. Unusually, the squadron brought its own aircraft, in the shape of a pair of P-38J-20s, modified to carry the navy APS-4 radar set. Suddenly night fighting had top priority, despite the lack of the 'right' aircraft. Brigadier General Paul B. Wurtsmith, commanding Fifth Fighter Command, gave the 547th's CO, Col William C. Odell, full backing for his experimental night operations.

As a high-performance fighter with the safety factor of two engines, the P-38 tempted Pacific field commanders to try the aircraft as a stopgap nightfighter when few other aircraft were available. Few doubted that the P-38 would be better able to catch enemy aircraft and destroy them than the A-20/P-70 light bomber conversions that otherwise equipped nightfighter units in the Pacific in 1942–43. The theory was one thing, but in practice the Lightning was not the ideal nocturnal interceptor for several reasons, not the least of which was its single seat and low availability in 1942.

Nevertheless, the 6th NFS operated two P-38Fs from Guadalcanal as early as February 1943. Fitted with radar, these nocturnal P-38s entered combat as the squadron's Detachment A, flying Lightnings unlike any others. An SCR-450 radar was installed in the nose, with rod receiver antennae on both sides. In addition, an 'arrowhead' transmitter aerial was positioned below the gun battery, which consisted only of machine-guns, a fifth such weapon being installed in place of the heavy 20mm cannon. This weight saving marginally increased speed, and five 'fifties provided more than sufficient firepower to bring down Japanese night raiders.

A great many USAAF nightfighter operations were carried out in 1943 in anticipation of the Northrop P-61's imminent availability. In the event the Black Widow's lengthy development period delayed its service debut until late 1944, with the result that most night-time kills of enemy aircraft accrued to interim types such as the P-70. This was one reason why Lockheed embarked on a nightfighter conversion of the P-38, but in this case the much larger Black Widow had the advantage of having been in service for over a year before the first Lightning conversion flew.

Time was against the P-38M. Had it been ready for service even six months earlier it might have been a more practical proposition, particularly to front-line Fighter Groups already operating P-38 single-seaters. Had such units had a flight of P-38Ms on standby to handle Japanese night intruders and 'bed-check Charlies' while the day fighter pilots rested, the Army would surely have looked favourably on the idea. Integrating a second, similar type into the Fifth Air Force's Lightning Fighter Groups would have served both maintenance and repair and reduced the need for a second servicing echelon to maintain P-61s.

On the other hand, the overriding factor militating against the P-38M, apart from Lockheed's more urgent commitment to building standard Lightning fighters, was the reduced activity of enemy night intruders over Allied bases. By mid-1945 the Japanese were still a presence, but in nowhere near the numbers that demanded a regular night-alert flight to be maintained.

The war had virtually ended before any P-38Ms could be supplied to units in the Pacific, but the Night Lightning did enjoy a brief period of service in that theatre. Several examples, issued only to the 491st NFS, flew patrols in the last weeks of the war, but no contact with enemy aircraft was reported.

Further flights took place during the first period of peace after the Japanese surrender, and it was a measure of the success of the P-38 day fighters that the bases used by the black-painted Lightnings were located in Japan.

Developments

Although the P-38M was the last variant of the P-38 to be built in quantity, there were earlier design projections of the basic twin-boom layout that might have made formidable combat aircraft. These were the two 'big brothers' of the P-38, the XP-58 and XP-49. To back-track a little on how a larger Lightning was conceived, it is necessary to return to Ben Kelsey's career in the 1930s with the USAAC Fighter Project Branch at Wright Field. Then a lieutenant, Kelsey had test-flown several multi-seat designs for a future 'heavy' fighter, a loosely-defined official requirement for what was alternatively known as an aerial destroyer or convoy fighter (escort fighter).

Kelsey had enough experience to convince himself that the concept had too many flaws to be successful. But when the dramatic Bell XFM-1 Airacuda appeared in 1937, Kelsey was duly impressed at such a radical approach. The Airacuda proved underpowered but was potentially heavily armed, with a pair of forward-firing 37mm cannon in two wing nacelles. The Bell concept was a bold attempt to meet the heavy fighter requirement.

When Lockheed made a bid with the multi-seat XFM-2 designed by one Kelly Johnson, Kelsey gave it his backing, though he remained unconvinced that a fighter really needed to have two or three seats.

The USAAC rejected the XFM-2, but Lockheed itself, then a tiny concern, had been the first manufacturer in the USA to secure a contract for aircraft for the RAF. Negotiations with the French government had also led to substantial orders, which prompted the US government to grant

Specification – XP-49 (Lockheed Model 522)	
Powerplant:	One Continental XIV-1430 (port) and one XIV-15 (starboard), providing 1,350hp (1,007kW) each for take-off. (Pratt & Whitney HX-2600 proposed for production aircraft.)
Weights:	Empty 15,410lb (6,990kg); gross 18,750lb (8,505kg).
Dimensions:	As for P-38, but length 40ft 1in (12.22m); height 9ft 10in (3.00m).
Performance:	Maximum speed 406mph (653km/h) at 15,000ft (4,570m); 361mph (581km/h) at 5,000ft (1,520m); time to climb to 20,000ft (6,000m) 8.7min; rate of climb 3,075ft/min (937m/min); range 679miles (1,093km).
Armament:	Two 20mm cannon, four 0.50in machine-guns (proposed).

The sole XP-38 was an attempt to fit a pressure cabin to the P-38F, only one aircraft being so modified. Engineering changes were considerable, and it would have been too disruptive to P-38 production to introduce the type. Lockheed

manufacturers *carte blanche* to supply the European powers with whatever they needed. Vital cash consequently flowed into the coffers of the manufacturers, many of whom were struggling in the face of very modest USAAC orders throughout the 1930s.

Having joined Lockheed in 1940, Kelly Johnson sat down with chief project engineer Jimmy Gerschler, chief engineer Hall Hibbard and managing director Robert Gross to design a Lockheed convoy fighter based broadly on the P-38 layout, but much more advanced. Designated XP-58, the new fighter was to be either a single- or two-seater powered by Continental engines. Much larger overall than the Lightning, it was to have a remotely-controlled armament system.

By the time the XP-58 had flown (on 6 June 1944), the USAAF had streamlined its requirements under the impetus of war, and it was soon realized that radical departures from convention would be costly, time-consuming and increasingly unnecessary. Lockheed was far from alone in proposing new ideas that ultimately proved impractical as far as quantity production went, but design exercises that may depart from the mainstream are an integral part of aviation progress and increased knowledge. Several US companies were able to build and fly prototypes that, at the very least, proved beyond doubt that they would not have filled a requirement during what turned out to be a very narrow timescale of less than six years.

Along with several advanced projects, Lockheed introduced a number of variations on the P-38 theme. Some extended the role of the aircraft without too many modifications, while others would have entailed a considerable degree of reworking. And by mid-1944 the company was planning the next generation of jet fighters, which would relegate the XP-58 and its ilk to historical footnotes.

Torpedo Lightning

Along with other manufacturers, Lockheed explored alternative roles for its successful aircraft designs; roles that would not require a radically altered configuration or disrupt established production lines. One aerial weapon that fired the imagination of air chiefs the world over before and during the Second World War was the torpedo. The difficulties of destroying or crippling enemy shipping and the high risk to the

Specification – XP-58 'Chain Lightning' (Lockheed Model 20-86-04)	
Powerplant:	One Allison V-3420-11 (port) and V-3420-13 (starboard), providing 2,600hp (1,940kW) for take-off and 3,000hp (2,240kW) at 25,000ft (7,600m).
Weights:	Empty 31,624lb (14,345kg); gross 39,192lb (17,777kg); maximum 43,020lb (19,514kg).
Dimensions:	Span 70ft 0in (21.34m); length 49ft 5in (14.95m); height 13ft 7in (4.14m); wing area 600sq ft (55.7sq m).
Performance:	Maximum speed 436mph (702km/h); cruising speed 274mph (441km/h); service ceiling 38,400ft (11,700m); range 2,250 miles (2,010km).
Armament:	Two 20mm cannon, eight 0.50in machine-guns, four 1,000lb bombs.

attacking aircraft in the early years of conflict brought about numerous proposals to improve the situation. One solution was to equip fighters with one or two such weapons, on the grounds that their high performance would make them into more effective anti-shipping strikers.

Lockheed adapted a single Model 322-60-19, AF221 (alias P-38F-13-LO 43-2035), to release a standard 22in dummy torpedo. Either one or two torpedoes could be carried, an oversize, 300 US gal (1,135ltr) drop-tank occupying the other pylon if a single 'tin fish' was fitted. This aircraft (incidentally, the only 'RAF version' to be fitted with turbosuperchargers) performed all the necessary flight tests with an offensive load unrivalled by any other type in its class. Several range-speed-fuel consumption sorties returned excellent figures, showing that the P-38 could have made a perfectly viable torpedo bomber. A final drop test was carried out at Muroc Dry Lake range on 8 December 1942, pilot Joe Towle staying at 3,000ft (900m) to allow for the torpedo failing to separate cleanly and striking the carrier aircraft. When the P-38's electrics failed to initiate release, Towle had to resort to the jettison handle to persuade the fish to fall away, but the trial was deemed a success. No combat use resulted, probably because the USAAF was perfectly satisfied that bombs were reliable enough anti-shipping weapons. They also had flexibility in that, in the event of a P-38 pilot failing to find a ship, the bombs, unlike a torpedo, could be used against other targets. Another factor preventing any P-38 from ever being operationally rigged to carry torpedoes might have been the notorious unreliability of the weapon in early-war US naval operations.

Ski Version

Another international fascination during the war was with the ski-equipped fighter, designed or converted to enable it to operate when conventional runways were covered in enough ice and snow to prohibit movements by conventional wheeled

Another experimental Lightning had a raised tail fitted, to clear the wake during water take-offs of a proposed floatplane version. Only one P-38F was converted.
P. Jarrett

aircraft; in Alaska, for example. Alternatively, there was the brighter prospect of continuing operations using makeshift runways on frozen stretches of water if specially-adapted aircraft were used. Several countries advanced similar ideas, Lockheed's proposal centring on the P-38F/G, which had three retractable skis manufactured by Federal attached to the main undercarriage legs in place of wheels, and which remained horizontal when folded. This allowed the skis to lie flush with the gear doors, creating as little drag as possible.

The converted P-38 was hardly damaged in a crash at Patterson Field on 15 January 1944, and it is understood that little further work was done because the need had all but passed. However, a P-38J was also fitted with skis; and Finland and Russia were among the combatant powers that did successfully adapt aircraft in this way rather then the US.

Seaplane Version

One of the most interesting aspects of World War Two-era aviation resulted from yet another international fascination, this time with the fighter floatplane. Dominated in terms of actual operational examples by the Japanese, this design philosophy was pursued experimentally by all of the fighting powers. Lockheed proposed a floatplane version of the P-38 that might have been a very potent aircraft had the USA been obliged, like the Japanese, to operate from water bases hundreds of miles from home. But that was not the principal reason behind the waterborne P-38. The Allied emphasis on floatplanes resulted from the need to ferry fighters over considerable distances. If they could temporarily be fitted with floats, landplanes could use relatively safe ocean waypoints to refuel, reverting to their conventional wheeled undercarriage upon arrival at their ultimate destination.

Long-range ferrying was certainly the reason behind the Lockheed P-38E Seaplane, which was to have featured moderately upswept tail booms to give adequate clearance of the spray during water take-offs. With its fully-operable land undercarriage retained (in the retracted position) ready for use once the floats had been removed, the Lightning Seaplane had an estimated range of no less than 5,000 miles (8,000km).

As a first step towards proving the floatplane's viability, P-38E c/n 5204 was modified to test the upswept tailplane. The

booms were lengthened by some 24in (61cm), and the fins had deeper fairings compared to those of a standard P-38. This machine was rolled out on 2 December 1942 and test-flown in this form before a second, more pronounced 'swoop tail' was fitted. Upswept by 33in (84cm) from directly aft of the Prestone coolers, and faired along the spine and into the lower fin area, the new tail was noticeably different from that of the standard Lightning. Flight data provided by '504 gave valuable results, the programme including dive testing to explore the compressibility problem further. The effect was reportedly no worse with the upswept tailplane, and it seems that, had production aircraft been fitted with it, floats could have been safely used for ferrying.

However, the US advance across the Pacific with a massive carrier force, and the rapid securing of island air bases, rendered the widespread use of floatplanes unnecessary. Along with other promising fighter floatplane designs such as the Grumman F4F Wildcat, Supermarine Spitfire and Hawker Hurricane, the floatplane Lightning idea was never pursued. Yet a floatplane was not the only maritime association considered for the P-38.

Testing of this unique Lightning continued, even after the floatplane concept had been shelved, the aircraft being flown most extensively as the first 'Piggy-back' P-38. This was a much more viable concept, requiring little more in the way of engineering changes than removing the radio sets and installing a seat. Consequently, Lightings with space for a passenger behind the pilot appeared in most war theatres. Adaptations were carried out on examples of most P-38 production variants, including several 'war-weary' airframes rebuilt by ground crews from cannibalized wrecks. In these, a second seat was almost de rigueur.

Shipboard Fighter?

It may seem ironic to recall the US Navy's reluctance to be associated with an aircraft that had been declared to be too large for wartime carriers when, at the end of hostilities, the Service introduced the Grumman F7F Tigercat, which was comparable with the P-38 in overall dimensions. Size, however, was not the navy's major problem with the P-38 and other aircraft powered by liquid-cooled engines. Air-cooled radials had long been favoured because of their proven ability better to withstand the

rigours of carrier operation, not to mention battle damage. Coolant loss, which could jeopardize both pilot and aircraft, posed a risk with engines such as the Allison V-1710 that the admirals were not prepared to take. Lockheed understood this, and put forward a 'paper' proposal to fit the P-38 with radial engines. Wing-folding provision outboard of the nacelles was incorporated in the projected design, as was an arrester hook, though the location of the latter appears not to have been finalized. Such a version of the P-38 might have been an impressive low-altitude performer, as it would have been by unhampered by turbochargers. Nothing came of the idea.

Assault Fighter

Another variation on the Lightning theme was an 'assault fighter' version. It may come as no surprise that this was a sub-type armed with a 75mm cannon, a weapon that seemed somehow to obsess (or haunt) the US industry for several years. There was, however, a genuine official worry that the US Army never possessed a purpose-built ground-attack aircraft that could also be deployed as a useful 'tank buster'.

A P-38G formed the basis of a preliminary study by Wright Field engineers into a version armed with a twenty-round T-9 75mm cannon (similar to that developed for the XP-58) and a pair of 0.50in machine-guns with 300rpg for ranging purposes. The study envisaged a P-38 with a short, steeply-raked nose section, with the cannon barrel blast tube running under the pilot's seat. A second seat was to be located behind the pilot for a cannoneer/loader, the elongated central nacelle also accommodating the cannon ammunition. In view of the bulk of the cannon breech, the P-38's nosewheel layout would have been revised, the unit being made to turn through 45 degrees to lie flat in its bay.

These plans for an 'attack Lightning' were apparently drawn up totally independently of Lockheed. Kelly Johnson knew nothing about it, and after the war was amazed to learn that such an idea was ever proposed. This seems to confirm that the project did indeed originate outside what Lockheed called its 'Imagineeering' department.

Had such an aircraft been built, it would probably have drawn more on the much modified P-38E Swordfish than on a standard airframe, which Johnson believed was

ABOVE: Hailed at the time as the only two-seat Lightning, the so-called Swordfish was an extensively remodelled P-38F for aerodynamic research. IWM

RIGHT: An internal modification that was quite practical in operation, the 'Piggy-Back' Lightning was in effect the forerunner of the P-38M, with a second seat behind the pilot in place of the radios. P. Jarrett

ABOVE: **Big brother. With the P-38 layout proven, Lockheed wondered what a really beefed-up Lightning might do with more power and advanced systems such as fire control for remotely operated turrets. Only two examples of the XP-58 were completed.** Lockheed

LEFT: **Photographic Lightning derivatives were still serving as late as 1963. This cockpit view shows the essential controls and some of the observation windows in the lengthened nose.** IWM

BELOW: **Although not a direct product of Lockheed's 'imagineering' department, the F-5G lent itself to considerable nose lengthening without any adverse effects on its handling. This example was seen in England in December 1955.** *Aeroplane*

far too light even to get off the ground with a modified field gun in the nose.

Most US manufacturers seemingly had to find a way of getting a 75mm field gun to fly, and this was Lockheed's attempt. Progressing no further than a provisional study, it remains something of a mystery, but it is interesting to speculate on how useful it might have been to the Army. The fact that such a warplane was proven by events to be unnecessary, and that standard fighter-bombers were more than capable in the ground-attack role, was one of the vagaries of war.

When the war ended, the career of the P-38 was as good as over. Innovative and highly distinctive, the Lightning had served long and well, but a new era was dawning for which no post-war developments were indicated. The P-38 was strictly of its era, with no life extension much beyond mid-1945. That was the end of its time slot, one shared with dozens of other fine aircraft that had been designed to fight, and win, the greatest war in history.

RIGHT: **Aero Service Corp employees unload a camera from the nose hatch of an F-5G of quite modest proportions compared to some other configurations.** P. Jarrett

BELOW: **An example of the P-38M that survived the mass scrapping after the war, 45-3097 is correctly identified as a P-38L by the wording under the tailplane, which also marked it as belonging to the 'Warbirds of the World' organization.** P. Jarrett

CHAPTER TWELVE

Memories and Memorials

One of the victims of peace, the P-38 had no American Service life beyond the end of 1945, but several had appeared under other flags while the conflict lasted. Those P-38s that inadvertently 'changed sides' during the Second World War did so as a result of pilots straying into the airspace of neutral countries which bordered or were close to Axis territory. Such navigational errors usually resulted in the aircraft being impounded and the pilot being interned. As detailed below, Germany, Italy and Portugal obtained first-hand experience of early P-38 models during the war.

At home and with the USA at peace, the P-38 was one of many warplanes that had to be 'turned into ploughshares' and valuable scrap metal for recycling. Hundreds of Lightning fighters, PR aircraft and trainers, including the surviving P-322s, were scrapped in the USA, and a greater number were smashed up and bulldozed into huge burial pits on Pacific islands after they had been abandoned by air- and ground crews eager to get home. The USA was awash with newly-built but obsolescent warplanes, and there was no requirement to bring thousands more of them back from the war zones.

The Army was obliged to cull its huge inventory of obsolescent aircraft before the formation of a separate air force and re-equipment with jets. There was, of course, a lengthy 'hand-over' period before the new types completely ousted the weapons of the recent conflict, and several piston-engine

fighters remained in service with the United States Air Force (USAF). Others were quickly stricken, and one of the reasons why the P-38 left the inventory rapidly was its high unit cost. In 1945 terms the US Government was paying substantial sums for each of its first-line fighters in flyaway condition per production example, and the Lightning was the most expensive single-seat fighter by more than $50,000. The postwar economies soon saw all fighters except the 'cheap' P-51 being declared obsolete, so the P-38 was not alone in this regard.

Unit Costs of Fighters, 1945			
P-61B	$190,000*	P-40N	$60,552
P-38L	$134,284	P-51D	$50,985
P-47N	$83,000		
*Approximate figure			

Honouring McGuire

An event that recalled the halycon days of the P-38 took place at Paterson, New Jersey, in the USA on 8 May 1946, when a posthumous Medal of Honor was awarded to Maj Thomas B. McGuire, Jr. The citation specifically mentioned three air actions, those on 25 and 26 December 1944, during which the local ace was credited with seven 'Zekes', and the fatal engagement of 7 January 1945.

A handful of late-production examples of the Lightning remained in inventory to take the post-war designations F-38J and F-38L in June 1948. Very few have been identified in USAF markings, but among them is F-38L-5 44-53236/PA-236, which was at one time earmarked to serve as a memorial to Dick Bong but was allowed to fall into disrepair. In any event, the armed Lightning was a 'single-role' type, not readily adaptable to the civil market. Running

OPPOSITE PAGE:
Air racing was revived in the USA after the war, and Jack Hardwick was one of the men who purchased a P-38 for a turn around the pylons. His aircraft was an F-5G-6 named *Batty Betty*, with race number 34.
Aeroplane

RIGHT: Gary Levitz (*left*) and Vernon Thorp were among the intrepid band of racing pilots who indirectly helped the P-38 to survive into the 'warbird awareness' era. H. Levy

costs were also high compared with those of light bombers, which were far more practical in terms of crew/passenger seating and equipment stowage. Almost inevitably, virtually all remaining P-38s had been stricken from the USAF inventory by 1949, but the type's wartime pedigree as a PR aircraft brought about a new lease of life, albeit a limited one, which ensured that the distinctive outline of Lockheed's most famous design would not completely disappear from the aviation scene.

The main post-war activity for the P-38 was as a photographic and survey platform, and a range of nose configurations appeared, some of which were unique to aircraft of the post-war period, with no direct wartime F-4/F-5 equivalent. It proved to be aerodynamically possible to lengthen the P-38's nose section several feet beyond the original dimensions, and this proved a practical asset. Space made available ahead of the pilot was used for various types of equipment, including a scanner for terrain-following radar, an assortment of cameras or more mundane items, such as the pilot's luggage. Aerial survey was big business in the early post-war period, particularly to support the expansion of civil air routes, which required much more detailed maps of the continental USA than had hitherto been available. Other areas of the globe remained almost uncharted, and business interests such as oil companies needed to chart new fields for exploration.

Lockheed had a hand in extending the useful life of the P-38, the company using at least one aircraft in the XF-90 test programme. This was the old Swordfish conversion of the P-38E used for boundary-layer-control and special aerofoil-section tests. As it had already been given a second seat, this particular Lightning had merit as a research vehicle, and models of the XF-90 jet fighter were borne aloft and dropped from high altitude to provide information on the behaviour of swept-wing design and aerofoils. Such work kept the aircraft busy until 1953, when it was retired.

Lockheed also retained the last P-38L it completed under wartime contracts, and in 1954 Hycon Aerial Surveys purchased this and the Swordfish conversion and took them to Ontario, California, to be modified to suit the company's work. The P-38L was given a very long camera nose, and there was some interchange of equipment between the two aircraft, including a cockpit redesign for the P-38L. What emerged was a hybrid with the US civil registration NB91300 and a dramatically ugly configuration.

What Might Have Been

Despite the mass cull of its fighter P-38s at home, the USAF apparently retained a substantial number of fighter Lightnings in storage in Japan, mainly those that had served the squadrons of the occupation air force between 1945 and 1950. These included the 421st NFS's P-38Ms.

When the Korean War broke out in 1950, some thought was given to passing the stored F-38s on to the Republic of Korea Air Force (ROKAF), which was badly in need of a combat aircraft. This was not to be, and the Lightnings were reportedly scrapped just at that time, a move that might appear badly timed at the very least. A speculative reason for this was the anticipated difficulty of supporting a friendly power flying an obsolete type. Spares would soon have become impossible to come by, as Lockheed had long since terminated the P-38 programme. Getting an air force organized is challenge enough in peacetime, let alone in the middle of a war, and the ROKAF eventually re-equipped with the far more plentiful F-51.

Widespread sales of surplus US military aircraft to other countries also did not include the P-38 in very great numbers. Fewer still desired to operate Lightnings in their original armed fighter configuration, Honduras being one of the exceptions. 'Armed' was a relative term, as there was a general lack of surplus machine-guns amounting to an embargo, and post-war military P-38s invariably flew with fewer than the specified number. This relatively small overseas usage almost certainly reflects the problem of keeping an older aircraft type maintained to the required standard

Keeping his P-38L in more or less stock configuration, Gary Levitz flew it with race number 38.
H. Levy

140

Just as the P-38 was on the verge of extinction the Confederate Air Force (CAF) of Texas made people realize that historic aircraft needed preserving. Lefty Gardner entered the CAF P-38L, in the original 'rebel' colour scheme, in the 1970 Reno races, and is seen rounding pylon 8.
Aeroplane

once production lines had closed and the number of flying examples in the USA had dwindled. This situation was far from unique to the P-38, but the lack of weapons must have seemed strange to governments who thought they were purchasing military aircraft.

In common with the P-47, which was also limited in US military and civilian markets, mainly owing to high operating costs, the process of extinction was swift and so nearly complete for the P-38 that, by the time museums and preservation groups wanted a representative Lightning, their choice was severely limited. Static examples to display were rare enough, let alone aircraft that were fit to fly.

In common with other US ex-military aircraft, the civilian market was the main source of museum and warbird P-38s, particularly examples that could be refurbished and eventually displayed at flying events. Almost without exception, all the flyable Lightnings eventually seen at air shows in the USA and Europe were returned to military configuration, which usually involved some degree of nasal surgery. Most airworthy airframes had been modified to PR configuration and operated by civilian survey concerns.

Warbird owners soon cottoned on to the fact that people wanted to see P-38 fighters in authentic wartime colours, and the F-5 noses began to sprout guns. This example was seen at Oshkosh in 1977. *Aeroplane*

RIGHT: As wartime nose art was usually applied to the port side of an aircraft, 44-53095 sported the well-known German slang term for the P-38. H. Levy

BELOW: An Abbotsford show entry in 1972 was Larry Blumer's P-38L, N74883, partly repainted as his wartime mount in the 367th FG. *Aeroplane*

BOTTOM: On the port side, Blumer's aircraft carried the elaborate artwork, name and scoreboard that once graced his personal P-38J-25. Purchase of an ex-Honduran Lightning gave Blumer a rare chance to relive old glories in the most realistic way. *Aeroplane*

Export Lightnings

A total of eleven foreign nations had a wartime/post-war association with the P-38, and details of their service follows, including extended French usage of the PR versions procured under Lend-Lease. To keep things tidy, those nations whose association with the Lightning was very brief or merely accidental are included below.

Australia

Although it operated three loaned USAAF F-4s in 1942, the RAAF did not acquire any Lightnings for its own use, despite the Australians finding the aircraft extremely useful at a difficult period of the war. (*See* earlier.)

China

A recipient of 1,249 US aircraft under wartime Lend-Lease agreements, Nationalist China took delivery of multiple hundreds of USAAF fighters before V-J Day, but the number of P-38s appears to have been very low, at only fifteen P-38Js and Ls, according to one source. Another states that Project *Bird* was a high-priority programme to get the new late-war Lightning models into Chinese hands as soon as possible, but it appears that this might have been revised, perhaps in the light of the low number of trained Chinese pilots available to fly them.

Contemporary photographs show P-38Js in Nationalist Chinese markings, though it is understood that few fighters were actually delivered. The Chinese also had access to over 1,000 aircraft of the Fourteenth Air Force when the US forces left the country in 1945, and additional P-38s would certainly have been available. However, PR Lightnings appear to have been the most numerous in the Nationalist Chinese Air Force (NCAF), these being operated in the immediate post-war period.

Some pilot conversion training was undertaken by the USAAF during hostilities, and the Chinese evidently received enough F-5Es and Gs (fifteen is the figure given in various references) to equip the 12th Tactical Reconnaissance Squadron, which operated from several bases including Nanking, Peiping and Shanghai in 1945–46. These aircraft were flown in both USAAF camouflage colours and unpainted finish.

The Chinese Nationalists had limited time before the march of communism made them leave the mainland and occupy the island of Formosa (Taiwan) from January 1950. Whether any P-38s made the crossing to form part of the 'new' NCAF in exile is unconfirmed, as indeed is the likelihood or otherwise of any Lightnings left behind on the mainland being absorbed into the Chinese People's Armed Forces Air Force.

Costa Rica

An air arm that was hardly worthy of the name, the Costa Rican Military Air Force acquired an F-5G, s/n GCR-01, in November 1948. Two were actually delivered out of a total of five authorized by the US State Department, but only the PR aircraft survived for long. The other machine, P-38L GCR-02, crashed in Texas before being flown to Costa Rica, on 26 December 1948. The F-5G was reportedly highly prized but infrequently flown before being sold to Honduras to become FAH 504 after the 'air force' was disbanded in December 1948.

Cuba

Cuba received six P-38L-5s in August 1947, these being 44-27145, 44-27258, 44-53082, 44-53100, 44-53010 and 44-53012. They were not Cuban owned, but were operated by what became known as the Caribbean Legion or Cayo Confites, after the island lying off Cuba upon which the legion had its main air base. Aircraft were 'loaned' to neighbouring nations in times of crisis and usually reverted to their original operator once the crisis had passed.

Since the 1930s various military operations in Central America had spawned the creation of several covert air arms that operated aircraft 'owned' by different countries in the region. The idea of loaning aircraft to friendly nations was that the donor remained politically independent of the combatants. In fact that was rarely the case, as factions tended to favour one or other of the warring sides. The idea did not meet with a great deal of approval or military success, but several Latin American aircraft took on new, albeit temporary, identities for the duration of their clandestine service. In the case of the P-38s they were flown by mercenary pilots and numbered 121 to 126 in Cuban service.

Owners of P-38s sometimes pick colour schemes that originally applied to a different model. Nearly all current P-38s are late models, but the name *Porky II* belonged on a P-38H (*see* page 45).
Aeroplane

An excellent view of a P-38L with traces of M series nightfighter conversion work that found its way to Dominica in 1947 and was recorded at Ciudad Trujillo Air Base. Note the Boeing Stearman in the background. P. Jarrett

Dominica

The *Campania de Aviacion* air arm of this tiny Latin American republic acquired its first relatively modern combat aircraft in the form of a single P-38L, which arrived at Santiago on 30 March 1947. Further deliveries are in some doubt regarding the sub-variants, particularly the four F-5s that appear in the accompanying list. All four apparently arrived that same March, most without the necessary export licences. Two more, identified as F-5Gs, arrived from Puerto Rico in August 1947.

The infant air arm had considerable difficulty in maintaining its P-38/F-5 fleet, the general lack of spares being only one of the problems. None of the Lightnings was armed, and it proved surprisingly difficult for the Dominicans to acquire even 0.30in machine-guns, much less the desired 0.50s to arm the Lightnings. In addition Gen Trujillo's agent, George C. Stamnets was the only individual qualified on type in the country. With inexperienced pilots having to come to grips with the P-38, the almost inevitable crashes followed, one occurring on 22 July at Andrews Field, California, when an aircraft's undercarriage collapsed on landing. This was one of two aircraft that had by then acquired a pair of 0.30in machine-guns. This P-38 (44-53167), believed to have been one of the first to arrive in Dominica, was subjected to a two-month repair, but a second crash on 28 July resulted in it being written-off.

As with most air arms, the *raison d'être* of Dominica's Lockheed fighters was national defence, which made any difficulties with the Lightnings that much more problematical, not to say embarrassing. Nine pilots were hired in the USA about the time that the country renamed its air force *Cuerpo de Aviacion Militar Dominica* (CAMD), on 5

February 1948. Attrition continued to take its toll of the P-38/F-5s, another being written off on 21 July 1948. Yet another was sold to Nicaragua at the request of Gen Somoza, leaving eight, only two of which were airworthy. A further setback occurred on 2 August 1948 when one of the US pilots out on a coastal patrol became lost and landed in neighbouring Haiti. This may have been the P-38L converted to a P-38M nightfighter but without radar fittings, a seemingly modified rear cockpit hood over the radar operator's position and predominently black finish, though most if not all of Dominica's Lightnings were reported to have been painted black in an attempt to mask their 'illegal' status.

Eight Lightnings were still included on the CAMD inventory on 10 January 1949. Three were described as airworthy (two being armed) and five were 'beyond repair'. That October the flyable trio was moved out to an isolated airfield, ostensibly to prepare two of them for sale to Nicaragua. The third machine was to be cannibalized as a source

of spares. In the event the Nicaraguan sale did not take place and Dominica remained one of the world's last P-38 users until late October 1950, when the aircraft were cut up and dumped. By that time the Lightnings had acquired national insignia and either two- or three-digit identification codes.

Dominica's Lightnings	
P-38L-5 44-53167	CAMD 501
P-38L-5 44-27200/N66808)	502
P-38L-5 44-53100	503
P-38L-5 44-5303	504
P-38L-5 44-27085	505
P-38L-5 43-51337	506
F-5G (?)	507
F-5G (?)	508
F-5G (?)	509
F-5G (?)	510

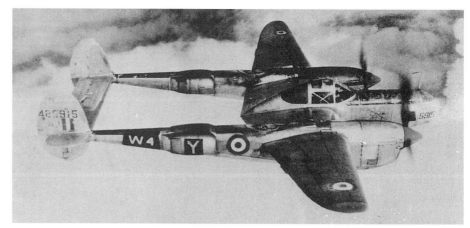

Although the French relinquished aircraft code letters for a time after the war, this F-5G of GR I/33 was probably in service after hostilities ceased. A. Pelletier

France

As related earlier, the F-5 remained a useful PR aircraft in the revived Armée de l'Air as it recovered from wartime chaos. Very many foreign aircraft types were pressed into service as the air force sought to rationalize its inventory. The PR Lightnings of GR I/33 Belfort at least retained continuity, in that the wartime unit continued to fly variants of the F-5 to carry out aerial survey work, primarily to prepare new maps of French West Africa (now Senegal and the Mali States) during 1946–47. Despite these lengthy flights over desert regions there were apparently few accidents. With wartime attrition having drastically reduced the number of earlier model F-5s, it appears that the A and G versions predominated in French service after the war, unit strength being a nominal sixteen aircraft. Becoming part of France's commitment to NATO, GR I/33 returned to Europe and was based at Cognac in France in August 1952, shortly before the unit was re-equipped with the Republic F-84G Thunderjet. Although GR I/33 was the only French PR unit up to that time, some F-5s were reported to have been on the strength of GR 3/33 for training purposes during the 1950s.

Germany

The Luftwaffe maintained a stable of fly-able Allied aircraft, the so-called *Beute-Zirkus Rosarius*, for evaluation by German test pilots and aircrew, similar in purpose to the RAF's Enemy Aircraft Flight. Among the US fighters was F-5E 44-23725, acquired via Germany's Italian allies. The Lightning was, rather unusually, 'delivered' undamaged to Milan-Linate airfield in Italy on 13 October 1944. The pilot, 2nd Lt Martin J. Monti, was an American of Italian descent who apparently had become bored with waiting for a posting from a replacement pilot pool in Karachi, India. Hitching a ride to Foggia and then Pomigliano, he attempted to join the 82nd FG, without success.

Monti then attached himself to the 354th Air Service Sqn and managed to talk his way into getting clearance to air-test the new F-5E. He duly took off and eventually landed at Linate, where he was taken prisoner. The Germans lost no time in repainting his PR Lightning in the high-visibility yellow undersides favoured by the 'Rosarius circus' and adding the unit code T9 and the identity letters MK. The aircraft ended

up at Schwangau in Germany, where it was 'liberated' by US troops in May 1945. Monti was court-martialled for desertion and 'wrongful misappropriation of a P-38 aircraft', and sentenced to be dismissed from the Service and serve 15 years behind bars.

Honduras

One of three countries in South/Central America to acquire fully combat-worthy Lightning fighters post-war, Honduras took delivery of seven P-38Ls in 1947/48 under the Mutual Defence Aid Programme. These included:

P-38L/FAH 500
P-38L/FAH 501
P-38L/FAH 502

P-38L-5-LO 44-53097/FAH 503/N9011R
P-38L-5-LO 44-26961/FAH 504/N74883
(*See* Costa Rica – F-5G)
P-38L-5-LO 44-53232/FAH 505/
P-38L-5-LO 44-53095/FAH 506/N9005R

These were ostensibly fully-armed combat aircraft, though the actual number of available guns was less than the seven 20mm cannon and twenty-eight 0.50in machine guns this number of aircraft would have normally been equipped with. The Hondurans instead managed to acquire a small number of 0.30in guns to give their Lightnings some teeth.

The USA was reluctant to supply P-38s to foreign customers, as the spares situation for an aircraft stricken from inventory was quite poor by the late 1940s. This

TOP: Out to grass but about to be snapped up by collections (including the USAF Museum) and collectors, the ex-Honduran P-38Ls found good homes. Number 504 sports an original squadron badge. Author

ABOVE: Back in the USA, Honduran Lightning No 506 had the transitional US registration N9005R crudely painted on its port boom. P. Jarrett

appears not to have worried the Hondurans, who successfully operated their P-38s from the country's main air base at Tocontin near the capital, Tegucigalpa. A good standard of maintenance was achieved, and it is believed that a number of 0.50in machine-guns were subsequently acquired to make good the armament deficiency. At some point FAH 504 was converted for PR duties and fitted with an F-5G type camera nose.

The Lightning remained in service long enough to became part of the new *Fuerza*

persuade the incumbent president, Julio Lozano Diaz, to resign.

More action for the Honduran P-38s followed when, on 21 February 1957, Honduras annexed the area known as the Mosquito Coast. Nicaragua, which had claimed the territory, lodged a vehement protest and prepared to seize back the disputed area, by force if necessary. As a prelude the village of Morocan was captured by the Nicaraguan National Guard in mid-April. To recapture it the Honduran Army launched an operation on 1 May, five P-38s

Seeking replacements for the ageing P-38s and P-63s, Honduras decided to acquire Vought F4U Corsairs. Broker Robert Bean agreed to supply the Corsairs in exchange for four P-38s, two P-63s and a Lockheed 10A. The deal was concluded in 1960, when Bean took delivery of two Lightnings on 2 February and one on 31 March, the last example arriving on 11 December 1961.

Subsequently P-38L 44-53232 (FAH 505) was acquired by the USAF Museum at Dayton, Ohio, and placed on public display.

Italy's P-38/F-5 fleet gave valuable service during the early post-war years when NATO faced an uncertain threat. This view shows some of these aircraft at the end of their Service lives. Italian Air Force

Aerea Hondurena (Honduran Air Force), formed in 1954. For the first time the national air arm was commanded by a Honduran national, *Teniente Corinel* (Lieutenant Colonel) Herman Acosta Mejia, but he was killed the following year when his P-38 crashed in the suburbs of the capital.

The surviving Lightnings remained as one of the nation's two primary fighter types, along with the Bell P-63 Kingcobra, and both took part in the country's 135th revolution since it gained independence, on 20 October 1956. The air force mounted a show of strength over Tegucigalpa to

and P-63s strafing and bombing Nicaraguan troops. Return ground fire damaged two aircraft (type unknown), which were forced to return to Tocontin.

Nicaraguan forces counterattacked on 2 May and retook Morocan on the 3rd. The Hondurans retaliated by attacking the disputed village (and Laymon) on the 4th, but by then the taste for an all-out conflict between the two countries had diminished, and a ceasefire was agreed on 5 May. The outcome of the short war was that the Mosquito Coast was restored to Honduran control.

As related above, a Costa Rican F-5G also joined the Honduran inventory, in early 1949.

Italy

Italy acquired an undamaged P-38G (s/n unknown) on 12 June 1943, when its American pilot landed in error at Cagliari-Capoterra Airfield, which was then in Italian hands. The aircraft had probably been on a ferry flight between Gibraltar and Malta, but owing to a 30-degree error in the P-38's compass the pilot flew over

Sicily and then Sardinia until, low on fuel, he had no choice but to land at the nearest airfield.

The Lightning was flown the following day by test pilot Colonello Angelo Tondi and demonstrated to the intrigued pilots of the 51 Stormo, based nearby. Italian national insignia was applied to the Lightning and Tondi sought permission to fly a combat mission to see if he could fool the USAAF heavy bomber crews and get close enough to shoot one down. This was duly sanctioned, and on 11 August the test was flown, Tondi indeed penetrating a fifteen-strong element of heavies en route to Rome and shooting one down over Torvajanica. Sources differ as to the type of bomber involved, the Italians claiming a B-24 Liberator but the Germans logging the kill as a B-17. The American crew were rescued by a PBY the following day.

After it was repainted in Regia Aeronautica colours the P-38 was flown to Guidonia, the Italian aircraft test establishment, for further evaluation. Tondi tried further 'deception interceptions' of Allied bombers, but without success. The Italians found some difficulty in maintaining the P-38, particularly as their low-grade fuel gradually ruined its Allison engines.

Post-war, after being on the receiving end of more USAAF P-38 combat sorties as an erstwhile enemy than they probably cared to recall, Italian pilots began flying a mix of P-38L fighters and F-5G PR versions from the spring of 1946. The previous April 100 dismantled ex-USAAF aircraft located at Capodichino were the subject of an agreement between the Allies and the AMI (*Aeronautica Militare Italiana* – Italian Air Force) under which IMM (Aerfer) would rebuild them at that location for use by the air force, the *Aeronautica Militare*. Lightnings and Mustangs were both acquired by Italy, which by then was running down its inventory of wartime vintage P-39 Airacobras. A high proportion of these P-38Js and Ls were PR conversions, including F-5E, G and H models. Seven airframes were not rebuilt but were reserved for use as spares, the remaining ninety-three being issued initially to the 3rd Stormo at Lecce and Bari and the Scuola (school) Lecce. Units operated a mix of fighter and PR Lightnings (of which there were at least twenty), and in time the 4th Stormo, 9th Stormo, 10th Grupo and 213th Grupo received examples.

Six Lightnings (MM4191–MM4196) were modified as dual-control trainers, with a separate cockpit with duplicated flight controls positioned forward of the standard cockpit in a lengthened nose. In this form these unique trainers, which served with the SCOT (*Scuoloa Caccia Ogni Tempo* – All-Weather Fighter School) at Lecce and Foggia, were identified as the P-38DC (Dual Control). It seems that the Italians continued to use the old 'P for Pursuit' designator rather than 'F for Fighter' introduced by the USAF in 1947.

Italian P-38s made their operational debut on 9 September 1948, a single F-5 taking photographs of objectives in the Balkans. These sorties continued but were not made public for reasons that remain obscure. On 27 October F-5E MM4175 crashed in Yugoslavia and was salvaged, almost certainly ending up in the Belgrade museum, as noted later.

Italian P-38s were quite plain in their natural-metal finish, each one being given a Matricola Militaire (MM) number, national insignia and necessary airframe stencilling. Ninety P-38s received the serials MM4144–MM4233.

The P-38 served the Italians until 1956, by which time a general lack of spares and increasing maintenance demands were taking their toll. Airframes were also approaching the ends of their lives, old age forcing an increasing number to remain on the ground, though the inventory had been depleted by several accidents. The last fourteen examples were scrapped following an official order issued on 17 July 1956.

Nicaragua

It was somewhat ironic that Nicaragua obtained P-38s some time before the country was engaged in a conflict with Honduras, which flew Lightnings in combat on the 'other side'. Two P-38Ls were acquired

The sole ex-1st FG P-38F-1 impounded by Portugal in 1942 was repainted in national markings and apparently highly prized. There would have been two Lightnings in the country's inventory had Jack Ilfrey not departed quickly after refuelling. A. Pelletier

illegally for service with the *Fuerza Aerea de la Guardia Nacional* in March 1949. The first of these was either L-1 44-24484/NL67745 or 44-53095, the latter a P-38L-5 that had been converted to P-38M standard (without radar or cockpit instrumentation) and came direct from the USA. A second P-38L-5, otherwise unidentified, arrived in the country via Mexico. Serialled G.N 50 and G.N 51, both Lightnings were armed with a pair of 0.50in machine-guns. At that time these were the only such weapons in all of Central America.

11 Portugal

As a neutral country during the Second World War, Portugal acquired several first-line US combat aircraft when pilots inadvertently violated her borders and had their aircraft impounded. The only P-38F-1 to wear the Portuguese Cross of Christ national insignia was an ex-1st FG aircraft that crossed into neutral territory in November 1942. (There would have been two, as related earlier.) It was subsequently given the code letters OK-T to denote the *Esquadrilha OK* at Base Aerea 2, Ota. Although well maintained by Portuguese air force personnel, the Lightning was apparently rarely flown. There was, however, apparent pride in the war prize, as it was rolled out to impress visiting generals and other dignitaries.

Museum Lightnings

Surviving P-38 airframes are far from numerous today, though a handful are maintained in flying condition. As is usual with the rarer wartime aircraft, the survivors are more likely to be seen in museums as highly-prized static exhibits. The saga of the Richard I. Bong memorial aircraft highlights the difficulties of finding a complete P-38. By the time this long-delayed tribute to America's 'Ace of Aces' was erected, in the form of a concrete plinth, the aircraft it had been built to support was almost extinct. However, P-38L-5 44-53236 was acquired in a virtually gutted state and mounted in Bong's home town, Poplar, Wisconsin. Painted as one of the ace's personal Lightnings, P-38J-15 42-103993, and named *Marge* after his wartime fiancé and later wife, the memorial is impressive, though the triple-pylon plinth upon which it is mounted appears quite utilitarian.

This, one of the world's few P-38s to be mounted in a flying attitude, was initially given 'USAF' titlings and red-barred national insignia. Before the aircraft was mounted, many useful items, such as engines, turbochargers and cockpit controls, were removed, presumably to lighten it. The memorial P-38 then suffered damage from a lightning strike, which, according to witnesses, 'burned out' the cockpit area and wrinkled the starboard wing. It was repaired and has since acquired correct wartime markings.

McGuire AFB in New Jersey conducted an even longer search for a P-38 to honour America's second-highest-scoring Lightning pilot. It was 4 May 1981 before a small aircraft in Second World War olive drab and grey paint was seen in the traffic pattern normally occupied by Lockheed C-141 StarLifters and C-130 Hercules. Piloted by Dave Tallichet, this P-38L/F-5G, 44-53015, was acquired from the Air Force Museum to be donated as a memorial to Tommy McGuire.

A restoration team from the 438th Military Airlift Wing undertook the considerable task of stripping off the camouflage and markings representing 44-53015/KI-W of the 20th FG and repainting the aircraft as *Pudgy* (V), McGuire's last regular mount in the 475th FG. As the P-38L was to be displayed outside, the refurbishing task included sealing all open ports. The decision to display the P-38 in the open caused some controversy at the time, but the finished aircraft looked magnificent. It was a fine tribute not only to a great pilot, but also to the diligent research by Tallichet and the painting skills of Don Spering. In addition, the gleaming natural metal finish P-38 was a clear testimonial to the dedicated work of Air Force men and women.

A fairly recent listing of surviving P-38 airframes puts the total at twenty-eight worldwide, the bulk of which are in the USA. The remainder are in Papua New Guinea, Australia and Alaska, the two latter countries having one each. Most of the extant Lightnings are later production models, thirteen having stemmed from F-5G conversions, though the P-38's passive PR nose, with camera ports rather than gun barrels, has not proved a popular choice for the modern warbird owner.

Glacier Girl

In 1992 came the exciting revelation that one of the six P-38Fs (plus two B-17s) that had been forced to put down in Greenland while en route to England as part of Operation *Bolero* in July 1942 had been in highly effective 'deep-freeze storage' ever since. Owing to the intervening years of hostile weather, what had been the surface in wartime was now 260ft (79m) down. An exploratory radar probe of the ice revealed P-38F-1-LO 41-7630 in a virtually complete state but about a mile from where it had originally crashed. The idea that the world's most authentic early-model P-38 could be brought to the surface was too tempting to ignore, and the Greenland Expedition Society, Roy Schofner and a recovery crew led by Bob Cardin set to work. After a careful, frustrating and expensive recovery operation the P-38 was raised from its icy grave back to the surface. It was found to be in remarkably good condition.

Having taken off from Bluie West 8, Greenland, in July 1942, the pilots of the icecap Lightnings had become lost owing to bad weather and German radio jamming, and opted to turn back despite their B-17 navigation escort. Several pilots found themselves too low on fuel to reach an airfield, including Lt Harry Smith, flying '7630, who was obliged to land his aircraft on the ice. Lowering the P-38's undercarriage proved to be a mistake, as the aircraft flipped over on its back. Smith radioed the following Lightnings and the B-17, all of which landed with their wheels up. Smith's machine was only superficially damaged, the propellers bearing the brunt of the impact. In common with all the other airmen who had crashed, Harry Smith was rescued unhurt.

When the recovered Lightning arrived safely back in the USA, its condition inspired warbird pilot Steve Hinton to undertake a restoration to airworthiness; a major task. It took more than ten years to achieve this goal, but on 26 October 2002 Hinton flew *Glacier Girl* for the first time. Now registered N5757, *Glacier Girl* is operated by Roy Schoffner and based at Middlesboro, Kentucky, where the restoration was carried out.

The Price

The grim downside of keeping vintage aircraft in flying trim has been the price paid in human terms. Putting aeroplanes that are three decades old, particularly single-seat fighters, back in the air is a task never undertaken lightly. The band of highly skilled modern pilots who take these warbirds aloft for the enjoyment of thousands around the world deserve the greatest of praise. They know that the aircraft preservation movement would be far poorer without their input, but sadly the toll of pilots lost has inevitably risen over the years as the number of flyable warbirds increases.

Among those lost in recent years, at the controls of a P-38 was Britain's 'Hoof' Proudfoot, an experienced and well-respected display pilot who crashed at Duxford, Cambridgeshire, on 14 July 1996. During the annual Flying Legends air show Proudfoot was flying P-38L *California Cutie*, belonging to The Fighter Collection. During a low pass he apparently entered the second of two aileron rolls at too low an altitude to recover. When the port wingtip touched the ground the aircraft ploughed in and exploded. Just over a year later renowned author and warbird display pilot Jeff Ethell lost his life when flying the recently restored P-38L N7973. Ethell took off from the airport at Tillamook, Oregon, on 6 June 1997 in company with a second P-38L (N2114L) to carry out a practice run for a P-38 pilot's convention scheduled a short time later. After a flight of some twenty-five minutes Ethell's silver-finished aircraft entered a flat spin from which it did not recover. According to the subsequent National Transportation Safety Board report the pilot, who lacked type familiarity, was unable to maintain minimum control speed after losing power on one engine due to fuel starvation.

The flying of vintage aircraft carries a considerable element of risk, despite the high standards of refurbishment and maintenance apparent in 2005. These increasingly rare warbirds occasionally succumb to other hazards without even getting off the ground. It was very unfortunate that the Musée de l'Air, having received P-38L-5/FG-5G 44-53247 from the Pima County Museum for display at Paris Le Bourget, lost the only known complete example of the Lightning in France. The aircraft was delivered from the USA on 26 May 1989, only to be consumed in a disastrous hangar fire in 1990.

New Guinea

Papua New Guinea has been a primary source for surviving examples of early P-38F and G models, plus (to date) a lone P-38H. However, the ravages of time, inaccessibility and a national policy of leaving wartime remains *in situ* have all contributed to the rediscovered airframes being in less-than-pristine condition, and in several more component parts than Lockheed intended. But salvage work has enabled these rare examples to form the bases for fully-authentic restorations, often by marrying components from a number of different airframes. It is to be hoped that these understandably long-term rebuild projects eventually reach fruition. Airframes that have to be recovered from long-abandoned airfields, open country and swamps provide the Papau New Guinea National Museum (PNGNM) at Port Moresby with an immense challenge, but the museum now has several early-model Lightnings

and plans eventually to place P-38F-5 42-12647 on permanent display. This aircraft has benefited from parts 'donated' by G-10 42-13084 and F-5A-10 42-13105, both recovered during the late 1970s.

In addition, the PNGNM has P-38H-5 42-66905, flown by ace Richard E. Smith of the 39th FS and named *Japanese Sandman* after a popular wartime tune, which was recovered from its wartime crash site in 1979. Papua New Guinea has proved a veritable treasure trove of wartime aircraft, though the government has clamped down in recent years to prevent wrecks being 'exported'. Now, it is hoped that the many rare examples of US and Japanese aircraft that still litter the territory, many of them unique, will ultimately find a place in the local museum.

Yugoslavia

The aviation museum in Belgrade has acquired P-38L-5 44-25786, though no Lightnings ever served with the country's air arm. The aircraft was last reported (in 1992) as being in storage in an incomplete state. As mentioned earlier, this might have been the Italian F-5E that came down in October 1948.

United States of America

The number of Lightnings to survive the post-war mass scrapping of surplus military aircraft was not very high, and, of the 'big three' US fighters of World War Two, the Lockheed twin became the rarest. This was partly due to high operating costs for civilian owners (a factor that also militated against the Thunderbolt), no large-scale peacetime military use (as there was with the P-51) and, to some extent, demanding handling qualities for pilots who lacked military P-38 flight time.

The Lightning made a brief appearance as an air racing entrant in the first post-war Bendix-sponsored cross-country event. Among the hopefuls on the flight line was one William P. Lear, Jr, a 17-year-old who had recently purchased an F-5G from the War Assets Administration for a thumping $1,250. Eager to race his new acquisition, NX56687, Lear was then the youngest pilot ever to compete in the Bendix. He finished 14th, which was no mean achievement for a racing 'rookie' up against the likes of Paul Mantz in a P-51.

The reborn Bendix-sponsored race from Van Nuys, California, to Cleveland, Ohio, lasted only four years, and although the P-38 was a desirable aircraft to use, it was unable to compete with the hotted-up single-engine fighters dominating the racing scene in the late 1940s.

Another event in which civilians could wring out a surplus Lightning was the Thompson Trophy pylon race. Both standard and modified examples of the P-38/F-5 were entered, but the dominance of the Mustangs and an increasing lack of spares led to the Lightning becoming less popular as a race mount, and its numbers declined during the1950s.

Ex-wartime Lockheed test pilot Tony LeVier picked up surplus P-38L-5 44-53087/NX21764, gave it a snappy overall red paint job after removing the turbochargers and tailplane tips, and went racing in the 1946 Thompson Trophy. Carrying race number three on his scarlet Lightning, complete with a white flash and his nickname, 'Fox of the Skyways', LeVier proved that he had not lost his touch by taking second place in the Cleveland event.

A high percentage of the flyable P-38s that did evade scrapping after the war had already been converted into PR aircraft. Those that survived long enough to acquire the type prefix FA-, allocated by the new USAF after 1947, thereafter passed on to the civilian market. Various companies were thus able to operate aircraft that had a good range and could be used for aerial survey work. It was occasionally surprising to see just how much the P-38/F-5 nose section could be extended to take cameras and instruments for the survey role, and examples could be seen in various parts of the world for decades after the war. It was indeed fortunate for warbird enthusiasts that several survived the rigours of civil flying to be (in most cases) converted back to P-38 fighter configuration.

Static museum aircraft (as opposed to flyable warbirds) in the USA include P-38J-10 42-67762, belonging to the Smithsonian National Air and Space Museum (NASM), Washington DC, which retains its stock military configuration, complete with armament, despite the ravages of the intervening years. This P-38 is currently stored at the NASM's Steven F. Udvar-Hazy Center at Dulles Airport. The curators decided to present the Lightning virtually as it was, complete with half a century of 'hangar rash'. It could well be the most original P-38 remaining, and they wanted to keep it that way.

P-38 Serial Numbers and Variants

AF Model	USAAF serial	Quantity	AF Model	USAAF serial	Quantity
XP-38	37-457	(1)		41-7539–7541	
YP-38	39-689–701	(13)		41-7544	
P-38	40-744–761			41-7548–7550	
	40-763–773	(29)		41-7552–7680	(148)
XP-38A	40-762	(1)	P-38F-5	42-12567–12666	(100)
P-38D	40-774–809	(36)	F-5A-1 (P-38F-5)	42-12667–12686	(20)
P-38E	41-1983–2097		P-38F-13	43-2035–2063	(29)
	41-2100–2110		P-38F-15	43-2064–2184	(121)
	41-2172		P-38G-1	42-12687–12766	(80)
	41-2219		F-5A-3 (P-38G-3)	42-12767–12786	(20)
	41-2221–2292	(210)	P-38G-3	43-12787–12798	(12)
F-4-1 (P-38E)	41-2098–2099		P-38G-5	43-12799–12866	(68)
	41-2121–2156		P-38G-10	43-12870–12966	(97)
	41-2158–2171		F-5A-10	43-12967–12986	(20)
	41-2173–2218		P-38G-10	43-12987–13066	(80)
	41-2220	(99)	F-5A-10 (P-38G-10)	43-13067–13126	(60)
F-5A-2 (P-38E)	41-2157	(1)	P-38G-10	43-13127–13266	(140)
P-322	(none) (RAF AE978–AF220)	(143)	F-5A-10	43-13267–13326	(60)
P-38F	41-2293–2321		P-38G-10	43-13327–13557	(231)
	41-2323–2358		P-38G-15	43-2185–2558	(374)
	41-2382–2386		P-38H-1	42-13559	
	41-2388–2392			42-66502–66726	(226)
	41-7486–7496		P-38H-5	42-66727–67101	(375)
	41-7498–7513		P-38J-1	42-12867–12869	
	41-7416–7524			42-13560–13566	(10)
	41-7526–7530		P-38J-5	42-67102–67311	(210)
	41-7532–7534		F-5B-1 (P-38J-5)	42-67312–67401	(90)
	41-7536–7538		P-38J-10	42-67402–68191	(790)
	41-7542–7543		F-5B-1 (P-38J-5)	42-68192–68301	(110)
	41-7545–7547		P-38J-15	42-103979–104428	
	41-7551	(228)		43-28248–29047	
F-4A-1 (P-38F)	41-2362–2381	(20)		44-23059–23208	(1,400)
P-38F-1	41-2322		P-38J-20	44-23209–23558	(350)
	41-2359–2361		P-38J-25	44-23559–23768	(210)
	41-2387		P-38K	41-1983 (conv. P-38E)	(1)
	41-7484–7485		P-38L-1	42-13558	
	41-7497			44-23769–25058	(1,291)
	41-7514–7515		P-38L-5	44-25059–27258	
	41-7525			44-53008–53327	(2,530)
	41-7535		P-38L-5-VN	43-50339–52225	(113)
F-4-1 (P-38E)			F-5A-1 (P-38F-5)		
F-5A-2 (P-38E)			F-5A-3 (P-38G-3)		
F-4A-1 (P-38F)			F-5A-10 (P-38G-10)		
			F-5B-1 (P-38J-5)		
			F-5B-1 (P-38J-5)		

TOTAL P-38 COMPLETED: 10,036

Note: Lockheed Burbank converted a total of 440 F-4/F-5s before Dallas continued conversion work to complete at least 828 aircraft, but the grand total probably ran to over 1,000 examples. These were the F-5C-1 (about 123 based on the P-38J airframe); the F-5E-2 (100 based on the P-38J-15) and the F-5E-3 (105 based on the P-38J-25). An unknown number of F-5E4s, F-5F-3s and F-5G-6s were converted from P-38L airframes.

P-38 Fighter Groups and Squadrons

Fifth Air Force

8th FG

35th FS (Black Panther)
36th FS (Flying Fiends)
80th FS (Headhunters)

35th FG

39th FS (Flying Cobras)
40th FS (The Red Devils)
41st FS

49th FG

7th FS (Screamin' Demons)
8th FS (Black Sheep)
9th FS (Flying Knights)

475th FG (Satan's Angels)

431st FS
432nd FS
433rd FS
6th NFS

Seventh Air Force

318th FG

19th FS
73rd FS (Bar Flies)
333rd FS (Coral Cobras)

Eighth Air Force

1st FG (to 11/42)
14th FG (to 11/42)
82nd FG (to 11/42)

20th FG

55th FS (KI)
77th FS (CL)
79th FS (MC)

55th FG

38th FS (CG)
338th FS (CL)
343rd FS (CY)

364th FG

383rd FS (N2)
384th FS (5Y)
385th FS (5E)

479th FG

434th FS (L2)
435th FS (J2)
436th FS (9B)

Ninth Air Force

367th FG (The Dynamite Gang)

392nd FS (H5)
393rd FS (8L)
394th FS (4N)

370th FG

401st FS (9D)
402nd FS (E6)
485th FS (7F)

474th FG

428th FS (7Y) (The Geyser Gang)
429th FS (F5) (The Retail Gang)
430th FS (K6) (The Backdoor Gang)

Tenth Air Force

33rd FG

58th FS
59th FS
60th FS
459th FS (Twin Dragons)

Eleventh Air Force

342nd Composite Group

33rd FS (Rattlesnakes)
50th FS

343rd FG

11th FS (P-38 1943–EoW)
18th FS (Blue Fox) (P-38 1943–EoW)
54th FS
344th FS (P-38 1944–EoW)

Twelfth/Fifteenth Air Forces

1st FG

27th FS (HV) (Black Falcons)
71st FS (LM)
94th FS (UN) (Hat in the Ring)

14th FG

37th FS (None/61-90)
48th FS (ES/1 -30)
49th FS (QU/31-60)

33rd FG

58th FS (Red Gorillas)
59th FS (Roaring Lions)
60th FS (Fighting Crows)

82nd FG

95th FS (A + a/c letter)
96th FS (B + a/c letter)
97th FS (C + a/c letter)

350th FG

345th FS (numerals)
346th FS (numerals
347th FS (numerals)

NB: Two P-38s per squadron only

Thirteenth Air Force

18th FG

12th FS (Dirty Dozen)
44th FS (Vampires)
70th FS

347th FG (Sun Busters)

67th FS (Game Cock)
68th FS (Lightning Lancers)
70th FS (White Knights)
339th FS (Sunsetters)

Fourteenth Air Force

51st FG

449th FS

EoW = end of war
NB: It was common practice for some P-38 squadrons to identify themselves by their regular radio callsigns when in combat theatres. Others used names based on their unit badge or nickname. In some cases Groups were only partly equipped with P-38s, as shown by the listing of one or two squadrons under the main heading.

Part of the last batch of Lightnings with the early engine cowlings, this H-5 has the red-outlined national insignia officially in use from 29 June to 17 September 1943. Lockheed

F-4/F-5 Photographic Reconnaissance
Units (solely or partly equipped)

Fifth Air Force

6th PRG

8th PRS (Numerical ID)
25th PRS (Numerical ID)
26th PRS (Numerical ID)
36th PRS (Numerical ID)

Seventh Air Force

28th PRS (Numerical ID)

Eighth Air Force

7th PRG (Numerical/colour ID)

13th PRS (Colour ID)
14th PRS (Colour ID)
22nd PRS (Colour ID)
27th PRS (Colour ID)

Ninth Air Force

10th PRG

30th PRS (I6)
31st PRS (8V)
33rd PRS (SW/2W)*
34th PRS (XX/S9)
155th PRS (O9)

67th TRG

12th PRS (ZM)
15th PRS (5M)
107th PRS (AX)
109th PRS (VX)

69th TRG

39th PRS (ETO from Jan 45)

Tenth Air Force

8th PRG

9th PRS (Numerical ID)
40th PRS (Numerical ID)

Eleventh Air Force

28th Composite Group

Twelfth Air Force

3rd PRG

5th PRS (Numerical ID)
12th PRS (Numerical ID)
15th PRS (Numerical ID)
23rd PRS (Numerical ID)

5th PRG

15th PRS (Numerical ID)
23rd PRS (Numerical ID
32nd PRS (Numerical ID)

GR II/33 'Belfont' French Air Force (W4)

Thirteenth Air Force

4th PRG

17th PRS (Numerical ID)
38th PRS (Numerical ID)

Fourteenth Air Force

21st PRS (Numerical ID)

Fifteenth Air Force

5th PRG

15th PRS (Numerical ID)
23rd PRS (Numerical ID)**
32nd PRS (Numerical ID)
37th PRS (Numerical ID)
154th WRS (Numerical ID)

Twentieth Air Force

41st PRS (no combat)

* Codes changed on transfer to the 363rd PRG, 30 Oct 44 with F-5?
** Post-war code introduced May 1945

NB: Some units operated a variety of other US PR aircraft, including the F-3 Havoc, F-6 Mustang, F-7 Liberator, F-8 Mosquito, F-9 Fortress, F-10 Mitchell and F-13 Superfortress as well as the British-built Mosquito and Spitfire. Relatively few flew only PR Lightnings.

Fates of RAF Contract Lightnings in the USA

Lightning I (AE978–AE999)

AE978 – surveyed, 20 Oct 1946

AE979 – scrapped, San Bernardino, CA, 13 Nov 1945

AE980 – scrapped, San Bernardino, 13 Nov 1945

AE981 – to CL-26 (Class 26)

AE982 – cr Bradley Field, CT 8 Apr 1942; pilot killed

AE983 – to March Field, CA, 26 May 1942

AE984 – to CL-26, 20 March 1942

AE985 – to CL-26, 10 Aug 1945

AE986 – to March Field, CA 30 June 1942

AE987 – c/landed Selfridge Field, MI; 12 Jan 1943; pilot safe

AE989 – cr into Puget Sound and sank, 22 March 1942; pilot killed

AE990 – to CL-26, Lincoln, NB, 25 Sept 1942

AE991 – to CL-26, Lincoln, NB, 11 Sept 1942

AE992 – condemned, Chanute, KA, 25 Nov 1942

AE993 – to CL-26, Lincoln, NB

AE994 – scrapped, Syracuse, NY, 23 Aug 1946

AE995 – surveyed, 7 Apr 1944

AE996 – to CL-26, Lincoln, NB, 22 Oct 1942

AE997 – surveyed, 7 Apr 1944

AE998 – surveyed, 8 March 1944

AE999 – wrecked nr Casa Grande, AZ, 10 Aug 1943

Lightning I AF100–AF220

AF100 – wrecked, Bradley Fld, CT, 22 March 1942; pilot safe

AF101 – scrapped, Cincinatti, OH, 12 April 1945

AF102 – scrapped, San Bernardino, CA, 28 Nov 1945

AF105 – condemned, 1 Jan 1946; to UK 25 March 1942

AF106 – condemned, 1 March 1946; to UK 25 March 1942

AF107 – surveyed, Williams Field, AZ

AF108 – (6 Dec 42) conv to P-38 for British use; to UK 25 March 1942

AF109 – (8 Oct 44) Chanute, KACL-26

AF110 – (5 Jan 44) surveyed, Williams Field, AZ

AF111 – (7 Apr 43) wrecked Williams Field, AZ, and surveyed, pilot cadet Robert G Stanley, fate unkn

AF112 – (6 Apr 42) cr Summerville; surveyed Windsor Locks, CT, 20 Aug 1942; 2nd Lt Raymond A. Keeney killed

AF113 – (8 Nov 43) surveyed, Williams Field, AZ

AF114 – (25 June 43) 981st ST Flying Grp; surveyed, Williams Field, AZ

AF115 – (8 Feb 42) CL-26 wrecked McClellan Field, CA, 18 March 1942; 2nd Lt Donald O. Starbuch safe

AF116 – (15 Jan 45) 65th Air Base Grp, Victoria, TX; 982nd Four-Engine Adv Training Sqn, Williams Field, AZ; 554th Air Base Gp, Memphis, TN; scrapped

AF117 – (13 Nov 45) 4th Air Force San Bernardino, CA; scrapped

AF118 – (15 June 45) 5th Flying GP, Love Field, TX; 981st Advanced Twin Engine Ftr GP, Williams Field; scrapped Syracuse, NY

AF119 – (31 Aug 42) 4th AF; North Isle, CA; CL-26

AF120 – (9 Mar 43) Love Field, TX; CL-26

AF121 – (15 June 45) Love Field Mod Centre, TX; scrapped

AF122 – (27 Oct 43) Williams Field, AZ; surveyed

AF123 – (29 June 45) Patterson, OH; scrapped

AF124 – (29 June 45) Patterson, OH; scrapped

AF125 – (26 Aug 43) Williams Field, AZ; wrecked and surveyed 29 Aug 1943

AF126 – (13 Nov 45); Newark, NJ, 928th Flying Sqn; scrapped

AF127 – (21 July 43) Willams Field, AZ, 981st Twin-Eng Adv Flying School; surveyed

AF128 – (13 Nov 45) 4th AF. San Berdardino, CA; scrapped

AF129 – (5 Jan 45) Williams Field, AZ, CL-26; surveyed, 26 June 1943

AF130 – (8 May 44) Williams Field, AZ; surveyed

AF131 – (15 June 43) Williams Field, AZ; CL-26

AF132 – (1 July 43) Williams Field, AZ; 5th Flying Group; surveyed

AF133 – (31 Dec 45) Kelly Field, TX; scrapped

AF134 – (31 Jan 46) Warner-Robins, GA; 981st Adv Fly Trg Sqn; scrapped

AF135 – (15 June 45) Warner-Robins, GA; 982nd AFTS; scrapped

AF136 – (10 May 43) Chandler Field, AZ; 535th Flyg Sqn; CL-26; wrecked 13 May 1943; Av Cad Herbert Brenner safe

AF137 – (13 Nov 45) 4th AF; San Bernardino, CA; scrapped

AF138 – (30 Nov 43) Williams Field, AZ surveyed

AF139 – (1 Aug 43) Casa Grande, AZ; wrecked in c/l and surveyed, 2 Aug 1943; Av Cad Russell W. Sly safe

AF140 – (16 Feb 43) Moore Field TX; CL-26; wrecked, 28 Apr 1943; Maj Fred E. Hild safe

AF141 – (7 May 43) Williams, Field, AZ; CL-26 wrecked 13 May 1943

AF142 – (13 May 43) Higley, AL; 981st FTS, Williams Field; AZ; 55th ABS; cr date unk but P/O Basil E. Park, RAF, safe

AF143 – (? June 45) Bolling Field, DC; 58th SETS; Syracuse, NY scrapped

AF144 – (? June 45) Syracuse, NY; scrap

AF145 – (15 Oct 43) Williams Field, AZ; 92nd FS, Craig Fld, AL; surveyed

AF146 – (31 Oct 43) 535th AFG; Williams Field, AZ; scrapped

AF147 – (2 July 46) 4th AF, Long Beach, CA; scrapped

AF148 – (9 Mar 43) Love Field, TX; CL-26; Love Field Mod Centre, Dallas, TX

AF149 – (9 May 49) Williams Field, AZ; surveyed

AF150 – (? Feb 45) Tinker Field, OK; scrapped

AF151 – (31 Oct 43) Williams Field, AZ; surveyed

AF152 – (7 Apr 44) Williams Field, AZ, 982nd AFG; surveyed

AF153 – (? May 45); Davis-Monathan, AZ; scrapped

AF154 – (9 Sept 43) Williams Field, AZ; surveyed

AF155 – (28 Nov 45) Austin, TX; scrapped

AF156 – (?) Williams Field, 982nd TEAFS; wrecked 3 Apr 43 Av Cad Benjamine G. Conrath killed

AF157 – (10 Oct 43) Williams Field, AZ; surveyed

AF158 – (10 Oct 43) Williams Field, AZ; 982nd FTS; surveyed

AF159 – (? June 45) Cincinatti, OH; scrapped

AF160 – (3 Aug 45) Will Rogers Field, OK; West Coast Flying Training; scrapped

AF161 – (19 Feb 44) Higley, AL; surveyed

AF162 – (19 Feb 44) Williams Field, AZ; 982nd AFTS; surveyed

AF163 – (6 July 43) Williams Field, AZ; 982nd AFTS; surveyed

AF164 – (13 Nov 45) 4th AF San Bernardino, CA; scrapped

AF165 – (9 Aug 43) Williams Field, AZ; 5th FG; surveyed

AF166 – (13 Mar 46) Brookley Field, AL; scrapped

AF167 – (13 Nov 45) San Bernardino, CA; scrapped

AF168 – (12 Oct 43) Williams Field, AZ; surveyed

AF169 – (?) Williams Field, AZ 981st FTS; scrapped June 1945

AF170 – (9 May 44) Williams Field, AZ; surveyed

AF171 – (16 Dec 43) Williams Field, AZ; surveyed

AF172 – (10 Aug 43) Williams Field, AZ; surveyed

AF173 – (? June 45) Syracuse, NY, scrapped

AF174 – (28 Oct 43) Williams Field, AZ, Chandler, AZ; surveyed

AF175 – (? June 45) Syracuse, NY; scrapped

AF176 – (?) Williams Field, AZ; 981st TEAFTS; scrapped June 1945

AF177 – (?) Williams Field, AZ; 981st TEAFTS; wrecked 28 July 1943

AF178 – (28 Nov 45) San Bernardino, CA; scrapped

AF179 – (28 Nov 45) San Bernardino, CA, 535th TEAFTS; dbr 29 July 1943

AF180 – (12 Aug 43) Williams Field, AZ; surveyed

AF181 – (13 Nov 45) San Bernardino, CA, 5th FG; 535th TEAFTS; scrapped

AF182 – (?) Williams Field, AZ; 981st AFTS, scrapped June 1945

AF183 – (13 Nov 45) San Bernardino, CA; 4th AF 982nd TEAFTS; scrapped

AF184 – (13 Nov 45) San Bernardino, CA; scrapped

AF185 – (12 July 44) Williams Field. AZ; 5th Ferry Group; surveyed

AF186 – (19 July 43) Kelly Field, TX; 55th Air Base Sqn; 535th TEAFTS; surveyed

AF187 – (18 Mar 44) Williams Field, AZ; 535th TEATS; surveyed

AF188 – No details

AF189 – (28 Apr 43) Williams Field, AZ; 981st FTS; surveyed

AF190 – (14 Aug 43) Williams Field, AZ; 982nd TEATS; forced landed 2 Aug 1943; surveyed

AF191 – (?) Williams Field, AZ; 981st TEAFTS; scrapped June 1945

AF192 – (17 Nov 43) Williams Field, AZ; CL-26

AF193 – (13 Feb 46) Williams Field, AZ; CL-26

AF193 – (13 Feb 46) Williams Field, AZ; FEAFHQ CL-26 26 June 1943; scrapped

AF194 – (30 Sept 43) Williams Field, AZ; crashed after in-flight fire

AF195 – (1 Dec 43) Williams Field, AZ; 982nd FTS

AF196 – (28 Nov 45) Williams Field, AZ; 982nd FS; CL-26; scrapped 8 May 1944

AF197 – (?) Moultire, Ontario, Canada, 75th Air Base Sqn; scrapped April 1945

AF198 – (13 Nov 45) Williams Field, AZ; 982nd FTS; CL-26, 8 June 1944

AF199 – (?) Williams Field, AZ; 982nd AFG; scrapped 20 April 1945

AF200 – (2 Nov 45) Williams Field, AZ; 981st TEAFS; CL-26; scrapped

AF201 – (17 Feb 44) Williams Field, AZ; 5th FG; 982nd FEAFTS; surveyed

AF202 – (?) June 45) Syracuse, NY; scrapped

AF203 – (8 May 44) Williams Field, AZ; 5th Ferry Group; 982nd AFTS; surveyed

AF204 – (?) June 45) Syracuse, NY; scrapped

AF205 – (18 Sept 44) Deming AAF; NM; CL-26

AF206 – (4 Mar 43) Williams Field, AZ; scrapped Feb 1946

AF207 – (10 Oct 43) ? surveyed

AF208 – (?) Williams Field, AZ; CL-26; scrapped Feb 1946

AF209 – (9 Sept 43) Williams Field, AZ; 982nd FTS; wrecked in c/l date unk

AF210 – (8 Sept 43) Williams Field, AZ; 535th TWFTS; surveyed

AF211 – (?) Glendale, CA; 473rd FG scrapped 13 Apr 1945

AF212 – (7 Mar 44) Williams Field, AZ; surveyed

AF213 – (9 May 45) Syracuse, NY; scrapped

AF214 – (29 May 45) Syracuse, NY; scrapped

AF215 – (29 May 45) Syracuse, NY; scrapped

AF216 – (8 May 44) Williams Field, AZ; 5th FTR; FEATG; surveyed

AF217 – (30 Aug 43) Casa Grande, AZ; 5th Ferry Group, FEAFTG; wrecked

AF218 – (15 June 45) US? scrapped

AF219 – (?) Williams Field, AZ; 535th FEAFTG scrapped 1 June 1945

AF220 – (13 Feb 43) Williams Field, AZ; FEAFTG surveyed

AF221 – converted to P-38F-13-LO

Key:

AAF – Army Air Field

AFS – Advanced Flying School (Sqn)

AFTS – Advanced Flying Training School (Sqn)

CL-26 – Class 26: a disposition classification believed to be equivalent to an RAF instructional airframe

cr – crashed

dbr – damaged beyond repair

FEAFTG – Four Engine Advanced Flying Training Group

FTG – Fighter Training Group

FTS – Fighter Training Squadron

ukn – unknown

TEAFTS – Two Engine Advanced Flying Training Squadron

TEATS – Two Engine Advanced Training Squadron

NB: Dates are believed to refer to delivery to first (or only) training unit or depot either for service or scrapping

P-38M-6 'Night Lightning' Conversions from P-38L-5

44-26831; 44-26863; 44-26865; 44-26892; 44-26951; 44-26997; 44-26999; 44-27000; 44-27108; 44-27233; 44-27234; 44-27236; 44-27237; 44-27238; 44-27245; 44-27249; 44-27250; 44-27251; 44-27252; 44-27254; 44-27256; 44-27257; 44-27258; 44-53011; 44-53012; 44-53013; 44-53014; 44-53014; 44-53015; 44-53016; 44-53017; 44-53019; 44-53020; 44-53022; 44-53025; 44-53029; 44-53030; 44-53031; 44-53032; 44-53034; 44-53035; 44-53042; 44-53050; 44-53051; 44-53056; 44-53062; 44-53063; 44-53066; 44-53067; 44-53068; 44-53069; 44-53073; 44-53074; 44-53076; 44-53077; 44-53079; 44-53080; 44-53082; 44-53083; 44-53084; 44-53085; 44-53086; 44-53087; 44-53088; 44-53089; 44-53090; 44-53092; 44-53093; 44-53094; 44-53095; 44-53096; 44-53097; 44-53098; 44-53100; 44-53101; 44-53106

TOTAL CONVERSIONS – 76

Glossary

A&AEE	Aeroplane and Armament Experimental Establishment	NACA	National Advisory Committee for Aeronautics
AFB	Air Force Base	NAS	Naval Air Station
AI	airborne interception (radar)	NCAF	Nationalist Chinese Air Force
BAD	Base Air Depot	NFS	Night Fighter Squadron
BG	Bomb Group	PG	Pursuit Group
BPC	British Purchasing Commission	PR	photographic reconnaissance
CAMD	Cuerpo de Aviacion Militar Dominica	PRG	Photographic Reconnaissance Group
CBI	China-Burma-India Theater	PRS	Photographic Reconnaissance Squadron
ETO	European Theatre of Operations	PRU	Photographic Reconnaissance Unit
FEAF	Far East Air Force	PS	Pursuit Squadron
FG	Fighter Group	RAAF	Royal Australian Air Force
FS	Fighter Squadron	RAE	Royal Aircraft Establishment
GFE	Government Furnished Equipment	ROKAF	Republic of Korea Air Force
HVAR	high-velocity aircraft rocket	rpg	rounds per gun
IFF	identification friend or foe	SWPA	South West Pacific Area
IJN	Imperial Japanese Navy	TAF	Tactical Air Force
JAAF	Japanese Army Air Force	TEL	tetraethyl lead
JNAF	Japanese Navy Air Force	TRG	Tactical Reconnaissance Group
KIA	killed in action	USAAC	United States Army Air Corps
LOC	Lockheed Overseas Corporation	USAAF	United States Army Air Force
MASAF	Mediterranean Allied Strategic Air Forces	USAF	United States Air Force
MIA	missing in action	VVS	Soviet Air Force
MTO	Mediterranean Theatre of Operations	WEP	war emergency power

Index